DWIGHT C. BAUM
- A MEMOIR -

BY DWIGHT C. "BILL" BAUM
AS TOLD TO KATE KITCHEN

ISBN: 1-4107-5952-0 (Dust Jacket)

Library of Congress Control Number: 2003094703

This book is printed on acid free paper.

Printed in the United States of America
Bloomington, IN

*This autobiography contains the recollections as dictated by the late Dwight
C. Baum. His heirs, co-author, and publisher 1st Books Library, are held
harmless from any liability with regard to possible inaccuracies.*

1stBooks – rev. 6/26/03

Acknowledgments:

Our thanks to: Nancy Stoehr, Library Assistant/Adult Services, Tompkins County Public Library, Ithaca, NY; Steve Kushman, California Historical Radio Society; Harry Eastman Kitchen, x-W8HOG, Consulting EE, for the editing of technical material; Barbara McGurn, Public Relations, Algonquin Hotel, New York, NY; The Public Information Office of the Whyte Museum of the Canadian Rockies; Alex Berliner of BEImages, Los Angeles, CA for photo reproduction rights and Nicole Follet, graphic designer.

Table of Contents

Introduction

Syracuse, New York - According to archives from the U.S. Weather Bureau at the Cornell Station, the morning of November 21, 1912 was *partly cloudy with moderate to brisk winds.* The temperature at nine o'clock was fifty degrees. It was a fairly mild day for that time of year, for which my parents were most certainly grateful, because that was the exact day and time that I chose to make my arrival into the world. Syracuse Memorial Hospital hosted my entrance—Dwight C. Baum, firstborn son of Dwight and Kitty Baum.

From early on I had a mind of my own. One of my first decisions was to change my name to Billy. My father's name was so unique that my playmates teased me incessantly. So I simply changed my name— problem solved. My parents must have been quite secure, for they honored my request without challenge. That kind of deductive reasoning appeared at a very young age and has served me well throughout my long and fascinating life. I have managed to take part in or witness incredible events through the years: the Spanish Flu Epidemic of 1918, the Great Depression, two world wars and four stock market crashes. For more than half a century, I enjoyed a challenging profession in corporate finance. I was on the ground floor of some of the most intricate mergers and acquisitions in American economic history. I was intrinsically involved in the early struggles of the savings and loan industry. I would like to be remembered as a man who was always thinking, working, learning, doing—the master of his fate. What an incredible journey—and what humble beginnings!

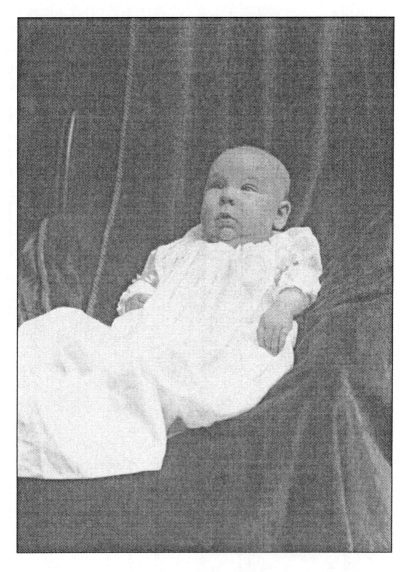

Dwight C. Baum born in Syracuse, NY

My mother "Kitty" and me, having an intriguing
conversation, probably about finance.

Grandfather's Farm

Homer, New York - In 1899, a friend of Grandfather Crouse wrote a novel about a country banker named David Harem. The book was named for its hero and became an enormous success, exceeded in sales at the time only by the *Bible* and *Ben Hur*. In the 1930s, the book was made into a successful movie of the same name. Unfortunately, the author died the year his book was published, completely unaware of its upcoming success. But for those who remember the village of Homer, New York as I do, the book left an indelible memory.

The author left behind a farm just west of Homer and a few miles north of Cortland. The farm was spread over more than five hundred acres. The pastures were pristine, laced with a sparkling brook perched alongside a luxurious meadow bordering the north side. When the land became available, Grandfather Crouse did not hesitate to buy the farm from the author's estate. It was more of a gentleman's farm than a moneymaking enterprise, and was primarily used to support a modest-sized dairy herd. Buildings were sparse, built for practicality, a sign of the times. There was a cottage-like farmhouse near the creek, a relatively small but efficient barn and a milking facility. As a small child I would sit with my mother in the tall grass, our faces warmed by the summer sun and she would tell me stories about her summers there as a girl. I particularly enjoyed the stories that included her pony, Daisy, who shadowed her closely all around the farm.

Today, more than a century later, Homer appears for the most part as it did in the mid-1800s, sporting a collection of white-pillared, neo-

1

colonial buildings along a wide village street. The area is well known for its sparkling Finger Lakes and is less than an hour's drive from several prestigious universities—Cornell, Colgate and Syracuse. The area's surrounding towns are clustered with country inns, large and small, from nineteenth-century Italianate farmhouses to rustic log cabins, still capturing the feel of more than a century past.

My favorite childhood memories were of summer visits to the farm. In my early youth, the farm was a two-day drive from New York City as we made our way across the corner of Pennsylvania. I remember one such trip in the summer of 1916 when we were only a few miles from our destination and a violent thunderstorm sprung up, pelting the car with a ferocious rain. I was only three-and-a-half, but still recall how relieved I was when my parents decided to take refuge for the night in a small country inn.

I recall so many odds and ends from those times. There was a one-lung pump at the farm. We had to pump water from the spring by the creek. It was brought up to a wooden tank above the house so we could have hot water. Mother would heat the water on the wood stove in the kitchen. Other amenities were rather upscale for the place and time. For example, our little farmhouse had a real flush toilet! For that I was grateful.

The crawl space underneath the porch was a perfect secret place for exploration by a curious little boy and I frequently took full advantage. One day I discovered the most wondrous mechanical device. It was a clay pigeon thrower and armed with a wrench borrowed from my father, I spent hours taking it apart only to reassemble it again.

The most exciting invention of the time was the telephone. There was the party line to deal with and the telephone had a handle that had to be cranked to summon the operator in order to make a call. There was no electricity in the house even though the cottage was only about a mile from the village of Homer. Some salesman had conned my grandfather into building a low dam on the creek and installing a low-head water turbine and generator, but there was rarely enough water to fill the pond and run the generator. A short bridge spanned the creek right on top of the dam; and I used to perch gingerly on the wall at the top and peer over the edge into the virtually empty pond.

Whenever I recall the apparatus, I remember the equipment lying unused, forever in disarray.

In 1920, Grandfather Crouse died and shortly thereafter, one farming disaster after another negatively impacted farming - not only in the immediate area, but all across the land. Bovine tuberculosis came first around 1921. It struck with a vengeance. The disease ran rampant and resulted in the widespread killing of cattle throughout the country. Our farm was heavily affected. Shortly thereafter, we were horrified to learn that all ten surviving cattle were killed instantly on one hot, summer afternoon during a thunderstorm. They were huddled together under a large tree when lightning struck.

Our farm never produced much corn or wheat, but there was ample crop equipment to fascinate a young boy. When I was eight, during one special visit, I was thrilled to watch the farm manager work the steam-powered, threshing machine. There was a huge silo filled with corn for the pigs, and I was always intrigued by the milking machines, especially the centrifuge that made cream separation possible. Of course, I kept bothering everyone around until they took the time to explain exactly how it worked.

On one especially warm and sunny afternoon, Mother and I sat together under a willow tree by the edge of the creek watching the fish swim around in the pond beneath our feet. Mother asked me to go down to make sure there was water in the tank surrounding the cylinder of the make-and-brake pump engine. I remember thinking that was a very important job. Those moments were precious moments that would last a lifetime.

My last memory as a boy at the farm was not my fondest. I jumped out of bed on one bright sunny morning to discover the most interesting bottle of pink pills. I quickly consumed a large amount of what I thought was *candy*. Shortly thereafter, I learned that the bottle contained laxatives. I spent the next couple of days *heavily involved*. No further punishment was necessary. In the mid-1920s, my grandmother sold the farm and I took the family memories with me, each one captured with care.

Many years later, after I entered Cornell—just forty-five miles southwest of Syracuse, I occasionally drove past the old farm on my way from Ithaca to Syracuse to visit my Aunt Margaret. Over the years, even as late as 2001, I returned periodically to see that most of the buildings were still there, although the dam had been breached and the electric generating facilities had long before been sold off as junk. The farm was, even then, very much intact and the town of Homer remained virtually unchanged.

Grandmother Crouse and me.

A Happy Childhood and Brandied Peaches

It was early spring in 1915. I was only three, but I recall that Mother was becoming impatient waiting for the birth of my little brother. She was doing everything she could think of to hasten the event. She had a light car, a Scripps-Booth. It was smaller than a Model T Ford, which was the bottom of the line in those days. She drove around a lot, explaining very carefully that going over bumps in the road might encourage the baby to come into the world a little faster. I enjoyed going for rides with her. One day I accompanied her as she went to do some shopping in Yonkers. In the middle of the square, the motor came loose, our stalled car creating havoc and causing traffic to scramble all around us. I was delighted at the excitement! Several men came along and pushed our little car to the side of the road.

The big day came on March 25. I noticed a sickeningly sweet odor in the house and ran upstairs to my mother's bedroom to investigate. A strange woman shooed me away. I later learned she was a midwife. I would never forget that pungent smell of ether. That was my introduction to my baby brother Jack—John Leach Baum.

I got to celebrate my baby brother's birth in a very special way. I remember sitting in the kitchen a couple days later, enjoying a special dessert the maid had prepared.

"Billy sure loves this treat!" the woman laughed happily as Mother walked into the kitchen. Mother had the strangest look on her face. After seeing the reason for my happiness, she was stunned to realize the maid had been feeding me brandied peaches –lots and lots of brandied peaches!

5

Even as a small child, my curiosity was piqued at finding out how things worked. One day I decided to examine the inner workings of the strange electric outlets. Prying open the flaps that covered one of the outlets in the living room, I experienced a sudden jolt throughout my entire body. I screamed bloody-murder, simultaneously wetting my pants – not a good thing to do with your finger in an electric outlet. Thankfully, Mother was in the next room. She came rushing to the rescue, yanking my fingers from the socket. Today, nearly eight decades later, I still wonder about that insane design.

My childhood wasn't all gadgets and technology, however. I decided one day, as every child in the universe does at least once, to use a handful of crayons to scribble all over a white cabinet. Aside from the look of horror on my mother's face as she discovered my artwork, I received no punishment for my misdeed.

My first life's lesson in disappointment came at the age of five. I was extremely upset to learn I was scheduled to have my tonsils removed. My grandmother promised me that if I went through with the operation, she would give me a *glasscutter*. Thinking I was getting a pair of shears all my own, the bribe worked.

I was shuffled off to the hospital to undergo the frightening ordeal made more painful due to the standards of medical care in 1918. When I returned home to claim my well-earned reward, I was presented with a tool kit that included a scriber—a *real glasscutter!* I am sure I behaved ungratefully simply because I didn't realize how unique a gift I had been given.

That year was very difficult for my parents and nearly devastating to me. I fell quite ill to the Spanish Flu, an epidemic that killed around thirty million worldwide. Deaths in the United States numbered nearly six hundred thousand. Comparing that number to World War II in later years, where less than three hundred thousand Americans lost their lives serving their country, this was an epidemic that struck fear in the hearts of people everywhere, especially parents as children were particularly susceptible. Friends and families could not even support each other in their grief as public funerals were banned in an effort to try to keep the virus contained. Someone would feel fine one moment and hours later be fighting for his life. I was in bed for months, but for some reason, thankfully, our entire family survived the winter. After a few months' bed rest, I was up and about again, mischievous as ever.

Even after all the trauma, I still held a very clear recollection of the end of the year that signaled the end of World War I. Even as a young boy, I was aware of the false armistice. A mistaken Scripps Howard news release reported that peace had come. But a couple days later, on November 11, 1918, the real armistice came. You could hear bells and whistles all over the place. There was so much excitement! Thousands marched from downtown New York City through a wonderful arch near Herald Square. I was awestruck as I watched throngs of people tear down the glory of that shimmering arch in celebration.

On May 14, 1922, my brother Peter joined our family but alas, there were no more celebrations with brandied peaches, so I wasn't so excited about his birth..

My father was a highly driven young man who was already on his way to becoming a world-class architect. Our family wasn't exceptionally wealthy, but in those days, even people of modest means could hire a cook for thirty-five dollars plus room and board, and with a family of three boys, a cook and a driver came in handy.

We had a Franklin motorcar at the time. It had an air compressor that was attached to the engine, so if the car had a flat, we could run the engine and pump up the tire. Our chauffeur enjoyed taking apart the assembly, but one time, after tinkering with the gadget a while, he reassembled it incorrectly and there was an incredible explosion! The air compressor destroyed itself and nearly blew up the car along with the garage.

Regardless of how upset Mother was, I was absolutely delighted to discover this rather unique invention and this thrilling incident was just one of many that fueled my later interest in science and technology.

~

My parents provided us with an extremely stable and happy household. They had fallen in love early on and had struggled to earn the right to be together. Their appreciation for each other was always evident.

Dwight James Baum and Lucia Katharine Crouse met in 1910 on the inter-urban line en route to Utica from Syracuse. The electric cars were much like trolleys, although built for higher speeds. The line carried passengers from city to city through the countryside.

Dad had graduated from college a year before and was already working in a prestigious New York firm with an architect by the name of Goldwin Starrett. In 1901, Starrett had joined his brothers to form the Thompson Starrett Construction Company. This firm designed and built the Algonquin Hotel for Albert Foster of the Puritan Realty Company. The hotel was located across from Pennsylvania station

An elegant woman, Mother was twenty-one at the time. Everyone called her Kitty. She evidently captured the attention of several rowdy young men on the train. As they began to tease her, Dad, although quite slight in stature, stepped up to rescue her. He firmly suggested to the fellows that they "back off," then he promptly took a seat beside her. They talked during the rest of the trip to Utica.

Dad was the perfect picture of an artist of the time. He was shorter than average and quite slender. He sported a neatly trimmed mustache and a prim and proper Van Dyke. Colleagues referred to him as a dynamo. Everyone who knew him agreed he was a brilliant man. Even his demeanor reflected a tremendously creative energy.

My father's parents were of modest means. Dad was born in 1886, the son of a merchant - near Little Falls, New York. On the other hand, Mother's parents, the Charles Crouses, were affluent New Yorkers. They, above all people, should have recognized the value of a self-made man. Jacob Crouse, Mother's grandfather, had begun his career as a grocery clerk. From a hard-earned savings of four hundred dollars that he invested in the wholesale grocery business, he eventually amassed a fortune of several million dollars. Born in 1824, the son of George and Maria Diefendorf Crouse, Jacob eventually became the largest owner of real estate in Syracuse.

Jacob died in 1900 and his family paid tribute in a dramatically unique manner. It took four years to place his memorial at its final resting place, but they did just that. Someone in the family had discovered an eighty-ton boulder, a relic from the ice age that had been moved by a glacier all the way to central New York from Canada. The boulder initially rested in Split Rock, west of Syracuse at Terry Road. After choosing it as a memorial to the multi-millionaire, the family made plans to load the boulder onto a sled to be pulled by a team of eighty strong, sturdy farm horses. It was to be taken to Oakwood Cemetery, a few miles away. One obstacle after another lay in its path. First, the horses had too much difficulty moving it on the sled over the snow. Then there were too many downgrades en route and it would have been impossible to stop on a downhill slope. After several weeks of trying to budge the heavy boulder and only accomplishing a move of a hundred fifty yards, all at great effort and expense, they abandoned the boulder by the side of the road. It lay there until spring. Obviously, no one was worried about it being stolen.

When spring came, movers signed up for double shifts to keep the boulder moving night and day. The family would not rest until they could honor Jacob Crouse in the manner in which they had chosen. The rock was moved at a rate of nine hundred feet per day. The Post-Standard reported in its morning edition, "Crowds lined the city streets to watch the progress, but only two accidents occurred, both to bystanders, neither of which was fatal, with settlements made out of court."

On June 18, 1904, four years after the death of Jacob Crouse, and at a cost of forty-five hundred dollars, the boulder reached its final destination to be inscribed by a stone cutter with this one word:

C – R - O – U – S - E.

Still, Jacob Crouse's legend as a self-made man did little to impress the Charles Crouses with my dad's circumstance. Realizing that he had worked his way through college, the Crouses took a dim view of any potential union he might try to forge with their daughter, a Syracuse debutante. Soon after Mother shared the joyous news that she had fallen hopelessly in love with this intense young man, her parents shipped her off to Europe with a lady friend for a year, hoping she and Dad would forget each other. This was a sign of the times and the normal solution to the problem faced by many well-to-do young women and their parents.

Dutifully, obediently - my mother did as she was told. Upon her return in November 1910, she and Dad once again declared their love. My father had spent the year creating a valuable reputation as an architect and the Crouses no longer doubted his abilities to provide for their daughter. And by now, they couldn't have dissolved the relationship if they had wanted to.

On Sunday morning, `Christmas Day, the Syracuse Herald announced their engagement. A year later, on January 3, 1912, at eight o'clock in the evening, surrounded by seventy-five family members and close friends, Lucia Katharine Crouse became Mrs. Dwight James Baum. The wedding was held at the Crouse mansion on West Genesee. Newspaper accounts reported that all the rooms, from the library to the parlor, were decorated with jonquils and other spring flowers even though it was early January.

From the moment he left college, Dad had begun to gain a reputation for his exceptional residential designs. Mother and Dad lived at 800 Riverside Drive during their first year of marriage and then moved to Fieldston, a new development in Riverdale-on-Hudson, in the Bronx, when I was a year old.

Dad was eager to design his own buildings, determined to be professionally autonomous. He began his proprietary career in earnest by designing his own house in 1913. The small Dutch Colonial was located at 4410 Waldo Avenue. The attic of the new family home became Dad's first office. It was so small that clients who came to look at his drawings on the drafting table could barely fit into the tiny room. He would stand in the doorway and point out features on the drawings from a several feet away. We lived there while he oversaw construction on our new family home, which was built on one of the highest points in the area. He finished the house at 5001 Goodridge Avenue in 1916, calling it Sunnybank. Our home became the subject of various feature articles, newspaper editors referring to the unique design as an "elegant, asymmetrical Colonial Revival frame house."

People quickly took notice of his work and he was soon surrounded by scores of unique residences he had developed. His style was referred to as eclectic-residential and became extremely popular in the United States during the 1920s and '30s.

\

"Billy" Baum

Fieldston: Riverdale-on-Hudson

Fieldston, located in the northwest corner of the Bronx, was the brainchild of Joseph Delafield. The entrepreneur had acquired the farmland in the early nineteenth century and named it Fieldston after an ancestral manor in England. In 1909, he began to develop it and sold the first portion to a teacher's college, which later became Horace Mann High School.

Unlike most developers who efficiently chopped their subdivisions into grids, Delafield insisted on developing curving streets that followed the contours of the land. Dad's design style complemented the unique plan. A fellow colleague of Dad's, Ludwig P. Bono, said of his work in Fieldston, "Dwight Baum always saved God's trees and rock formations." Dad was known for his respect of the topography and the natural layout of the land and many of his houses sat in unique positions that did not squarely face the road.

Fieldston was a perfect neighborhood for a young boy growing up in the early 1900s. Jack, Peter and I, along with the neighborhood kids, used to run through the wooded areas that were plentiful throughout the development. As a child, I desperately wanted to climb the pencil-thin limbs of the newly planted chestnut trees in the parkway nearby, but Mother wouldn't let me. Today you can't get your arms around them.

Early in his career, Dad had wisely connected with a local real estate agent, acquiring commissions to design a number of houses in the Fieldston development. First he designed a small three-room Elizabethan building for office use. In order to expand his business, he required far more space than the attic provided. The real estate office was located at one end of the building and Dad moved his office into the other end. We visited the office many times, and throughout my life, I never forgot the poignant scent of Dad's drafting room, the aroma of the erasers and the ink used on those large blueprints that lay spread out all over the drafting tables. Eventually, there were one hundred forty houses erected at Fieldston, a good half of them designed by my father, who at the peak of his career employed more than twelve draftsmen.

The Delafields later sold the property where the office was located and as a child I watched with fascination their struggling attempts to move the building. The workmen jacked up the building, carefully placing large wagon wheels underneath. But the heavy structure quickly collapsed. Jacked up again, the building was set onto large twelve-by-twelve inch beams. They slowly maneuvered the building down the hill to the corner of Spuyten Duyvel Parkway and Waldo Avenue where it remains to this day, although it's hardly recognizable after multiple renovations.

Spuyten Duyvel was Dutch for "in spite of the devil" and was also the name of the creek connecting the Hudson and East Rivers waterway that formed the tip of Manhattan Island. It was named so because you could get through it, "in spite of the devil." In later years, it was dredged and the creek no longer remains.

On the southwest corner of Spuyten Duyvel Parkway and Broadway was a very large IRT subway with an elevated yard used for car storage and maintenance. The 242nd St. Subway station was elevated, of course, and we had to climb the stairs to get up to it. My earliest memory was that no matter where we were going, we would buy a ticket for five cents and pass through the turnstile. The subway was double tracked in those days, so there would almost always be a train waiting. We'd get on and wait for it to start on its way south. It was a dead-end station. There was no turn around. The subway would pass over the ship canal to the northern tip of Manhattan Island on the swing bridge. We'd love to stand on the front of the subway train looking out the window and watch the train stop whenever the bridge had to open. The bridge was lifted a few inches hydraulically, then swung ninety degrees so the ship could go through, then was swung back again to settle down so the subway train could go forward over the bridge.

The area provided an endless collection of memories. I have vague recollections as a very small boy sitting on a hill on the east side of Van Courtlandt Park watching army maneuvers being conducted down in the park. Once my buddy and I found a dummy bomb and managed to get it home in my wagon.

On the west side of Broadway, there was an amusement area with a merry-go-round. You had to go up a number of steps to get to it.

The New York Central Railroad ran on the east side of the Hudson River past Riverdale Station, used for commuters from the city. The line swung around the curve and ran parallel to the ship canal, down to Grand Central Station.

Every Christmas our family went to Syracuse to celebrate with my grandparents, the Crouses and the Baums. Around the twenty-second of December, we would drive up to Yonkers and park the car. We would board the express train, always first class. The train proceeded up to Harlem where the electrified portion of the New York Central line started. The electrification was by a third rail alongside the track. The third rail had a wood cover that kept people from stepping on the 600-volt hot wire, which charged the electric locomotive that pulled the trains. There, they would disconnect the train, back up and connect the beautiful, shiny steam engine. The New York Central was very proud of their equipment, and kept it immaculate.

There were an endless number of sites along the Hudson River that delighted a young boy. The train passed right next to Sing Sing. As a kid, it always fascinated me. I would watch out the train window as canal boats would float along the river beside us, hauling tons and tons of coal. We would see the occasional remains of an icehouse. There was a tremendous problem with typhoid in the early 1900s because all the towns along the Hudson dumped their sewage into the river. They eventually discovered one of the primary causes of typhoid was the contaminated ice from the Hudson River.

There was an island barely off shore of the Hudson with a sort of castle on it. The owner had a store down on lower Broadway that dealt in arms. He bought surplus guns and ammunition and sold them primarily to Latin American revolutionary countries. I was fascinated by that as a kid and visited the store a number of times. There were rifles from before the Spanish American war as well as civil war rifles, cannons and lots of different kinds of antiquated ammunition.

The owner guaranteed us that seventy-five percent of it would still fire.

In the glory days of the New York Central, everything along the line was neatly cared for. Workers continually lined up the gravel roadbed under the railroad ties so there would be a nice straight parallel line to the tracks. Everything was based on efficiency. There was a water trough between the rails and the locomotive tender would reach down and scoop the water up so he wouldn't have to stop the steam engine.

Our family would leave Yonkers around nine in the morning and arrive at the outskirts of Albany on the east side of the river minutes before twelve o'clock noon. By this time, we would be seated in the dining car. Lunch was a great experience. Shiny silver lay on white linen and crystal goblets were filled with iced water. All the waiters were black and dressed to the hilt in their formal uniforms. The kitchen was along one side of the dining car. The cooks used charcoal in the stove and the aromas that came from there were wonderful. And at the end of our scrumptious lunch, we would be presented with a lovely bowl of pistachio ice cream, sometimes vanilla. Once I saw black specks in the ice cream and I thought it was soot from the train. Mom and Dad laughed and laughed. Mom said, "That is pure vanilla and that's what makes it *sooo good*!"

The trains stopped at Albany so they could add an extra locomotive to climb the grade up to Little Falls and Schenectady.

Schenectady, located at the top of the grade, was not only the home of the General Electric Company, but also the American Locomotive company, the largest manufacturer of steam locomotives in the country. They had huge yards and I was fascinated by some of the old locomotives being brought in. They were either trade-ins or waiting to be rebuilt. There were large numbers of them.

My dad grew up at Little Falls. There was a big bend in the rail line there and he often told the story that as a newsboy, he would go down there to pick up the morning papers. Once, a high-speed mail train had tried to make the curve, but careened off the track and wrecked. Many people were killed. Curiously, maybe twenty-five or so years ago, there was a similar accident in the very same spot.

There were many factory towns along the river, manufacturing companies that made typewriters, rugs and all sorts of things.

The country was usually snow covered at that time of year and it would be getting dark around four-thirty in the afternoon, about the time we got to Syracuse. Our arrival was always exciting. The main line for passenger trains on the New York Central Railroad went right through the heart of the city. Every now and then the train would have to stop because some one would have parked their car too close to the tracks and they would have to get someone to move the car so they could go on to the Syracuse station.

The station was a huge open shed with six lines of tracks that ran through it. The waiting room was on the south side. But the ends of the shed, both east and west, were open so the trains could pass through it. When the wind picked up and blew through there, it was *cold*! Grandmother Crouse's chauffeur would pick us up at the station in the big Packard to drive us to 416 West Genesee Street – to that huge old house. Grandmother always had a Packard and once she even added a Dodge to her collection. Of course there was no heating system in the cars in those days. We would jump out of the car half frozen and run inside the house. There we would all gather around the warm floor register until we got warm.

There was always a Christmas tree already decorated at Grandmother Crouse's house. And there would be a huge pile of beautifully wrapped presents around the tree. Aunt Margaret was crippled and couldn't live alone, so she lived there as well. On our first morning, we would have breakfast and the Barnums would come over -- Uncle Joe and Aunt Eleanor and their family. Uncle Joe (Jerome) was publisher of the Syracuse Post Standard, the morning paper.

The second day, we would visit my grandparents Baum in the small house that Dad had designed for them. We would have a modest Christmas there and a wonderful dinner. Then the next day we would have the Crouse family Christmas at the big house. I was always embarrassed to be asked by the Crouses what I wanted for Christmas. One year I couldn't decide, so I asked for books. Boy, did I ever get books! Since many of them were inappropriate for someone my age, I probably only read half of them. But it was a great gift.

The Crouses had a very large, formal dining room table, but there were so many us that they had to put up a card table for the children. After Christmas Day, we spent days playing with our new gifts. We often played downtown. The original Erie Canal ran right through the center of the city and in the center block there was a large canal basin where canal barges were unloaded. When I was a kid I would watch them clear snow off the streets and dump all the snow and ice from the streets into the huge basin. There was a weight lock on the canal where barges were weighed and the tolls assigned. The basin has long since been filled in and a museum now stands in its place.

And then came New Year's dinner with another huge turkey with all the trimmings. Shortly thereafter, we would be taken to the station where we would board the train to take us home, loaded down with presents.

Our house in Fieldston was heated by a gravity-circulating, hot water system. The source of the hot water was a large, cast iron furnace. There was a large space on top where one dumped in the buckwheat coal and it was fed by gravity down into the grates where it burned itself down. Mom would shake the ash out every other day. The furnace was controlled by dampers driven by battery-powered motors. On the living room wall was a Honeywell Regulator Company clock, which could control temperatures and time as well. This was very much state of the art in 1916. The furnace room was always very heavily wooded and the anthracite coal had to be dumped through a chute into the coal bin. At the bottom of the coal storage area, you would grab a couple of shovels full, toss them into the top of the furnace and they would be fed all the way down. The Bradley Mahoney Coal Company was our supplier. Coal was delivered in huge trucks by two big, strong, husky black men. They would dump the coal into large canvas bags and haul them on their backs to the crawl space in the basement.

In the laundry room was a very small, anthracite-fueled furnace that made the hot water for the laundry room. The washing machine, manufactured by EZ Washing Machine Co. was a big copper tub. There were two very large ceramic tubs - one for hot water and one for cold water. Later on, Dad bought a huge, gas-fired mangle iron, which could press large sheets. In the 1920s, many homes converted from anthracite fuel to fuel oil, but Mother and Dad said that was too sooty and a nuisance. It wasn't until probably the 1940s when Mom had the furnace converted to manufactured gas. There was no natural gas in New York until some time in the 1950s.

17

Jack and Peter and I built the most magnificent tree house out in the back yard. There was none other like it in the neighborhood.

~

Fieldston was a rather prestigious place to live but hardly diversified. The house on the northwest corner of 250th Street and Goodrich Avenue was occupied by the Hughes family. Mr. Hughes was a New York lawyer and the son of Charles Evans Hughes, also a lawyer who earned national recognition for his investigation into insurance fraud. He became governor of New York, defeating William Randolph Hearst in 1906 and was re-elected two years later. In 1916 he ran for the presidency against Woodrow Wilson. It was a very tight race. For a while, it looked as if Hughes might have won. The swing vote was cast by California.

When newspaper reporters came to Hughes' hotel room, his son answered the door and said, "I'm sorry, the president is asleep." The reporters had come to tell him that he hadn't won after all, that California had gone to Wilson. He had lost the election by 23 electoral votes. In 1930, President Herbert Hoover nominated Hughes to serve as Chief Justice of the U.S. Supreme Court. Hoover was to play a large part in my Dad's life a few months later.

There was a large piece of property down the street. It was a spread consisting of several acres, bought by a rather weird church group who built several houses and fenced in the area. They called it Chapel Farms and had services there, although we weren't quite sure what kind of services they provided.

Butting up against Chapel Farms, there was an adjacent lot that Mom and Dad bought to use as a vegetable garden. They tried to grow corn, but the squirrels always got to the corn days before it was ripe enough to pick. I still can still visualize squirrel sitting on the fence holding an ear, stripping the husk, and munching away at the corn. Fortunately, there was a two-acre farm nearby where an old farmer grew the sweetest corn. Mom and Dad would buy corn from the farmer for ten cents an ear. It was wonderfully sweet and his farm was one of the last farms in the city of New York.

Another family nearby in Fieldston was the McNitt family. Frank's father was a journalist and went off to Europe in 1919, returning home with German army supplies, including ammunition. Fascinating stuff for kids aged seven or eight. Frank and I were not particularly close but kept busy exploring the neighborhood. We would take kerosene lanterns down to basement of the house and play army, hiding away in the closets down there. We even kept white mice down there at one time. Of course they escaped and Mother was catching them for years, all around the house.

Mom and Dad would have wonderful dinner parties. I got to meet such interesting people as Frank Lloyd Wright and Fiorello LaGuardia, the colorful mayor of New York City. It was their world and they never thought a thing about it.

Sometime in the early 1920s, we got rid of the icebox and bought a mechanical refrigerator. It operated with a gear-type motor compressor and heat exchanger, which were separate. The evaporating unit was placed in the refrigerator itself. Subsequently, we got one of the first GE turret-top refrigerators, standard for the 1920s and '30s.

In the early '20s, stores were small. The drug stores sold drugs and only drugs, grocery stores sold groceries, and the meat market sold meat, unlike today. Products were typically placed on counters and on high shelves behind the counters. The clerk would take long tongs and reach for the cereal and other requested items. There was no parking area and apartments were over the stores. There were about five stores in a row all on one street.

The A & P store chain opened a store on the corner of Spuyten Duyvel Parkway and Broadway. The manager quickly realized he had a number of wealthy clients up the hill and he rapidly expanded the store and increased the merchandise. On his own, he arranged for delivery service and credit accounts. You could phone in an order and it would be delivered on credit. When the A&P district manager discovered what the store manager was doing, he was absolutely horrified and the ingenious young man was immediately terminated.

When you bought ice cream, it didn't come pre-packaged. Rather, it came in large paper tubs and there were only a few flavors. The clerk dished it out into a cardboard box, using a big spatula, heaping it as high as he could. He closed the box and you ran as fast as you could to get it home before it melted.

19

You didn't buy milk at the stores. Milk was delivered daily by the milkman and came in glass quart bottles or half-quart bottles, a healthy supply of cream settled on top. You could open the bottle, pour out the cream for coffee or whipping, or shake the bottle and distribute the cream into the milk. The milkman also brought eggs to the house. There was even a man who came around in a wagon and delivered fresh produce, fruit and vegetables.

There were no banks in the area and some of the big New York banks had no branches at all. You had to go down to 200th Street. The assistant manager was told that if he were to obtain a certain number of deposits, he would be given his own branch. Dad helped him and my grandmother, among others, transferred some accounts down to his bank. He got his award and opened his branch on 207th St, only seven blocks closer.

One of Dad's clients was Mr. Campanion, a successful real estate investor and contractor in New York. He was Italian and a colorful man. In 1929, he contracted with Dad to design a very expensive executive home. It was to be a magnificent house. I remember being with Dad in Campanion's office one day as they were discussing various phases of the design. A man came in, indicating he wanted to borrow some money. Campanion told his secretary to draw up a note and after she did so, without a word, he handed the man a check for ten thousand dollars. That's how wealthy he was.

As the depression hit, real estate construction dropped precipitously and Campanion's vacancies in real estate increased. He went from being a very wealthy man to losing all his properties except one. He stopped construction on the big house and he sold his house down on the circle by the Riverdale Country Club. His family moved into the garage. On the northwest corner of 7th Ave and 42nd St, there were some intrinsically valuable lots with FOR SALE signs on them for about three years. Somehow Campanion managed to put himself back in business; he started making money again and he and Dad finally built the house. It exists even today as a gorgeous Italianate house, and belongs to some highly orthodox Jewish sect.

There weren't many Catholics in the area when I was a boy. We were members in the Presbyterian Church but we were not active, although Mother did enroll me in Sunday school. I was rather intrigued watching the Episcopal kids run past the house waving palms on Palm Sunday. A neighbor girl encouraged me several times to switch to her Episcopal Sunday School because she would be awarded with little gold medals for bringing converts.

One odd thing I remember from that church was how the roof beams in the church were put together. And I didn't like the idea of hanging my head to pray. I always believed you shouldn't hang your head as if in shame, you should look up to the Glory of Heaven. I always refused to look down to pray.

I only recall one Jewish family moving into the community. It was in the 1930s. We had no antipathy toward them; they just weren't part of the community that my family happened to know socially.

Down the street, in the mid-'30s, an African-American musician by the name of Cab Calloway bought a house. He kept the place up even more nicely than the neighboring houses, although everyone kept their houses up there. At the time, his music was thought to be very far-out. Of course, in later years the neighborhood would house the family of singer Carly Simon. They lived on Grosvenor Avenue.

In addition to designing at least half of the Fieldston houses, Dad was offered a number of noteworthy commissions, one of which was an elaborate estate in Sarasota for John and Mable Ringling. Ringling was the famous circus magnate and owner of "The Greatest Show on Earth." The five million dollar mansion was built seaside, directly on the bay and called Ca' d'Zan (house of John). It was constructed from 1922-1926 and situated next to the Ringling Museum of Art. Its design reflected that of a Venetian palace. Dad was recognized throughout the world and said to be one of the leading figures in the development of Florida in the 1920s. A courthouse he designed in Sarasota was of Spanish style, complete with campanile bell tower that stood one hundred twenty feet high and had a pool fifty feet in diameter. Many of his plans were exhibited in Paris, London, Berlin, even South America. He was Architectural Editor of Good Housekeeping Magazine and wrote numerous articles on architecture in America.

He designed multiple structures for colleges and universities throughout upstate New York and New England. In the 1920s, he built what was at the time the longest house in New York, a home of Georgian design. The beautiful building still stands as an embassy for an African nation. He designed the parish for Christ Church in Riverdale, pro bono.

Perhaps one of Dad's most noteworthy projects was the West Side YMCA in New York City, built adjacent to Central Park in 1930. The massive buildings were designed in fifteenth-century style, fashioned after the Italian provinces of Lombardy and Tuscany. He used pastel-shades of bricks manufactured in South Carolina but never before used in New York. The effect was the same as those used in northern Italy. This was at the time, the largest institutional building of its kind in the world.

A 1932 article in New York's Herald Tribune heralded his architecture, stating, "He looks the part of the artist and dreamer and scholar—unusually small and slight of build, with the artist's small pointed beard and mustache and gentle blue eyes."

Dad built several exhibition buildings at the Chicago World's Fair in 1933 and the New York World's Fair in 1939. He earned an Honorary degree as Doctor of Fine Arts from Syracuse University in 1934 and won various gold medals from the Architectural League of New York City. In 1932, he was awarded the "Best Small Home Design" from 1926-1930. That particular honor was for a home designed for Francis Collins at Fieldston and was presented to him in person by President Herbert Hoover and sponsored by the American Institute of Architects. In 1931, 1932 and 1933, he won the bronze medals awarded by Better Homes in America.

One of his most unique designs was the Renaissance Italian villa for the estate of Anthony Campagna. It reflected the Tuscan style with materials shipped over from Italy. The owner was so pleased, he commissioned Dad to design a school to be built in his native town in Italy. The building had to be drawn in the metric system for the Italian builders, quite an unusual project for an American architect. When the school was completed and donated by Campagna, Mussolini was so pleased that he made the Italian gentleman a count. Another was the Great War Memorial tower in New York City.

Just days prior to his premature death, a new project was announced, which included a million-dollar building and modernization program for Wells College at Aurora. His life's work was heralded in a book entitled, *The Work of Dwight James Baum* by Matlack Price.

Our family home in Fieldston. Dad's office was in the attic.

Dad and me with the family dog.

Dwight James Baum, architect

Barnard School for Boys

In the fall of 1917, Barnard School for Boys, which was located on the Fieldston development, had one hundred fifty students. At the age of five, I was sent there to attend kindergarten. There were two schools in the development, Barnard School for Boys, which was affiliated with Teachers College at Columbia University and the Horace Mann School. Both schools were close to the end of the subway that shuttled our fathers into Manhattan every morning. Horace Mann boys referred to the Barnard boys as the *Barnyardites* and we in turn reciprocated vociferously by taunting them with the name *Horsemanure.*

Miss Weed, a typical head mistress of the day, ran the school with a proverbial iron rod. Classes were of modest size. I rode my bike the five or six blocks down the hill from the house. In the winter when biking was prohibited due to snow, I walked to school. As more families began to discover the popular community, one particular family by the name of Englehardt bought a house at the bottom of the hill. It was a move that would one day change my life. Little did I know, nor would I have cared at that age, that my future wife was residing right down the street in a house my father had designed. Hildagarde was the little girl's name and it pleased me to no end that we were bitter enemies throughout my boyhood. I had absolutely no reason to permit girls to enter my very busy, interesting life and I may have known somehow, even then, that she would change all that.

Mother tried desperately to teach me how to ride a bike. I continued to fall off, time and again, often bruising my knees *and* more often than not, running into my mother in the process. Finally, the boys in the neighborhood took pity on my poor mother and after parading me around the road a couple of times, perched atop my bike, guided me to the top of the hill, and gave me a healthy shove. Suddenly on my own and now fully committed, I found myself actually riding down the hill. By the time I got to the bottom and landed safely right in front of the Englehardt house, I knew how to ride a bicycle.

What an unbelievable thrill it was to have that freedom! There was no fear of anything, not of traffic or danger of any kind. It was a carefree world for boys especially, who, on our bikes, felt absolutely immortal. The entire area, from Broadway and the Hudson River to Spuyten Duyvel was open to us. There were no apartment houses around at the time. We would chase garden snakes through the neighborhood, then jump on their bikes and ride down to the Hudson River to watch the trains go by on the New York Central Railroad. The area provided as close to a country setting as one could be without actually living in the country.

Throughout my life, I would always remember the freedom and joy of that time, and would especially recall my dad telling us to always forget the bad times and remember the good times. And good times were plentiful.

~

In the summer of 1921, my parents enrolled me at Camp Iriquois for two months. It was a boys camp located near Burlington, Vermont, somehow connected with Barnard. My first camping experience gave me incredible memories I would never forget.

Campers would all meet on July first at Grand Central Station. The train had sleeping berths, quite a novelty to us. Once delivered safely to the camp, we were delighted to learn there was no running water. Toilets were simple latrines referred to as two-holers and four-holers. And near the property line was a rather unique contraption called the funnel. Quite useful for young boys.

Early each morning, the camp counselors would roust us out of bed and we would dash naked down to the ravine and across the beach into Lake Champlain for rather informal bathing. The chilly water had not yet been warmed by the sun, and we would scamper out quickly so we could dry off, get dressed, and begin our day of adventure. It was my first time away from home alone and I found myself a little homesick for the first two weeks. My parents had thoughtfully shipped my bike to me. Once that arrived and I assembled it, I never was homesick again.

A month later, the counselors announced that we were all going to take a wonderful four-day bike trip. There were no paved roads around the area. The roads had been covered with marble dust and crushed marble chips and were smooth as glass.

We stayed at a farm and were delighted at the opportunities that venue allowed us, from playing and jumping in the hay to watching the farmhand milk the cows. One morning I was gazing intently at that wonder of nature, when a great big squirt of hot, rich cow's milk splattered all over my face. The farmhand had grabbed the cow's teat and had pointed it toward me. Then just as suddenly, my shock turned to pleasure as I tasted the warm, fresh milk.

After another day of hard peddling, we arrived near Mount Mansfield. Together we trudged up the mountain, which reached forty-two hundred feet into the sky. Exhausted but happy, we spent the night in the loft of a roadhouse. The next morning I caught my very first trout in the cool, clear stream and was so proud. Moments later, after watching the trout struggle for air, my mood changed and I felt so sorry for the fish, I never ate it.

The summer I was nine, we were allowed out of our bunks in the middle of the night for a very special treat. We got to lie on the grass, flat on our backs, and watch a meteor display. We were so overcome that we were totally silent. It was fantastic and I never saw anything again so spectacular as that incredible artistry from the heavens.

Everyone had names sewn into their clothing. All my clothes had *Billy Baum on them* with red thread sewn onto white ribbons. There were twelve cots in my cabin, each one with a navy-colored surplus blanket on top. This was shortly after the end of World War I and there was no electricity in the cabins, so for light, counselors used gas lamps. Those lamps gave a lot of light once they got going. There was no hot running water except in the kitchen. Each cabin had a faucet with ample amounts of cold, running water.

After we climbed into bed, we would tell stories until we fell asleep. Once I decided to tell a ghost story. Naturally, I decided to use props. At the side of the cabin I rigged up a board in a tree, put a big stone on it, then attached the board to a rope. The apparatus was hidden among the limbs and leaves. The idea was that I would pull the rope so the stone would fall down and crash some bottles underneath, for effect. The problem was that as I was balancing the stone and arranging the bottles, I fell, crashing into the bottles, breaking them all. Of course I managed to break the fall with my head. There was blood everywhere. As it turned out, I only had to have two stitches, but the counselors were very upset. Two days later, it was long forgotten in a *boys will be boys* attitude.

I had been taught to swim going to the Lake Placid Club in the summers but I always objected bitterly. I must have been a terrible learner. The first year at camp, I remember I was so afraid I'd step into the water from the beach and there would be a gaping hole in the water and I would drop from sight. I fought the instructor all the time but finally at the end of the summer, I was able to swim a modest breaststroke.

One of my camping buddies was Gurnsey Gurnsbach. His father was Hugo Gurnsbach who was famousfor introducing *Popular Electronics, Popular Radio* and lots of magazines of that sort in the very early part of the century, around 1907. Then in the middle 1920s, he introduced a pulp magazine called *Amazing Stories* that popularized science fiction.

We were allowed to take a canoe or rowboat out on the water. At the south side of the bay, there was a peninsula with a swamp. We would maneuver the boat into the swamp and hunt for frogs and tiny catfish. There were lots of birds around and we felt quite like pioneers. Once we went down to Burlington, took the ferry across Lake Champlain, went over to the west side of lake and watched the trolley that went up the marble chasm . I was amazed to see where the marble had been eroded over time by the running water.

On the way in from Burlington to camp, halfway to the covered bridge where the road went around a cliff or a ledge along the river, there was a soft drink stand where they sold magazines. There was even a slot machine that we weren't allowed to use, but of course we did. Sometimes we would win a token and be able to buy a candy roll. There were also punch boards that were forbidden for kids to touch but I never let that stop me. The odds of winning anything, of course, were lousy. There was a candy stand nearby where they sold the most wonderful all-day suckers in various great flavors. They took hours to eat. They were made by the Crystal Confectionary Company of Burlington.

In August 1923, while at camp in Vermont, President Harding died during a trip to San Francisco. Vice President Coolidge was at his family farm in Vermont and was sworn in with a family Bible by candlelight. He went on to run again and win a full term in 1924. He'd gotten in trouble for talking too damn much and when elected, he remained "silent Cal" for years, having discovered it was better to remain quiet.

~

Even as a child newspapers had a monumental effect on me. I could hardly wait to learn to read. Some of my first memories were reading such incredible events of the time, such as the assassination of the Russian czar and his family. Reading about the Russian revolution *as it happened* influenced my desire to continue to study current events.

I was seven when the newspaper announced the enactment of the Eighteenth Amendment to the Constitution. It was to become effective January 12, 1920. The amendment prohibited the manufacture, sale or transport of intoxicating liquors. But there was a year's grace period and my father took advantage of it. I remember Dad and the family chauffeur driving to Wanamaker's. They proceeded to load the car with whiskey and wine. Although my parents were not heavy drinkers, there was a principal in his action. He obviously thought prohibition was nonsense.

Community amenities at Fieldston included a country club complete with tennis courts, even a two-lane bowling alley in the basement. Also in the basement was a dance floor which I stayed away from whenever possible. Although dances were sponsored for the youth, from time to time, I had a natural aversion to girls and to dancing and the combination was horrific for me. Although I eventually and happily would change my mind about girls as a young man, I never did change my mind about dancing.

Every now and then the movie theatre owner would bring silent movies to the club. And then something wondrous happened, something that was invented to break the silence, the development of the wireless. In 1921, there were two stations on the air, although they were not yet assigned frequency allocations, as such. The radio had been born and no one was more excited than I. The first radio delivered to the Baum house was the Paragon RA10, with an amplifier and horn loud speaker, made by Western Electric. It had a multitude of dials and I became instantly hooked to the intriguing world of radio. That intense interest has lasted a lifetime. The first radios were so primitive that when our family sold the house in 1969, there were still burn marks in the floor where battery acid had scored and scarred the wood.

Here I am in my new suit, all ready
for Barnard School for Boys.

The Harvey School and My Introduction to the Wonderful Technology of Radio

I attended Barnard until 1923, when at the age of eleven, my parents sent me off to boarding School in Hawthorne, New York. The Harvey School was located in Westchester County. My brothers, Jack and Peter, followed suit.

Harvey School had been founded several years earlier. Of course, the students referred to the nearby monastery as *the monkey house.* The school was originally built to serve as a large farmhouse and was located on quite a bit of land. But in 1923, there was already a dormitory, a large dining room, an ample kitchen, several classrooms, plus additional classrooms in the farmhouse itself and a modest-sized building that housed my least favorite places, the gymnasium. The grounds had a soccer field and a baseball field. I literally hated athletics and only participated when required to do so. One of the perks of our school being located on a working farm was a generous arbor loaded with delicious Concord grapes.

A Danish farmer who managed the property completed the pastoral setting. We had horses, a donkey, and even a pig that was fed from the school's garbage. We were nearly traumatized the day the pig was declared *surplus* and later served for dinner.

I was one of the youngest at the school, but after mastering several years of summer camp, I handled the transition well. In addition to basic courses, I took uniquely challenging courses such as Greek mythology. Unhappily, I was saddled with a course in music with which I was less than thrilled. On a weekly basis, a man came in to

31

teach about the great composers. It was a mandatory course that made absolutely no sense to me.

One silly thing teases my memory. In my first year at Harvey, when my youngest brother Peter was just learning to walk, Mother and Dad came up to school. Peter must have been a year and a half old. He was barefoot and I was terribly embarrassed. I remember thinking that all my classmates would wonder why the poor Baums couldn't afford to buy shoes for their youngest child.

Family vacations were treasured by all of us. At the end of summer camp in 1926, Mom and Dad arranged for a camp counselor to take Jack and me to Quebec City where we spent two nights at the Chateau Frontenac. We saw St. Ann de Bupre' Catholic Shrine and I thought it was phenomenal.

After we returned home to New York, our family went by train to Philadelphia to celebrate the Sesquicentennial marking the signing of the Declaration of Independence. On our way home, we took the train to Washington D.C. where I saw the impressive Capitol Dome for the first time. We stayed at the Mayfair Hotel that had recently opened.

Back at school, now thirteen, I discovered a friendship that would last a lifetime. Jim Wyld was the son of the vice-president of Foster and Wheeler, then one of the major power boiler companies in the country. Dad had designed their family home in Garden City, Long Island and while visiting my school, he recognized Mr. Wyld. Within minutes, his son Jim and I were on the road to becoming great pals.

Jim was hampered by a chronic heart murmur and had to be careful about over-exerting himself. That malady, coupled with my impatience at athletics, rapidly redirected us to other interests. Jim had a brilliant mind even then, and we became mutually fascinated with engineering, science and technology. At school, we'd wander down to the creek, take hours to build elaborate dams and locks, then just as we were leaving the site, would take great pleasure in destroying our work so we could watch the rushing water flood back into the creek.

It wasn't long before we were inseparable. On school vacations, we would take turns visiting each other's homes. I would take the Long Island Railroad to visit Jim and the next time, he would come into the city to visit me. We were separated when I went on to

Berkshire to complete my last four years of high school and Jim was sent to another school. We met whenever possible and took for granted our get-togethers during holidays and other school vacations. Jim developed a talent for writing lengthy, creative correspondence, a talent that would one day capture the interest of none other than the Smithsonian for his discussions of rocket technology interspersed with quickly drawn sketches detailing the mechanics of his thought process.

~

Long before I had a radio set of my own, I used to carry a catalog around. The catalog primarily sold radio parts, but also offered kits so you could build your own which was the practice of many people in those days. The company also made a very high quality, three-stage tuned-radio-frequency set that was actually state of the art at that time. Unfortunately, they spent so much time improving it that it broke. That's probably why I was able to buy my first set so cheaply.

Then came Christmas 1926 and my family really splurged. Dad built a little enclosed radio shop for me in the attic right above my bedroom.

In the far end of the attic, directly above the maids' rooms, Dad constructed another small area where Jack could put his incipient insect museum. Jack and some friends in the neighborhood had become interested in entomology and minerals. One of them had secured the loan of a used garage stable on the other side of River Avenue, and the neighborhood gang started their own little kids' museum there. From that exposure, Jack became so interested in minerals that he later earned a degree from Harvard in mineralogy.

My other big present that Christmas was a complete set of parts to build a Remler superheterodyne receiver. RCA had the patent for superheterodynes tied up and would not allow anyone to make them commercially, but those who were able to build their own equipment could buy kits. The RCA was the top of the line receiver—too expensive for people of modest means. The Remler Company was based in California [*Remler Company Ltd.; in the late 1920s also known as Gray and Danielson Mfg. Co. –ed*]. In many respects, I believe they were unique. They made variable capacitors and both sets of plates moved as they intermeshed. The shape of the plates varied from the conventional ones, but they made pretty much a straight-line frequency. Remler also made 45-kilohertz intermediate-frequency transformers necessary for those radios.

In those days all radio tubes were three-element: filament, grid and plate. The circuits were straightforward; one had only to look at a circuit diagram and could tell immediately what every part was supposed to do and why it was there. A superheterodyne radio in those days would be comprised of a detector, an oscillator to drive the detected signal to a 45-kilohertz intermediate frequency or IF, three stages of IF in increasing amplification, a second detector to turn it back into audio, and two stages of audio to turn it into what could be heard. The tubes were standard 201As; five-volt quarter-amp filament, a grid and a plate, designed to operate on 90 to 135 volts, all from dry cells, that is except for the *lovely* acid-filled 36 volt storage batteries.

By 1925, there were already more than five hundred radio stations, almost all of them independent. NBC was just starting out and Columbia had not yet been created. The FCC's predecessor had sorted out the frequencies reasonably well and the broadcast band ranged from 550 to 1500 kilohertz. This was before FM, of course, and television was only a dream. There were a handful of worldwide short-wave stations as a consequence. I had become an avid broadcast band DXer [*DX is ham radio jargon for "distance" –ed.*] whenever I was home from school and early that summer I was working for Jack.

Before we took our big trip, my radio died. I finally determined the problem was that an intermediate-frequency transformer had opened. There was no way to fix it so I went down to buy another transformer, but I didn't realize at the time that the transformers were sold as matched trios. The one I bought turned out to have a somewhat different peak frequency than the balance of the set. I knew that the Remler Company was in San Francisco so I bundled the three transformers up and took them on our big trip.

While in San Francisco, Dad and I went to Montgomery Street, where they had a laboratory although the manufacturing plant was not located there. They checked out the transformers there and found the one had a different frequency, so they got some wires together, wrapped them into a spiral, hooked them into the transformers, cut a little bit off here and a little bit off there, and *voila`*! - they're all tuned in line. So I got home, installed it back in the set, and they worked beautifully. One of the first DX stations I heard - mind you, this was in September 1925 and I was in New York - was KGO in San Francisco!

It was an exciting time. The world was on the brink of so many inventions, so many exceptional feats. I had become an avid reader and was thrilled to see the name of Charles Lindbergh spring up in the headlines in 1927. Imagining about a man in a small airplane flying all the way across the Atlantic to land in Paris, France created a watershed year in my life. My eyes had been opened to endless possibilities and I could think of nothing but technology.

When I arrived home from school that summer, I happily discovered that Dad had been talking to Jack High, a radio afficionado and amateur ham radio operator. Jack made radio sets that you couldn't buy in the stores. RCA had the patent on a certain circuit and the best radio sets had those particular circuits, by far. So no one could commercially make those with the patented RCA circuit. For years, in our home, we'd had radios privately made with that circuit. I had been interested and had built some sets. Jack and was developing loudspeakers in his garage on the Hudson River.

Radios had by this time developed from ear-phone and horn-type speakers to cone speakers. But cones were large, with a free-mounted driver behind them. And the quality was terribly poor. Jack had found out he could mount a cone in a baffle, which protected sound waves from interfering with each other—thus improving the sound.

Hour after hour, I would help Jack disassemble the horn speakers, remove the drivers, and mount the magnet and driver on a bracket connected to the cone. We experimented with everything we could find and I began to be of real value around the shop. It was a learning process and took an inordinate amount of time, but we ended up with a product that was a vast improvement over what was available at the time. And best of all, I was bringing home a whopping five dollars a week that summer and savoring the sweet taste of challenge and achievement for the first time.

~

My parents had adopted Mrs. Jessie Case, a wonderful companion for Mother, expanding us to a family of six. The woman quickly became an integral part of the Baum family and traveled with us on all our vacation trips from that point on.

One hot August day, in 1927, we all packed up and headed to Grand Central Station where we took a night train to Montreal. The country was still in the throes of prohibition and Dad scouted around Quebec looking for a liquor store. Finding one, he went in and asked for a "nice old port." He took his bottle with him on the train and we returned home with his illegal contraband several weeks later.

We took several trips across Canada. There was no air-conditioning in the 1920s and observation cars were open, filthy with soot, and smoky. But that little inconvenience did not mar our trips across the expansive wasteland, especially the moment I experienced my first view of the Rockies. We stopped at the Continental Divide and my brothers and I enjoyed the moment of realizing exactly where we were standing, as if on a map.

While in Banff, Alberta Canada, the family met a most colorful man by the name of Tom Wilson. The rugged pioneer was credited with discovering Lake Louise, which was originally formed by a glacier. He was searching for a stray horse at the time when he came upon the most beautiful lake he had ever seen. He named it Emerald Lake but the Canadian government renamed it years later.

Banff National Park was Canada's first national park and remains to this day a year-round protected wilderness area. The scenery offers alpine beauty surrounded by the Rocky Mountain landscape. Lake Louise is now one of the finest ski resorts in the world and the terrain is spread over four separate mountain faces. In the mid-1920s, the area was basically untouched and its natural beauty remarkable.

On one such trip, after arriving in Seattle, we were strolling through a hotel lobby when several gentlemen recognized my dad. They were attending a convention for the Northwest Society of Architects and instantly adopted him into their activities. A lumber company executive from the Long Bell Lumber Company also recognized him and made arrangements for Dad and me to go up into the mountains in Longview, Washington to watch the fascinating logging operation.

The family went on to Portland, then to Mt. Hood and northern California. On one glorious summer day, we took the Oakland Ferry to San Francisco. It was nine o'clock in the morning. Coming into the bay with the sun behind us, I stood at the front of the boat and saw San Francisco for the first time. There were no high rises to spoil the scenery.

I was astounded at the number of cable cars. We took the trolley out to the site of the 1915 Exposition, then the ferry to Sausalito and marveled at the incredible expanse of water that did not yet include the Golden Gate Bridge. The next day we went to Los Angeles and stayed for a week at the Biltmore Hotel.

Every morning we would walk through the park at Percy Square, marveling at all the lush tropical plants, on our way to a spectacular cafeteria for breakfast. The cafeteria was Clifton's. Today, the enterprise is better than ever and still fully operational. The family who has owned it through five generations has fed the poor since the early days surrounding the Great Depression. No customers were ever turned away and during one ninety-day period, ten thousand ate free of charge. Our family certainly enjoyed our meals there and we three boys delighted in being able to choose from such a wonderful variety of foods displayed out on a huge buffet table.

Parked along the streets were big, open tour buses, operated by shills for real estate development. They would drive the tourists around and pressure them to buy lots and houses. Vacations turned out to be quite an education for us, as kids.

Our family, which of course included Mrs. Case, spent an entire week taking in the sights of Los Angeles. We went to MGM where we watched films being made, took a trip to an ostrich farm and another to Gay's Lion Farm. My brothers and I were delighted when Mother allowed us to swim in the Pacific Ocean. It was a first for us. In Santa Monica, Dad, Jack and I strapped ourselves into an airplane and got to fly up and down the coast. It was exhilarating! It was August 1927 and that five dollar airplane ride was my first experience in the sky. And now I had another reason to love technology. I would have to fly again - and again.

We ended our summer trip by traveling through the Panama Canal back to New York by way of Havana. I took something very special back with me. I earned some money by betting on simulated horse races. We had left Los Angeles on the SS Manchuria. I spent two days watching the adults bet on the fake horse races by rolling the dice and moving their horse around the track. I suddenly realized that once a horse won, no one would bet on him again. I figured he had as much change as any other, so I started betting on the horse that won. After all, the odds favored my horse, I thought. Proceeds for the races went to the Seaman's Fund. But I pocketed twenty dollars, which I quickly spent. I bought a parrot—cage and all. I wasn't even questioned when I re-boarded the ship, parrot cage in hand. At the time, the Panama Canal had been open for twelve years. I was fascinated by the locks as Dad explained how they worked.

My return to New York at the end of vacation was a return to my last year at Harvey. In one summer, I had acquired a lifetime of experiences and enjoyed immeasurable moments chock-full of wonder!

~

Upon returning to Harvey School, I had built a battery-operated, one-tube single-circuit oscillating receiver. I think it used the 201A receiving tube, the standard at the time. There were five or six volts in the filament and 45-90 volts from a B cell. It used a variable capacitor across a coil, connected to the grid of the tube. There may have been a grid leak resistor in there, the capacitor across the earphones, six volts in the filament and 45 volts on the plate. Since the circuit was oscillating, it was alive all the time and I couldn't really tune in the capacitor. So I put a nail on the little pedestal, and moved it in and out of the conducting coil so I could zero out the oscillator and listen to the station without the squeal.

In what must have been one of my first forays into Courtlandt Street radio row, I had brought three Edison nickel-alkaline storage battery cells. These were rechargeable. I bought a charger to keep them charged from time to time, rather than using a dry cell to run the filament off the tube. Each student had a small storage closet that had no door. I stored them on a shelf in the closet, standing upright, preparing to see how I could arrange the circuit to recharge them, and to see what voltage I should use.

Before going to school that year, I had bought a new suit, a horrible blue-olive-green color, which my mother hated. Why she let me buy it, I don't know. In any event, the pants were hanging in the closet directly under the shelf. Somehow one or more of the batteries tipped over, and the alkaline content leaked out and ran off the shelf and onto one of the pant legs, a couple inches above the knee. When I saw the stain, I was in shock. I picked it up and it disintegrated in my fingers. It was only the one leg that was affected, so I found a pair of scissors and very carefully cut off the whole leg just above the part that had been destroyed.

When I told my mother about the problem, she was very unhappy with me. I thought she had begun to cry, but she hadn't. She had started to laugh and laugh and couldn't seem to stop. In those days, one didn't wear short pants, especially not at my age. One time I heard her telling her friend about her son who had saved half a pair of pants by cutting off the damaged leg. Every time she mentioned it, she laughed so hard I never did get punished for the event.

The next Christmas, Mother and Dad really bought me something special - the parts to make a Remler Infradyne set. This was two stages of tuned radio frequency, plus all the rest of the superheterodyne form. It used some low current tubes, 199s, so the battery drain wasn't too terrible. I got myself a very unique product, especially for those days. It was an A-battery eliminator, which plugged in to generate the power for the tube filaments. The kit had a preformed color-coded wiring harness which made wiring it up a separate task, but it was still a real exercise in complexity. The set lasted me for two years, till I bought my first real manufactured radio - a Silver-Marshall set, again, state of the art.

My next radio, which I must have purchased in the winter of 1932, was an E8 Scott all-wave radio, short wave as well as broadcast. The short wave was in plug-in coils and you had to open the set, take out cans, and plug in several short wave coils. It was really very sensitive, a very satisfactory radio.

I had that for two years, then really splurged. I bought myself the next model of the Scott radio, a switchable long wave-short wave receiver, which I still have. Wouldn't dare turn it on now. The capacitor had to be replaced, but it's still built in there—it was a great radio, with push-pull output stages, and great loudspeaker. Of course all loudspeakers in those days were electromagnetic and the field coil of the loudspeaker was part of the filter system. One learned how to make powerful permanent magnets to do away with the field coil.

~

Harvey had an athletics program, of course - soccer in the fall, basketball in the winter and baseball in the spring. As I have admitted freely, I was never athletically inclined. There was nothing wrong with my eyesight, but I could never follow moving objects accurately, so ball games were simply not an option. I finally talked my way out of even attempting to be on a team and during my last two years at school, officials let me go for walks in the woods around the school, which I loved. I would wander down along the river looking for birds. That was much more fun to me than struggling to play a sport and knowing I had no talent for it, or sitting on a bench for a team and doing nothing. I remember one time while wandering through the woods I found a whole patch of lady slipper wild orchids. I dug some up, brought them home, planted them on the hill behind our house, and they took hold. For years and years we had wild orchids growing behind our house.

Sometimes with friends we would do a bit of archaeology. Running between the Selmo River, south of the school, and Rockefeller Hill, there were the remains of a road that appeared to have been the original Albany Post road. There were bits and pieces of foundations marking the places where houses had once stood. Somehow we would dig around a bit and find shards of pottery, which was a great discovery.

Wandering through the woods north of the school, we came across a turf battle between squirrels and flying squirrels, and I couldn't believe what I saw. The large squirrels were chasing the flying squirrels who had the advantage because they could jump from limb to limb in a way that the bigger squirrels could not. It was absolutely fascinating. I also found that the big squirrels were endeavoring to neuter the flying squirrels. I spoke to the headmaster at the school about that, and he looked it up in a book and said yes, those things did happen.

Another time, under some bushes, I saw the remains of a rotting wood box. On the side you could see it was dynamite. It was a well-built box. The lid came away easily and there were some greasy brown tubes, which I easily recognized as being dynamite from the times when the workers were dynamiting rocks in Fieldston. We did not touch them, but we did report the incident, and the principal must have sent somebody out to recover the box because I never heard anything more about it.

On Sundays, Harvey held a brief non-denominational Sunday service in the common room library in the main building. Everyone was required to attend except the Catholic boys who went off to mass somewhere. Only one Jewish boy was registered at school and I never knew what he did to worship.

Mr. Carter would slide the vertical piano out for the hymns. The gentleman who ran our little store and also kept the books for the school was a former minister and he would give a brief sermon. The service was very informal. In later years at school, I found I could get a taxi, go to North White Plains, catch a train into Harlem, get off at 125th Street, and Dad and Mother could come down to meet me. I could be home for the balance of Sunday and still return to school in time for dinner Sunday night. Every few weeks, I'd take a seat near the door and when I'd see a taxi outside, I'd sneak out while Mr. Carter was playing a hymn. I just did it. I never got specific clearance. I had been successful in my stealth four or five times and returned one time to be called into Mr. Carter's office. I explained to him what I had done, and he said "you never had permission to do that."

I replied, "I never thought I needed permission to do that." He obviously wanted to make a real example of me, so I was grounded for two months. I couldn't even take my walks in the woods. I thought that was most unfair, although I admitted I had been doing it for some time and had never been caught.

In the spring of 1928, my parents had found a new boarding school that would take me the rest of the way through high school. Located west of Hartford, Connecticut, it was the pride of the Northeast, having recently been founded. Unfortunately, when I visited the school to look it over, I had a severe case of influenza that evidently distressed the headmaster. The gentleman wasn't impressed and I was not accepted. I returned to the Harvey School and was immediately put to bed in the infirmary where I remained for five long days.

After graduating from Harvey, our family took another memorable, summer trips, starting with a train trip to Buffalo where we stayed at the Statler, a rather prestigious hotel. After checking out of the Statler, we ran down to the docks to catch a steamer when Mom discovered she had lost the diamond out of her ring. Dad scurried back to the hotel and found it on the lobby floor, directly in front of the cashier's window. We went on with our plans to board and were soon steaming through Lake Huron, then on through the Sioux Canal at Sioux Ste. Marie, Michigan and on into Canada.

Heading west, we found ourselves a few days later at Yellow Stone Park and were awestruck by the hot springs. After visiting Old Faithful, we took our driver's suggestion to see The Grand Tetons where Dad snapped a picture of Mom feeding a bear.

Berkshire School
and How the Wall St. Journal Changed My Life

Once again I returned home from summer vacation just in time to pack and head off to my new high school. My parents had enrolled me in Berkshire School in Sheffield, Massachusetts, south of Great Barrington. It was only three and a half miles from the Connecticut line. Founded in 1907, Berkshire had a roster of one hundred ten students. The campus was spread over two hundred acres. Academically, Berkshire had already earned a reputation for excellence as a college preparatory school that offered French, Latin, mathematics and physics: all the courses required to challenge a college-bound student.

Being a boys' boarding school, there was basically no contact with young ladies save for heavily supervised dances once or twice a year. Girls were invited from the nearest finishing schools but I hardly noticed, being unabashedly timid where the opposite sex was concerned.

When I attended dances at all, I would stand and watch the other fellows dance with girls and wonder what all the fuss was about. It was a strange ritual, dating, and I was far too interested in other things. In addition to my love of electronics, I had found photography to be another interest and my mind was already occupied.

One weekend when I was home from Berkshire and Peter was still at Harvey, Mother and Dad decided to drive up to Harvey school. I was learning to drive, so I got to drive Mother's Packard part way. I can still visibly recall almost every inch of that road from Fieldston to

43

Hartsdale and Thornwood, then through Hawthorne and finally arriving at the Harvey School. In those days, the roads were all two-lane roads and you had to drive through each and every town. There were no bypass roads or highways, as we know them today. We got into one of the towns, I think it was Thornwood, and I had to make a quick right-hand turn. Somehow I nearly lost control of the car. No damage was done, but about a hundred feet on, I was relieved of my driving responsibilities.

A number of years later, well after I learned to drive but before I had my own car, I wanted to drive up to visit Harvey School, so I borrowed Dad's car. Dad had an older Franklin, a bit *long in the tooth* by the early '30s' standards. On the way home, I was stopped for speeding. The police officer wanted to know if I had a right to drive the car and I said, "No one would steal a car as old as this," to which he agreed. He sort of *putzed* around for a bit, then indicated that if I were to purchase a couple tickets to the local policemen's charity event, I might be able to bypass a speeding ticket. So I paid five dollars, a lot of money in those days, for two tickets to the policemen's ball, and away I went, driving more carefully.

~

1929 was the peak year of the great boom of that decade. Every time I visited Jim Wyld on Long Island, I would invariably pick up Mr. Wyld's Wall Street Journal. I became an avid reader of this tremendous resource for business and finance. In March of 1929, I learned that the Federal Reserve Board had tried to quash excessive speculation. They had raised the discount rate to a higher percentage to quell the economic boom. Under pressure, the Fed dropped the re-discount rate and the boom continued. Little did they realize how the stage was set for the ensuing crash that would come months later.

I was home on vacation at that time and while riding home to Riverdale on the suburban bus from downtown New York, was listening to riders discussing the iniquity of the government trying to kill the stock market boom.

But a Baum family trip had been planned for the summer of 1929 and the world hadn't yet gone topsy-turvy. My uncle was Jerome Barnum, publisher of the Syracuse Post-Standard. His son Jerry was invited on our family vacation and we all hopped the train in Montreal to ride clear across Canada again.

We took a boat to Victoria then on to Seattle and on July 3rd, I remember standing in a brokerage office watching the ticker tape. The market was going wild. July 4th, we left Seattle on the SS Admiral Rogers, bound for Alaska.

We stopped in Vancouver where Jack and I discovered a pool table on the lower floor of the Vancouver Hotel. One afternoon we were happily playing that *wicked game* permitted for men eighteen and older, when a member of the hotel staff discovered our sin and shooed us away from the pool table. Fairly mild antics for a young man compared to today, I'd say.

In Juneau, Mom and Dad found an oil painting of a tall ship at sea and fell in love with it, paying the astronomical price of three hundred dollars or so. The piece, now over seventy years old, was painted in 1929 by Sydney Laurence and was recently appraised for somewhere between thirty-five to sixty thousand dollars. It graces my dining room wall to this day.

We went on the narrow gauge railroad through the famous Yukon Pass to Whitehorse in Yukon Territory. Then we took a side trip via rail, boarded a lake steamer, and finally took a short portage railroad to Atlin Lake, British Columbia's largest natural lake, which was hauntingly breathtaking. The little town of Atlin is located a few miles south of the Yukon border. One particular highlight of our trip was visiting a virtually deserted gold mining town nearby.

Returning to White Horse, we took the stern wheel Yukon Riverboat down to Dawson. Though it was also virtually deserted, there was one gold mining dredge still operating.

One moment that took our breath away was on a steamer up the Yukon where we had to stop momentarily for a huge herd of caribou to migrate across the river. There were thousands of them.

There was word that an American Curtis plane was coming in. The pilot was trying to make a record run all the way from Washington DC up to Nome, Alaska and back again. The pilot stopped for an hour or so to refuel, barely giving me enough time to get to the Whitehorse Airport, buy an envelope with a special Yukon stamp on it and hand it to the pilot who promised to mail it when he got home. Later on, we learned that the plane had crashed somewhere in British Columbia. Fortunately, the pilot survived. I eventually discovered that even my letter survived the crash when I received it, weeks later, in the mail.

~

Then Armageddon struck. It was late 1929 and the Great Depression struck so hard, the impact would affect the country for nearly a decade. Excessive stock speculation had kept the stock market on an artificial high and this, coupled with the uneven distribution of wealth between classes brought the economy crashing down. It seemed that the only businesses remaining unaffected were those depending on radios. In the mid-1920s, major broadcasting companies such as NBC had begun to appear. By the 1930s, forty percent of American families had radios in their homes.

At Berkshire, students were not yet allowed to have radios at school and the boys all brought their wind-up phonographs from home. Already an entrepreneur-in-the-making, I built an electric phonograph for myself, then started selling them to my schoolmates. In the last two years at Berkshire, I made enough money to take the sting out of the depression.

The Great Depression had fiercely grasped the heart of the country and Dad's business began to suffer from the impact. The era of designing really grand homes was dying off. Large construction projects were few and far between. Non-essential building had nearly come to a standstill. Luxurious estates were for the most part a thing of the past. Dad had designed several large estates such as for the president of Richfield Oil Company and other executives. But even before the depression, people had begun to turn to more modest homes and a less opulent lifestyle. Times were changing.

At Christmas 1929, my Grandmother Crouse presented each of us three boys with ten shares of stock from a very special company. It was a wonderful, quality investment. Stock had come down from sixty-seven dollars a share to thirty-seven dollars a share during the great crash. It paid a dividend of a dollar sixty. I was intrigued. More than intrigued. What had happened to me was the beginning of a fascination I would carry throughout my entire life. I had made a little money from selling phonographs at school and desperately wanted to have my own investments, to be completely in charge of my own destiny, and finance was where I could find that incredibly unique and rewarding challenge.

I always had trouble with foreign languages. I had taken French at Harvey and it was also required at Berkshire. I always used to say it took me four years to learn the first year of French and still, not very well. I was the despair of Dean, the French language instructor who came from northern Vermont. Everyone used to say he spoke French with a Canadian accent. But even more difficult for me was Latin, which I failed in the school year 1929-30, so during the summer of 1930, I was required to be tutored. My poor mother arranged for the sister of some famous novelist who worked for Columbia University to tutor me that summer. I was not a good student.

Once, Jim Wyld gave me some assistance, and the tutor said I did very well indeed, but two weeks later, when I did poorly again, she complained to my mother that I wasn't working hard enough.

For some reason, in early September, I desperately wanted to go up to Syracuse to attend the state fair - God knows why. Mother said that unless I could get clearance from the tutor, I could not go. Well, that was enough to get me by. I did make it to the state fair and the reason I remember that is because the racing cars all used castor oil lubricant. That's a smell you never forget any more than you forget the first time you hear the rattle of a rattlesnake. I had worked hard enough to be allowed to go to the fair and returned to Berkshire to take the make-up exam. I barely squeaked by and that was all the Latin I ever had to take.

~

In the summer of 1930, the family decided not to travel. Since the beginning of the depression, orators would stand at Union Square and 14th Street in New York City, preaching Communism to the crowds. As a young capitalist, I loved to stand there and argue with them.

And I was just as happy working on amplifier power systems through the summer, with some of my dad's colleagues. The amplification systems sold for thirty-five hundred dollars and were used for large institutions such as a large church close to Columbia

University, a church that Rockefeller supported. I spent my summer steeped in electronics and technology and learned a great deal.

My work also entailed converting Stromberg Carlson radio sets into quality sets that could drive loudspeakers and required customer installations. We built power supplies and power amplifiers and did custom installations. We installed a system at the chapel at Princeton. We also built a phonograph system with a 100-watt amplifier for one of the Dupont's estates. We even built remote control radios and remote control record changers. These things were revolutionary at the time.

As the depression deepened, the Kruegger and Toll stock my grandmother had given me dropped to seventeen dollars a share, but I still believed in it. So I went down to Wall St. and bought additional shares of K and T with my own money. In March of 1932, my stock had dropped to nine dollars, and while home from school again, I traipsed back down to Wall Street to buy even more K and T stock.

En route to Wall Street on a Saturday morning, I got sidetracked and for some inexplicable reason, got off the subway at Thirty-second Street, ending up in Macy's Record Department. My eyes caught sight of something that literally made me catch my breath. On the floor before me was a rare, very expensive record changer with a ticket price of sixty-four dollars. I could hardly believe it. I knew they were selling for more than a hundred dollars and was certain it had been marked down by mistake. I never got to Wall Street that morning. Instead, I invested in something even more exciting and I never regretted that purchase. But I went home that afternoon without buying more K and T stock.

The next morning in Paris, the president of Kruegger and Toll put a pistol to his head and blew his brains out. The public came to find out the man was a crook. He had milked his own company by using the firm as collateral for his personal investments.

As stock in his company would go down, the banks would call in loans. The owner became so desperate to get the price of his stock up that he manipulated his own company to buy his own shares. As the company was finally running out of money, he actually had counterfeited thirty-five million dollars of Italian government bonds. He had taken the bonds to one of the New York banks and actually convinced the bank manager that the deal for the bonds was a secret deal between Kruegger and Toll and Mussolini, the dictator of Italy.

He had told the banker that the bonds were good, but the fact that they were issued by the Italian government would have been very upsetting to the public, so it was very important that word not get out. The banker bought the story and accepted the bonds as additional collateral for allowing more funds to be loaned to Kruegger and Toll. The company's basic business was the manufacture of matches. They had a monopoly on matches in several countries around the world. The business was a strong business but the owner ran it right into the ground.

When the story finally got out and the house of cards came tumbling down, the man put a pistol to his head. In due course, Kruegger and Toll stock went to zero and I framed the stock certificate and hung it on the wall of my home. It remains there to this day. I had been taught a lesson I would never forget. From that moment on, I became a value investor, never again a speculator. My grandmother had given me the initial shares, but I'd kept buying it because it was cheap. From that moment on, I always made a point of studying a company's background.

On the other side of the coin, the Alaska stock I bought on my own started making money as the depression forced operating costs down and the price of gold went up with Roosevelt's devaluation of the dollar. I did quite well on that stock.

~

In the summer of 1931, still not realizing the full depths of the depression, my parents signed us up for another incredible family trip. We took off from New York on the SS Resolute of the Hamburg-American line for a cruise to Iceland and Norway, with plans to cruise back down the beautiful coastline of Norway. But en route to Iceland, we ran into such a ferocious storm, everyone stayed in his cabin. Everyone, that is, except me. I had convinced myself that even though the seas were extremely rough, I was not going to be sick. When we finally got to Iceland, seas were still so rough, we were unable to anchor and disembark for quite some time.

When the ship was finally cleared to leave, we went on to North Cape, Norway where Jack and I raced each other up to the top of the bluff. This spot is the northernmost part of Europe. Then we went down the coast of Norway to Oslo, then to Stockholm where Dad was impressed with the quality of modern design, then on to Helsinki where he admired the city's architecture. Then on to Leningrad we went. Even though there were no diplomatic relations between the USSR and the United States at the time, Dad had managed to get a visa for himself, Jack and me, allowing us to leave the ship and actually go inside Russia.

After docking at Leningrad, a bureaucratic nightmare kept us ship bound until issues could be unraveled, but we three willing explorers were finally permitted off the ship. I recall the thrill of seeing the winter palace. We took a night train from Leningrad to Moscow, traveling in cars that were surely built prior to World War I.

A taxi took us from the train station to the Metropol Hotel and I added another special memory to my family scrapbook. The quaint entrance opened into an elegant and spacious dining room surrounded by glass walls. An all-girl orchestra was playing "The Waltz" from the opera *Evgenij Onegin* by Tschaikovsky. It was eight o'clock in the morning and that moment was indelibly implanted in my mind. I never forgot it. Anytime I heard that piece, the entire incredibly exquisite scene completely replayed in my head.

Soap was evidently hard to come by in Russia. Permanently etched in my memory was the smell of the unbathed populace as Dad and I strolled through the streets of Moscow. Returning to Leningrad, we traveled by ship to Helsinki where the transition was remarkable. The city was fresh smelling, clean and lovely. We moved on to Copenhagen, and finally via trains and ferry to Berlin. The depression had deepened, first to Austria, then to England, then throughout Germany. The Nazi party was building up its strength fighting socialists and the democratic people, and was struggling for power. It was a difficult time and a lot to take in, I thought, for a privileged young man from New York.

We took the train to Nuremberg, and the family went on while I stayed over in that incredible city for one more day to see my very first opera. It was Mozart's "Magic Flute." I flew to Cologne on a Tri-Motor Fokker passenger plane to join the family. En route, as I was taking pictures from the window, a German passenger became very upset with me. I told him that I was an American and since there could be no military targets, no German should object to my taking photographs. This was three years before Hitler's rise to power and the start of German rearmament.

I arrived in Cologne before the family and was able to explore the city on my own. I was enormously impressed by the Cologne Cathedral. After we joined up, the family went on to Amsterdam. We delighted in experiencing Edam, the cheeses and all the girls in wooden shoes. We went on to Hamburg, then home. It was the fall of 1931 and I was ready to start my last year of high school at Berkshire.

It was 1932. I had graduated from Berkshire and the country was in the depths of the depression. I spent the summer touring the United States with Jim Wyld in a very tired first-edition Model A Ford. We drove to Washington DC during the Bonus March. Veterans of World War I were protesting, demanding that they be paid a bonus to help them through the depression. Some politician had become an advocate for the cause and organized the march on the nation's capitol.

They even set up a shantytown in DC. Hoover was president at the time and the Democrats were in control of Congress. There was no way, in the throes of the depression, a bonus of any kind could be offered from the federal government. The general public became upset with shantytown, and Congress laid blame directly on Hoover. General Douglas MacArthur took it upon himself to disburse the marchers, and with one fell swoop, disbanded shantytown. It had been an effort in futility but an interesting experience for us to witness firsthand.

Jim and I toured all the museums in DC then went on to Richmond. We made our way down to Asheville, North Carolina, then across the Appalachians to Tennessee where we spent a night in Crossville. Gasoline was thirteen cents a gallon and wherever we chose to stop, we stopped. At twenty, we weren't concerned about being stranded. Every day offered us a new adventure. We knew we could roll up in a blanket somewhere or stay with a family.

People often rented out a spare room in their homes for a dollar and twenty-five cents. Since motels weren't available, homeowners would advertise vacancies by putting a sign in their windows. For a night, weary travelers could be part of a family, sit in the living room and listen to the radio, sometimes even share a family breakfast for twenty-five cents, then move on rested and relaxed.

One rainy night, we stopped at a coffee shop and visited with the locals. One fellow asked us, "Hey, kids, ever seen a still?" Of course we hadn't. The man took us into the hills and showed us a Kentucky still where he made moonshine.

In Kentucky, we stopped near Mammoth Cave, after which we drove to Lexington, Kentucky where we visited Jim's uncle on his tobacco farm. He raised hogs on the side. We stayed two weeks and spent the lazy summer days touring the countryside.

While we were there, we came across a flash flood that had washed a bunch of hogs out into the stream. Fortunately for Jim's uncle, his hogs were ready for market and as we quickly learned, *a fat pig floats!* Within a couple of days, we had helped him gather up all the hogs and off to market they went. We became enthralled with his uncle's dog. The silly dog had been trained to amble through the tobacco patch, find the worms that threatened to destroy the crop, grab them, shake them, kill them, and hunt for more. Smart dog.

Jim and I came across the trolley line that ran from Lexington to Versailles. The flood had caused the wire to be downed. For some inexplicable reason, maybe a throwback to my fascination with outlets and electricity, I picked up the wire. It must have been providence that I had on rubber shoes. I received quite a jolt and was a little stunned, but I wasn't hurt as badly as I could have been.

As a bona fide, card-carrying Republican, I had attached a Herbert Hoover sticker on the front bumper of the car. Jim, however, was a Norman Thomas Socialist and had carefully placed a Norman Thomas sticker on the back bumper. "The hell with the democrats," we had decided, foregoing a mule or some such party sticker. After spending some time touring around central Kentucky, we drove up through Detroit to visit the Ford factory. The manufacturing plant was making the first V-8s.

It was still during prohibition. One evening, we stopped at a coffee shop and quickly discovered it was a speakeasy.

We picked up my dad in Syracuse and the three of us drove back to New York together.

The summer's events were capped off quite dramatically. Jim and I drove up to southern New Hampshire to visit a classmate from Berkshire at Squam Lake and got to witness a full eclipse of the sun. How could we have known that a movie called "On Golden Pond" starring Henry Fonda would be filmed at this very site more than fifty years later? We returned home exhausted and exhilarated from a full summer's exploration. Jim left to begin his sophomore year at Princeton and I was preparing to enter Cornell.

CORNELL UNIVERSITY

It was the fall of 1932. I had returned from a wonderful summer, packed up Mother's Franklin and my parents drove me to Ithaca for my first view of Cornell. I'll never forget it. Actually, I had originally tried to get into MIT but that school had required two foreign languages. Oddly enough, I had two: French and Latin. But the *powers that be* refused to accept the latter as a foreign language. No one thought to question the decision. It was MIT, after all. But I had been easily accepted by Cornell and would remember forever my first drive onto the Cornell campus, coming in from the east, down by a power plant. That road would eventually become the location for the engineering part of the campus. I had rented a room in a rooming house at 517 Stewart Avenue, right on the edge of campus. The house remains a rooming house to this day.

Days later, I walked across campus, taking it all in. Bells were ringing and the campus was absolutely beautiful. How happy I was to feel as if I were an integral part of this prestigious university and this, I thought, was all part of me.

Once on campus, I quickly noticed that only one block from the rooming house was a building that I thought was most probably a broadcasting station. The station was probably housed in the Unitarian Church, I figured, because that structure had two radio towers on the roof. As I went through my registration process, I was asked my religious affiliation. Without hesitation, I responded, "Unitarian!" I thought I might be permitted to do some work with the radio station if I were involved with the church. Little did I know the radio station had been closed down for three years.

54

I enrolled in the College of Engineering and began immediately to enjoy college life. There was no hazing at that time and the worst humiliation I had to suffer was to wear my little gray beanie during my freshman year.

The first year, my courses were all mandated - machine shop, foundry, surveying, math courses, and drafting. In a required course of physical education, which included a section on hygiene, I've always been fond of saying, "I learned the facts of life and what my heart was for."

As a boy, while visiting my grandmother's house, I had discovered the physics books my grandfather had used at Yale in 1880. Fascinated, I had read all his textbooks, just for fun, and was happily ahead of the curve during my entire time at Cornell. The books had provided me with the mechanics of physics, including pendulums and the acceleration of gravity, everything I needed, as basics had remained the same. I hated drafting but loved physics. I recall suffering enormous embarrassment upon opening my hygiene book, however, to see the explicit drawings relating to an anatomy lesson.

It didn't take me long to know that engineering was not my calling. Although I enjoyed it somewhat, I found that I was so interested in business, I decided to use engineering as a background. So for a while, I pursued a physics major.

I had pledged Phi Delta Theta and had been accepted. This was the same fraternity my dad had belonged to at Syracuse University thirty years before. The fraternity house was a nice one, located north of the engineering quadrangle, across a ravine and suspension bridge. I stayed in that house from my sophomore year through graduation. It was still Prohibition and for house parties, beer was delivered in big gunnysacks marked PEANUTS...from some brewery in Pennsylvania. The brewery had been operating all through Prohibition. Farmers would go into Canada and buy liquor, smuggle it back, and sell it. There were always ways to get around the law.

John Dobson was my fraternity brother and roommate for my last three years. We shared a two-room suite that included a study and a bedroom. In addition to being a mechanical engineer major, John was an editor of the town's daily morning paper, the Cornell Sun. Once a week John would stay up most of the night putting the paper to bed.

The one thing I was not terribly excited about at Cornell was their mandatory ROTC. Students were given a choice of first year infantry or cavalry. I had never been on a horse in my life and had no intentions of getting on a horse at college, requirement or not, so while John signed up for Cavalry, I signed up for the Infantry. I strongly believe, to this day, that I was most probably one of the worst ROTC students Cornell University ever had.

In my second year, I was thrilled to find out that the ROTC program had a Signal Corps, and with my interest in communications, quickly signed up for it. But alas, after one glorious semester in the Signal Corps, from which I brought home an A+, I had a scheduling conflict with other required courses and was forced to return to the Infantry. The three semesters in the Infantry gained me three C-minuses. My A-plus was lost in the shuffle. But after two years of ROTC, I finally celebrated the completion of that requirement.

On March 4, 1933, Franklin Delano Roosevelt was inaugurated. Herbert Hoover's term had ended. I celebrated that date by being inducted into the Phi Delts at a formal dinner.

The first thing Roosevelt did was to issue an executive order to close all the banks so people wouldn't make a run on them. The President needed time to organize the country's economy.

Banks near campus used to let students sneak in through the side door to cash checks for ten dollars or so. The stock markets had also been closed. Roosevelt took the United States off the gold standard, which had been valued at twenty dollars and sixty-seven cents per ounce. The public was told to turn in all their gold coins. I had a few coins and decided to keep them. Once the stock market and banks reopened, the market took a sharp rise upward, for three or four months until the top dropped off again. Jim Wyld's dad had made a couple of very sharp speculations, one of which was in Franklin motorcars. Stock went from almost nothing up to a very fine value, although the company was doing nearly nothing at that time. He made quite a lot of money.

In the summer of 1933, after the end of my freshman year, Jim and I hooked up again. Jim's father had bought a brand new 1933 Chevrolet and offered to let us use the car for a summer trip. My dad wasn't faring as well, as the depression had taken hold of the building industry and Jim's dad kindly loaned me three hundred dollars for the trip. Full of youthful exuberance, we took off in the new sedan and headed straight for Chicago to see the World's Fair.

Driving into Chicago in a blinding rainstorm, I could hardly see in front of me and slammed on my brakes too late to miss the car in front. I hit a beat-up Model T Ford truck. The Model T was destroyed and the driver distraught. Not knowing what to do, I offered the man all of ten dollars. He accepted the money and we drove off. We went to the Phi Delt house on the campus of Northwestern University and stayed with our Chicago fraternity brothers for several days.

The Chicago World's Fair was celebrating the hundredth anniversary of the founding of Chicago. There was a huge railroad exhibit among other fascinating sights and we took our time exploring it all, including the talents of the famous Sally Rand, Fan Dancer.

We took our time roaming through the Dakotas and stood in awe at the Black Hills Memorial below Mount Rushmore where the presidents' faces were being sculpted. We drove to Yellow Stone National Park then went on to Salt Lake City. On our way to Salt Lake, we passed a fireworks manufacturing company and joked about what a *"bang!"* it would be if that place were to catch fire and blow up. Arriving there nearly twelve hours later, we picked up a newspaper to see that it had, in fact, blown up!

We drove on across the desert to Reno, then to Tahoe and started up into the mountains. We hadn't gotten far when a car headed the other way flagged us down. It was a beat up Model T Ford. They were heading east. The family inside was an 'Okie' family who had given up on California. They were heading home, but their car's brakes had given out. We jumped out and moved the Chevy around behind the Model T, tied the bumpers together and literally lowered it down the hill. Passersby would have seen what looked like a Model T towing a brand new Chevy down a hill. The family seemed destitute, but tried to give us twenty dollars. We refused.

After waving them off, Jim and I turned the Chevy sedan around and headed back up the mountain. Although it was August, the weather was icy cold and we were nearly freezing. Even while we drove, we had to wrap ourselves in blankets, as the car had no heater. After visiting Sacramento, San Francisco and Los Angeles where we spent a week, we drove across the desert to northern Arizona where we visited a huge meteor crater and the petrified desert.

As Jim and I were driving back from the coast, we found ourselves caught in a flash flood in the middle of Kansas at night. What had looked like shallow water turned out to be higher than we anticipated. It came all the way up to the floorboards. The car stalled and the engine wouldn't start, but in those days without automatic transmission, you put the car in gear and pulled the starter. We made it somehow to higher ground, dried the spark plugs and distributor and got the engine started, but then found the engine was full of water. We finally got to a service station three miles down the road and drained all the oil out, flushed it, drained it and flushed it again, and things were as good as new.

On the way back home, we stopped off at Jim's uncle's house in Kentucky before driving back to New York. Jim returned to Princeton and I went back to Cornell. I moved into the Phi Delt house for my sophomore year.

As much as I liked my roommate, John, being in the cavalry, would return to our room late in the afternoon, smelling like horses. Horses and sweaty leather being an acquired smell and I having never acquired it, I accepted that challenge as the only negative in an otherwise satisfactory relationship.

In November of my sophomore year, I turned twenty-one. I happened to be visiting Aunt Margaret in Syracuse one weekend when my grandfather, who also lived in Syracuse, became extremely ill. Dad was in New York and rushed to Syracuse to see him. My grandfather held on until Dad got there. He died that weekend.

The following spring, I was given several thousand dollars from Grandfather Crouse's estate. I was eager to invest the funds and quickly picked up some stock in GE, some General Motors stock and a little US Steel.

All during school, I had kept in close contact with Jim Wyld, who specialized in copious correspondence. His letters were chock full of hand-scribbled rocket designs and mechanical explanations. For decades, I collected what eventually became a voluminous file of correspondence, Jim's first rocket reference having been received by me at Cornell in a letter dated Oct 25, 1934. In the lengthy letter, Jim talked about borrowing a book from a professor at Princeton, a book entitled *Raketenfahrt* by Max Valier. Jim referred to it as "the only really scientific and well-written book on rockets I have even seen."

In a letter dated January 28, 1935, after a lengthy discussion of various direct and indirect love affairs he had experienced, there appeared the phrase, "A friend and I have been getting up a lot of new schemes in connection with rockets but haven't worked them up yet for sure." Jim eventually became the inventor of the counter-flow, cooling principal liquid motor.

(The engine Jim designed and built ended up featured in Air & Space, a publication of the Smithsonian, issue Dec. 1988-Jan. 1989. The article was entitled "Bringing up Betsy" and referred to the rocket engine known as Black Betsy that propelled the Bell X-1 rocket faster than the speed of sound on Oct. 14, 1947, creating the first aircraft-generated sonic boom over the Mojave Desert. The pilot was Chuck Yeager. The rocket engine was a 210-pound, four-chamber engine designed and built of principles developed by Jim and the three other founders of Reaction Motors, Inc.)

~

It was a time of change. With the Eighteenth Amendment repealed, in part, the public was allowed to buy beer. At first, anything 3.2 percent or less was considered non-alcoholic. Finally, in the fall of 1933, the amendment was repealed in its entirety and people were permitted to buy bona fide alcoholic beverages. My first experience ordering a drink was rather radical. I ordered a liqueur and the waitress was so inexperienced, she brought me a glass tumbler, nearly filled to the top with liqueur.

No fraternity man was complete without a car. In those days, the NRA stood for the National Recovery Administration. The NRA began fixing prices and I ended up buying a brand new 1934 Ford V-8, 93 HP coupe' for six hundred and nineteen dollars. It was a two-passenger car with no rumble seat nor heater, but it ran like a jackrabbit. I installed a heater and a Motorola radio. I bolted an antenna onto one of the bumpers and fell in love for the first time - with a car!

Occasionally, on weekends, I would leave campus to go to Syracuse, about forty-five miles away. I would visit my Aunt Margaret and return to campus rested and well fed. Aunt Margaret had a three-car garage that was fitted with a huge turntable. The garage even had its own gas pump. You could drive the car into entrance of the one-car garage onto the platform then rotate the turntable to drive out whichever car you chose. I was fascinated with that curious invention.

After my sophomore year, during the summer of 1934, my brother Jack and I decided to tour the country in my little car. We drove to the World's Fair again, drove south to New Orleans and forever I would recall a wonderful dinner in that city so famous for its cuisine. We paid some extravagant price that was considered ridiculous at the time, but never forgot the meal. We went on to Texas and decided we would drive to Mexico City. We hadn't realized there were only trails, not real roads.

Once in the bowels of Mexico, we discovered too late that we were on a road that had been washed out. Natives tried to help us and pull our car out of the mud, but all they ended up doing was stripping the battery from the car. Finally pulling free, we headed back up north and spent a day as a guest of a rancher who took us dove shooting. I shot my first dove and made up my mind in that instant I would never shoot another animal for the rest of my life. I never broke that promise. It reminded me of the trout I caught. I was not born to be a hunter.

Driving through a mining town, we came across a group of children who were Mexican by lineage, but who all had bright red hair. Inquiring about the strange anomaly, we learned that the children were descendants of a group of redheaded Cornish miners who had worked the area years before.

We made our way up through Texas and on to the Colorado River, where we stayed for a while to watch a dam being built. It was the Hoover Dam. After a while, we drove on to Los Angeles then down to Tijuana, which we considered to be a dump. The summer before, Jim and I had stayed at the YMCA in Pasadena and Jack and I decided to do that again. Then we drove up Mt. Wilson and stayed in a little inn up in the mountain, for the night. We watched the city lights of Los Angeles, totally unspoiled and free from smog. We drove back across country and headed home, another summer spent in happy wandering.

In my junior year at Cornell, I decided to switch from a physics major to electronics communications to avoid some courses I didn't want to take. I wanted to pick up some courses I was really interested in. The counselors were quite flexible. I ended up taking a course in High Vacuum Phenomena and took some courses in business I thought would help me more in a profession.

In the fall of 1934, I traded in my car, which had suffered tremendously from the trip to Mexico. I got four hundred dollars for it, a bargain considering its condition. I picked up another Chevrolet coupe' that cost seven hundred dollars and installed a radio and heater in it so I would be prepared for the winter in New York. I liked the car but its performance wasn't as *zippy* as my first.

The threshold of my heart had not yet been crossed, but all that was about to change. I became friends with a fellow by the name of Bill Harry who lived in Broomfield, northwest of Detroit. His dad had done well in the auto supply business. His biggest customer was Ford Motor Company.

Back at school, we formed a triad. Bill Harry had a room in a house nearby, Ted Ellis, a Beta, stayed at his fraternity house and I lived at the Phi Delt house. We quickly became fast friends. I decided to string a wire between the three houses so we could talk back and forth. I bought a few thousand feet of wire and first, walked over the roof of the Phi Delta house, stringing wire and inadvertently breaking tiles along the way. Next, I strung the wire through the woods to the Beta house, then on over to Bill's house. During the experiment, Bill's girlfriend Bobbie Frederick was helping out and caught her skirt on a bush. We were all laughing so hard at her embarrassment, I suddenly had an epiphany—I liked girls! I had suddenly discovered that the opposite sex might be kind of fun. At least I was having a good time talking to Bobbie.

The wire never worked well and the telephone set up was a disappointment. The weather destroyed the set up with the first hard rain. But as Bobbie and Bill visited together, playing cards at his rooming house, I would find myself dropping in and joining them, all the while becoming more comfortable as we three chatted away the evening.

Once, Bill, Ted and I went down to New York to see some power plants. They had commissioned the largest power generator ever built. It was built by the Alice Chalmers Company of Milwaukee and called *Big Alice*. It was out of service quite a bit but was still most impressive. The system worked but capital costs were out of line. I doubt they ever built any more of them. It was turbine powered. We were awestruck, particularly when they put some mercury in a glass, washed the glass out, tossed it into the boiler and the alarm went off. In those days, they were worried about mercury vapor as they are today.

~

In the summer of 1935, armed with a brand new Chevy, I decided to take my brother on another summer trip. We repeated New Orleans and Texas. But Dad had connected us with a fellow by the name of Esteban Cerdan. He was traffic manager of the New York, Rio and Buenos Aires Line, Inc. Esteban wanted to return to Mexico so we decided to give Mexico another try with Esteban as our guide.

We headed south into Mexico and stopped at the river. The only way to cross was to put our car on the ferry which was tied to the trunk of a tree by a rope. The whole ferry was then carried across the river by the raging current with young, strong brown boys on either side holding on to the rope. Feeling adventurous and immortal as young men do, we decided to navigate across the river, taking this one available route. The alternative would have been to turn back. The frightening river crossing safely behind us, the three of us spent the night in some nondescript little town.

In the middle of the night, we were startled awake by a frantic screeching. It sounded like some poor soul screaming, "HELP! HELP!" in a high-pitched wail. The screamers turned out to be peacocks demonstrating their night call.

There was no highway leading into Mexico City. Driving up into the mountain, we came onto a ledge, probably six to seven feet wide. It was literally carved into the side of the mountain. Men were reconstructing the new highway into Mexico City. We were told it would be another month or so before the road would be passable as a highway. We had no choice but to brave the mountain's ledge. After navigating the makeshift road successfully, we spent a night at a ranch.

Whether it was the ability to sit and relax after such a harrowing experience or the coffee beans, I would forever remember the most wonderful cup of coffee I ever had in my life at that little ranch in the mountains of Mexico. The roads were miserable and we had to drive very slowly, finally stopping to take a break at a small town in the village square where we watched the local fiesta.

Finally arriving at the YMCA in Mexico City, we spent the first night there. Rested and ready to explore the town for more permanent, albeit temporary quarters, we solicited Esteban's assistance and rented an apartment. That mission accomplished, we visited the local museums. Then we found a local pawnshop where Jack bought a .45 caliber pistol.

We decided to head on down to Acapulco, at the time an unspoiled little bay on the Pacific coast. It took us two days and two new tires to get there. En route to Acapulco, we met a couple of young schoolteachers who were floundering with a flat. We changed their tire for them and we all had a hot beer together, as there was no refrigeration and the cantina had no ice. My experience of seeing Acapulco for the first time was printed indelibly into my head. We found a small hotel in town that was so ancient and decrepit, we figured it had to have been built at the time of Cortez. We chose the alternative, a guesthouse on the hill, complete with a personal cook. We stayed at that pristine beautiful house on the hill overlooking the sea for nearly a week.

Finally deciding to return to Mexico City, Jack and I again used up two days and two tires getting back. It became immediately obvious, upon our return, that Esteban had thoroughly enjoyed the apartment in our absence.

We began to worry that the road may be closed, so we decided to leave. Of course, we were forced to make our way across the narrow ledge once more. Our rear tire blew out and along the way, as luck would have it, we found an abandoned truck tire. Ingeniously, we cut it apart, took some of the fabric out and put the fabric over the blowout. We put the tube back in and we were off!

Once again on level land, we were traveling pretty fast when suddenly we noticed a large horse standing in a ditch beside the road. As we came up alongside the animal, the horse spooked and ran onto the road right in front of us. Slamming on the brakes wouldn't have helped. There wasn't a thing we could do. The car hit the horse head on, and up and over it went, head over rear. We had learned that if you had an accident in Mexico, you didn't stop. You kept going! Shaken, we looked back to see the horse climbing out of the trench it had been thrown into.

Not a soul was around. We drove around a couple of corners, stopped the car and reviewed the damage. The headlight was demolished, full of horsehair and horseshit. The left front fender had been pushed back about a quarter of an inch. Otherwise, the car was in fairly good shape for all it had been through. We made it to the border in Laredo and bought new tires then headed to New Mexico, then on to southern California, all the while enjoying saner driving conditions.

~

Returning to Cornell for my senior year, I decided I needed to take a course in public speaking, believing speech was the area in my life that would require the most improvement. I worked hard and made such headway that my professor considered me the most improved student in his speech class. I was delighted when I was amply rewarded. I was excused from the final exam. I always had a full range of opinions about everything in my busy world, and soon found that speaking extemporaneously was not only challenging, but also quite enjoyable.

For my course in physics, I built an X-ray tube, dabbled in X-ray spectography, and even made a photocell. The course that was most problematic to me was Powerline Theory, the interrelationship between power lines, capacitance and circulating currents. But I thrived on the challenge.

Still enjoying my avocation in the radio business, I decided one day to run the power amplifier I had built to the top of the library tower so I could play classical records at high volume. Perhaps it was standing there that day, surrounded by powerful music composed by the masters and looking up at the sky, that made me decide to take flying lessons.

I drove to the small airport down by the lake and signed up. The FAA had yet to be formed, so when an instructor said you could fly, you could fly. I learned to fly a WACO OX-5, powered by a World War I engine used in lots of planes in the 1920s and '30s. And after only five or six hours of flying, my instructor, who must have weighed all of three hundred pounds, got out and said, "Take it around by yourself, Bub."

Without a moment's hesitation, I, weighing a mere hundred forty pounds or so, at five feet eleven, taxied down to the end of the runway, turned the plane around and pushed the throttle forward. Off I went, making a wide circle around the field. I had never before experienced this kind of freedom. When I eventually descended to start the landing, I realized that it was the instructor's weight that had made the other landings so smooth. Being as slight as I was, the plane floated - and floated - and floated. But I was finally able to set it down. I loved flying and flew any small planes available. The rental fees were nominal and it was a great pastime, especially for a college student.

I had been watching my investments carefully and continued to buy stocks whenever I could. The next time a stock paid off, I spent nine hundred and seventeen dollars and bought a brand new Buick coupe'.

There were radicals and "pseudo Reds" at Cornell at that time. I was so curious about one particular group that I figured the best way to find out what they were all about was to join them. I learned quickly when they assigned me the job of passing out Communist flyers. Of course I refused. I had seen how dictatorially they conducted their meetings, as the politburos did in Russia, advising students no discussion would be allowed, telling them what they could and could not do. That was enough for me, being a freethinking young capitalist. I had learned enough.

My fraternity brothers had decided they would no longer permit me to be a hermit so they arranged a date for me with a freshman named Lois Peters. In February 1936, at the age of twenty-three, I had my first bona fide date. As a boy, I had refused to take dancing lessons, so this date to go dancing wasn't all that successful. Nevertheless, Lois was a nice girl and made the evening quite pleasant. I had dipped my toe in the water and returned to the dorm that night unafraid of girls. Regardless, I continued to be especially aware and highly appreciative of the way that Bill Harry and Bobbie Frederick got along.

The next weekend there was another dance. Bill and I ended up in the library with Bobbie. Lois had gone off with someone else. Bill went downstairs for something, leaving me sitting on the arm of Bobbie's chair. When I looked down, our eyes met. My heart nearly stopped as she asked quietly, "Aren't you going to kiss me?" It took no further persuasion. I kissed her and for the rest of the evening, I was in a daze. Realizing I had fallen deeply in love with my friend's girl, I could hardly think. The rest of the weekend was a blur. By Sunday night, Bobbie had gone home and I was left in an emotional turmoil.

For two nights, I agonized over writing her a letter. Finally, several days later, I discovered a letter addressed to me. It had been left on the piano at the fraternity house. It was from Bobbie. She told me that the boys had set up our kiss in the library as a prank. She realized I had taken it seriously and she was very upset. With the door open to communication, even slightly, I decided to write her immediately. Of course, I accepted her apology. Nevertheless, I explained to her, I had fallen indeed, but I realized she was Bill's girl.

It was 1936 and my focus was changing. I had become a man. I bought a journal and wrote out my feelings, starting a process that would stay with me throughout my life.

Our friendship none the worse for wear, in late March of 1936, Bill and I decided to spend our final spring break together. We drove all day and all night, finally arriving in Jacksonville, Florida. On our way to the beach, we watched a prison chain gang working on the road. Naturally, the men were dressed in unmistakable prison garb. The unusual thing was - one of the prisoners was carrying the guard's shotgun! They all seemed very relaxed and the scene seemed so strange and out of place. It was a memory I wished I had captured in a photograph.

Two months later, nearly finished with school, we were looking forward to a long weekend to celebrate Memorial Day. I asked Bobbie if I could visit her and she agreed. I drove from Ithaca to Buffalo, over to Canada, then on to Detroit. Bobbie was by now employed. She worked in a department store as an assistant buyer in the glove department. She and her mother lived in a large old house and were very gracious to me. Nonetheless, I was heartbroken to realize that she still was Bill Harry's girl, plus she already had another fellow she was seeing in Detroit. Alas, our relationship was not to be.

At least the home fires had started burning and I was quickly introduced to another girl at school, also a freshman. Her name was Ena Cuypers. Early one afternoon, Ena and I drove around the north end of the lake and stopped for a lovely lunch. As I put my arm around her, I realized that life might turn out all right after all.

Graduation from Cornell did not end merely with my diploma that affirmed a degree in electrical engineering. As I walked out of the auditorium, Mom and Dad handed me a thin envelope. I opened it to see the first thousand-dollar bill I had ever seen. What a graduation present in 1936! Ena was going to return home with me, so I quickly loaded up the car and we started back. For some reason, the family delayed their return until the next day, and Ena and I arrived at Fieldston at three o'clock in the morning. Even though Mrs. Case was at the house as chaperone, we had several hours to *visit* before my parents came home.

After four years of college, it was time to celebrate. Jim Wyld, Bill Harry and I decided to get passports and head off to Europe. I arranged to have my car shipped as well so we would have transportation upon our arrival. We booked tourist class tickets on the Rotterdam of the Holland-American line. Capping off our incredible voyage was docking at Plymouth, England to watch the workers unload my car, which had been placed in a big sling, onto the dock.

Piling into the car, we felt so free. School was behind us and the summer was before us. We took our time driving through Cornwall then on to London. We quickly found a place to rent near Marble Arch at Hyde Park. We were impressed upon seeing the BBC studios in London, but decided to leave the city and go exploring.

Our first unique European experience happened almost immediately. Driving north through the countryside, we noticed a huge broadcasting transmitter. Suddenly, as we were looking up at it, a thunderstorm came up and one of the antennas took a direct hit, nearly paralyzing us with fear.

Jim had graduated in mechanical engineering from Princeton the year before. Early on, he had become interested in rockets. He lived, breathed, slept rocket-talk and while in Great Britain, had decided to visit G. Robert Pendray in Liverpool. Pendray was the leader in

British rocketry and of course a member of the British Rocket Society. Whereas Robert H. Goddard, PhD, his American counterpart, had been quite secretive about his rockets, Pendray loved to talk about the technology. All it took to get Jim and Pendray together was the knowledge that Jim was active in the American Rocket Society. We thought it absolutely fascinating to listen to Jim Wyld and G. Robert Pendray talk on a collegial level. What an inspiring visit.

Traveling on, we met a family who expressed tremendous concern about potential war with Germany. Little did they know their world would soon be turned upside down. We drove on up to Edinburgh, Scotland to visit a relative of Jim's who was a Lord and Chief Minister of the Scottish Supreme Court.

We put the car on board the Bosle, a small steamer, and set across the North Sea, heading for Norway. When we disembarked, we drove on to spend three days with another of Jim's distant relatives. We explored Sweden, Denmark and Copenhagen and were heartily greeted in Germany by a "Hail, Hitler!"

The Olympics were going on in Germany but none of us were interested in athletics, even at this level. We all experienced a slight, chilling fear at the Nazi greetings as we spent a couple of days in Berlin. Everything was decorated in Nazi flags, everything that is, except the stores owned by Jews. We were happy to move on and toured Prague, then Vienna, the Nazi greeting still very much a presence in our thoughts. Rushing along a road in northern Italy, we nearly ran down the Italian army, but we all escaped without incident, including the Italian army. We went on to Rotterdam where we caught the ship to the States. Another glorious summer.

Jim returned to the U.S. where he found a job making heat exchangers for a company in Ohio. But all his free time was spent in doodling rocket designs. Every letter I received contained elaborate scribbles and graphics, all focused on his rocket mechanics.

Bill got a job working for Bell Telephone Laboratories in microphone design. He eventually would design the standard radio broadcast microphone that was used by broadcasters for many years.

Harvard Business School

It was September 1936. I had enrolled at Harvard and was eager to start on my master's degree. At Harvard Business School, I settled into D-32, my single room, surrounded by my radios, electric phonograph and other paraphernalia students normally bring to college. Having gone through engineering school, unlike many students who had gone to a liberal arts college, I was highly disciplined, already used to deadlines and I had developed solid study habits. As a result, I found the academic regime at Harvard less of a chore than many of my classmates. One of my professors in Business Administration was none other than George Dorio who went on to achieve great fame as a general in World War II.

Cars still spoke to me as if they were living breathing works of art. I had become totally enamored of a new car introduced in 1935, the Chrysler Air Flow. The car had a rounded, somewhat ugly nose in its first incarnation, but in '36, engineers had redesigned the nose, attaching a radiator grill, improving its appearance tremendously. After searching for a while, I finally found one and without hesitation, traded in my Buick. The car had the world's worst headlights. As it turned out, the car obviously had been abused by the former owner. On the upside, the tires were blowout-proof.

I took a couple other students on a trip to Florida, but in Wilmington, North Carolina, we discovered a broken piston. Luckily, we found a Dodge piston that would work and drove on to Sarasota.

Dad had given me the name of an associate, a fellow named Burns and as luck would have it, Mr. Burns had a daughter, Leah. She became our tour guide and we got to see some of Dad's work first-

69

hand. It was amazing to see the Sarasota courthouse and the elegant estate of John Ringling, both of which he designed.

Traveling on to the Keys, we were fascinated by the remains of what had been begun as a luxurious Biltmore. Development had begun in 1926 in boom time, but when Florida real estate collapsed the same summer, due to gross over-speculation, work was halted. Only part of the roof had been completed. Reinforced concrete, left to the elements, was crumbling into disrepair. And now it was 1937, with no work done on it for more than eleven years. The Keys showed effects of the depression throughout. Streets were partly overgrown with foliage gone wild. There were lots for sale throughout the area and an occasional cluster of houses. No one was building.

We tried to limit our night driving because the headlights in the Chrysler were less than adequate, to say the least. On the trip home, we purchased wiring and doubled the headlights but that quick fix was of little help. Eventually, we returned to Harvard without major incident, ready to resume our studies.

Occasionally I drove up to Lake Winnepasocki, New Hampshire for a weekend. Friends of our family, the Arnolds, owned a house there. He was a commodities broker and was cleaned out in the depression. His summerhouse was in his wife's name and they had sold their house in New York and moved to the lake. They had a daughter Natalie, who was my age. They started taking in guests at the lake, as did others in the area. I would periodically drive up and stay with them for a relaxing weekend.

After my first year at Harvard, I was encouraged to find an internship for the summer. But my parents invited me to go on a family trip that sounded too good to pass up. It took little persuasion to forego the internship. The professor was not happy with my decision. To appease him, I suggested that I could write a paper in great depth on a company that I would visit over the summer. Reluctantly, he agreed.

So the family, which still included Mrs. Case, packed up and boarded the USS President Pierce, heading from New York through the Panama Canal then up to Los Angeles and San Francisco. The only family member missing was Jack who had remembered his violent seasickness on a previous trip and elected to drive to California to meet us.

The passengers were all older than Peter and I, all except for one of them—a very special passenger indeed. An attractive young woman by the name of Kay Louden was bound from Boston to San Francisco. She worked for Eaton and Howard, a mutual fund. The company had experienced such a good year in business that they had given Kay her trip as a bonus.

Deciding to get off the boat on the Caribbean side, Kay and I took the train across the Isthmus of Panama to Panama City. We rented a car and driver. Kay had heard fascinating stories about the red light district and wanted to see it. It took some time and rather wild gesturing to get the idea across as to where we wanted to go, but our driver finally got the picture. Driving through the area did not prove to be very exciting and Kay was a little disappointed although the process had been entertaining - and so much fun!

We went back to the Canal to watch the ship go through the locks, then got on board and cruised onward to Los Angeles. Good friends by now, we knew we were going to be docked in Los Angeles for two days but neither Kay nor I wanted necessarily to go into town. We found out we could fly over to Catalina on an amphibian plane. We took off from Long Beach Harbor and took the fifteen-minute flight to Catalina, landing at Avalon. The plane taxied onto a little ramp and we strolled off to find two rooms at the St. Catherine Hotel.

We decided to take the town's seaside walkway to the Casino, which was not, in fact, a gambling casino but rather a dance hall. The island was beautiful and remote. We returned to the hotel where we talked over cocktails until the wee hours of the morning. After a few hours rest, we caught the plane and went back to Long Beach. My father was appalled when he found out we had spent the night in a hotel in Catalina. I quickly assured him that we had stayed in separate rooms. My conscience was clear and Dad calmed down.

We boarded the ship once again and took a luxurious day and a night to get to San Francisco. It was a beautiful sight to see, slipping into the bay under the Golden Gate Bridge. On May 28, 1937, the Golden Gate Bridge had opened to vehicular traffic at precisely twelve o'clock noon when President Franklin D. Roosevelt pressed a telegraph key from the Oval Office at the White House to announce the event to the world. For a while, it looked as if their ship's mast wouldn't clear the bridge, but of course it did. The height of the two towers that supported the two main cables reached seven hundred forty-six feet above the water and the length of the bridge stretched a full 1.7 miles across the bay. It was a massive structure and Dad and I especially marveled at the incredible feat of engineering.

Arriving in town, we discovered there was a hotel workers' strike and we wouldn't be able to stay at our favorite place, the St. Francis, so we had to scout around to find another hotel. We went on to Los Angeles, shortly thereafter, and Jack joined us at the Biltmore, now that we were safely on land.

While there, we had the most unusual experience. Peter came prancing into the hotel room where Jack and I were sleeping. He began to shout, "You'll never guess what! You'll never guess what! Dad's lost Mum's car! Dad's lost Mum's car!"

Dad had visited the Hearst ranch for a couple of nights. The ranch was also an animal preserve with semi-automatic gates. In leaving, he hadn't closed the second gate properly. He got out of the car to close it and looked back to see his car slowly rolling down the road - without him! He hadn't secured the brake. He dashed after it, but it was too late. The road took a turn, the car didn't, and it hurled headlong into the bottom of an arroyo with a great crash. His hosts got a tractor and pulled the wrecked car out of the arroyo. It had every bit of our family luggage inside. The car was totaled and the Hearsts kindly sent Dad and his luggage by air to Los Angeles.

Mom and Dad had to go car shopping to get the family back home. As they all began their cross-country trip back to New York in their brand new Packard, I stayed behind in Los Angeles. I still had to find a company to write about for my graduate school assignment.

I discovered a steel fabrication company that made towers for power lines. I thought for certain they would be interested in having a report written about them by an eager young student. Unfortunately, they wanted no part of me nor any part of my grand idea.

Heading back to San Francisco, still in search of a viable project, I learned there were three small pulp companies that were going to be merged into one company called Rayoneer. Their major product was making pulp for paper manufacturing but also dissolving pulp for the rayon industry and their principal market was Japan. Blyth and Company, an investment banking firm based in San Francisco, heard about the potential merger and became the underwriter.

I located a copy of the red herring prospectus on the deal and began inquiring about this merger, thinking that would be the basis of my report. I knew virtually nothing about investment banking nuances at that time, certainly not enough about corporate finance to ask intelligent questions. When I started interviewing the head of Rayoneer, he became very upset.

As it turned out, one of their biggest problems was that the United States was beginning to tighten the screws on Japan. We were starting to embargo exports to Japan. The deal was in big trouble. And the company needed the money. They were building a new plant in Georgia and expenses were running over what was originally anticipated. It was a complicated merger and the head of the company wasn't thrilled about a green Harvard business major questioning their solvency and current business dealings.

Meanwhile, Kay Louden was still hanging around and I found her to be great at typing report drafts as I put them together. My report included quite a lot of detail about the merger of the three companies, proposing a new stock offering, adding everything I could learn about the economic problems and political nuances they were experiencing. There were serious problems. The deal was *sticky* at best.

I was staying at the new YMCA in downtown San Francisco at a rate of two or three dollars a night, although I could have stayed at the St. Francis or any other upscale hotel for ten or twelve dollars a night. Kay and I would meet at a bar near the Clift Hotel in the evenings and talk over scotch and soda, purchased at the hefty price of twenty-five cents. Together we found a beautiful spot on the north side of the Golden Gate Bridge. Often we would park the car and look out over the bay, the water shining in the moonlight. All was right with the world.

In the fall, I returned to Harvard Business School and handed in the report. It was accepted as barely adequate and in retrospect, through the years, I came to realize how relatively simplistic it was, not really touching on anything of value.

In the spring of my second year, I read a short item in TIME Magazine that reported how some local utility holding company had a manufactured gas plant serving a small city in Massachusetts. The company had only five hundred customers or so and was losing money. They wanted to get permission from the Securities and

Exchange Commission to sell the company to local buyers for a couple dollars each, just to get rid of it. The thought of buying a small utility company and running it completely intrigued me. That single article planted a seed of interest in me that never went away.

In June 1938, I graduated from Harvard with an MBA. Students didn't seem to care about the pomp and circumstance and hardly anyone hung around for graduation. I was no exception. My diploma was mailed to me.

My First Professional Job
The Mine Safety Appliances Company

In the summer of 1938, the country was still trying to recover from the depression. Corporate America was not sending recruiters all over the country to hire business school graduates, even those with master's degrees. A good two-thirds of my class already had jobs, most of which resulted from their summer internships. I spent the summer trying to find something of interest, some foundation on which I could build a career. I was finally successful in scoring an interview with Juan Tripp, founder of Pan American Airlines.

The airline was offering the strangest deal for employment. I was *invited* to purchase a round trip ticket to South America with the understanding that I could stop off wherever I wanted. I was encouraged to figure out any improvements I might want to recommend and upon my return, write a report. Based on that report, I might or might not receive a job offer.

I wasn't thrilled with the audition aspects of it and turned it down. Then I applied at Vanity Fair, manufacturer of ladies intimate apparel. During the interview, they demonstrated more interest in what car I drove than my professional skills or career goals. They offered me a job at a hundred dollars a month. Even at the time, it was the lower end of the pay scale, especially for someone who had invested the last six years in higher education at highly prestigious universities.

Finally, I made two solid connections with companies in Pittsburgh and set up a morning interview with Crucible Steel Company, which was a steel mill, and in the afternoon with the Mine

Safety Appliance Company. With regard to the latter, I had dropped by their office on Fulton Street in New York City to talk with the local sales representative and was given a catalog of their products. The company manufactured such safety equipment as gas masks, safety goggles, hard hats and miner's safety lamps among other items. MSA was the worldwide representative of the Edison Company for production of alkaline battery-powered safety lamps.

Encouraged, I headed off to the Pittsburgh plant for an interview at Crucible Steel. I was fascinated during the tour at the magnitude of the operation. Right off the bat, I was offered a job as an electrician's assistant at the mill. I thought it might have been a good starting place because of my engineering background. There was a hitch, however. The plant paid by the hour, a good rate in and of itself, but I would be given only two and a half shifts per week. I wouldn't be able to make a good living on what amounted to part-time work.

In the afternoon, I met with J.T. Ryan, Sr., one of the two founders of the Mine Safety Appliance Company. Although Ryan had my resume at hand, he began to ask me about the universities I had attended and other things he obviously already knew.

When I told him I had earned an engineering degree at Cornell, Ryan said, "I want you to know I'm a University of Pennsylvania man." I was too polite to respond.

The inquisitor asked, "What fraternity did you join?" When I told him I was a Phi Delt, he said, "I want you to know I'm a Beta. My son also had the stupidity to join the Phi Delts." Then he paused for moment, looked straight at me, and right out of the blue asked, "How does one-and-a-half sound?"

I had absolutely no idea what he meant but came to find out I was being offered a hundred fifty dollars a month; plus, I was to work as the assistant to Ryan's son.

Stunned, I quickly accepted. That was a good starting salary for 1938. In September, for the first time in eighteen years, I would be going to work instead of to school.

A few days later, I packed up my car and drove to Pittsburgh to work as assistant to Jack Ryan, Jr. who had graduated from business school two years before. We hit it off right away and before long, I was referring to myself as *chief assistant to the assistant chief.*

I was a stranger to Pittsburgh. Through the fellows at the plant, I found an apartment that was quite convenient, only two blocks from work. I rented a furnished apartment with three other guys. My first day in the apartment, I attended to the usual housekeeping duties. I made a hurried trip to Sears Roebuck to buy sheets and blankets for my bed. Roomers usually made their own breakfasts and sometimes dinner as well. The landlady Mrs. Gagler believed in minimal amenities and believed even less in maintenance.

There was certainly no distraction by women at work. MSA founders were staunch Catholics who believed women belonged at home and refused to hire a woman whose husband was employed. Certainly, few single women were in search of a job in a manufacturing plant in 1938.

I drove to New York on occasional weekends to visit my two girlfriends, Ena and Lois. Lois Peters worked for a large advertising agency in New York and had been living with her family in Forest Hills. Her family was exceptionally strict and Lois wanted desperately to move to New York. She found an apartment on the East Side on Thirty-eighth Street. I had driven her around to look at apartments and evidently the landlady thought I was keeping her because she asked me where I wanted the key sent. We had a good laugh and only one key was issued.

On one weekend, I returned to New York to find that both Lois and Ena had other plans. *Enter Hildagarde Engelhardt, my former neighbor.* Hilda had grown up in the house at the bottom of the hill, the house that my dad designed and the hill where I landed unceremoniously the day I learned to ride my bike. Hilda had attended the Horace Mann School for Girls, which was perched at the edge of Fieldston in Riverdale. She had gone on to Randolph Macon Women's College and eventually graduated from Sarah Lawrence College.

Desperate for a date, I called her. As luck would have it, Hilda was hosting a sledding party that weekend and invited me to join the festivities. To my total surprise, we had such a good time that I dated her a couple more times. Whenever I could spare the time from my job and return to New York, I would call her. But I didn't work fast enough, for just as I was really getting to like her and wanting to see more of her, I popped back to New York for a weekend. I stupidly hurried to her house without calling and was surprised when I was introduced to an older gentleman named Walker. I quickly learned he was Hilda's fiance'. I stayed for only a minute. I heard later that she married him and they had taken in his two daughters from a previous marriage.

Returning to Pittsburgh, I realized I was less than thrilled with my environment. A thick layer of smog frequently covered the city and coal dust was prevalent in the air, especially during the winter. There was rarely any hope of enjoying a clear, sunny day.

Bars were not allowed to operate on Sundays, and the state operated the liquor stores. Thankfully, clubs were permitted to serve drinks, so the city wasn't entirely dry. I finally found something I could do on Sundays.

Although I had learned to fly at Cornell, I had rarely pursued it. Airplane rentals were relatively inexpensive, still, the hobby was costly to a full-time student. But now I was working. I soon discovered Pittsburgh's Turtle Creek Airport. Part of the airport was perched on a hillside.

Six months after my arrival at MSA, I noticed a little Taylor Craft Cub someone had listed for sale for seven hundred dollars. I couldn't resist the purchase. The airplane was a tandem two-seater but I never flew with a passenger as I only had a student license. I had logged five or six hours of flying, then soloed and was able to soar over Pittsburgh, certain that if I were going to have to crash land, I could surely land on the smog.

Within months, my solo hours totaled upwards of two hundred hours. The forty horsepower airplane had no brakes and a somewhat dysfunctional tail wheel. But at that age, young men are indestructible and I was having far too much fun to worry about no brakes and a poorly working tail wheel. Flying into the north-south runway, pilots had to fly over a little power line. But there was plenty of room before running out of runway and running into Turtle Creek. The airport even had a hangar where I could keep his airplane out of the elements.

One day I decided to check out the compass in my plane. I flew due east for twenty-five minutes, then banked, turning a full hundred eighty degrees. I flew due west for the same amount of time only to discover that I was nowhere near where I had started. The little plane was frequently buffeted about in storms, but I enjoyed flying so much, the occasional storm didn't bother me.

I enjoyed my work analyzing the sales potential in industries and corporations. The MSA newsletter referred to me as *a walking ticker as far as stock market quotations are concerned.* They also dubbed me a lady's man and suggested that I had been seen calling frequently at a local ladies finishing school. The article, lifted from the 1939 company archives, continued-- *Dubbed the fender-bender, his wild-eyed driving kept the fenders of his car in constant need of repair. Maybe his airplane piloting made it hard for him to resume his earthly ways.* I must say, I strongly disputed that last claim, only having had one accident.

My grandmother died while I was working at MSA, but my grief in saying goodbye to Alma Elizabeth Ackerman Baum was nothing compared to what I was about to experience eight short months later. In the middle of December 1939, now twenty-seven, I returned to my room after dinner one evening and settled in for the night. Someone knocked on my door and called to me, "Phone call for Baum." I ran to the phone and my world changed forever. Mother had called to give me terrible news.

Dad had walked out of the Astor Hotel lobby at West 45th Street and 7th Avenue to catch the private Riverdale suburban coach home. He collapsed on the sidewalk, suffering a fatal heart attack. A neighbor of ours, a physician, happened to be on the coach and saw it happen. The doctor dashed over to Dad, but to no avail.

They carried Dad's body to the West 47th Street Police Station nearby. Jerome Barnum, his brother-in-law and publisher of the Syracuse Post-Standard, was in New York staying at the Cornell Club while attending a meeting of the board of directors of the American Association of Newspaper Publishers. Someone called him to go identify Dad's body so they could release it and take him home.

He had taken a physical in Syracuse only a few weeks before. That day, the architect had been downtown conferring with YMCA officials. He had designed the New York City YMCA years before and now was bidding on the YMCA in Greenwich, Connecticut.

I booked a flight immediately and arrived home in the middle of the night. Jack was at Harvard at the time. Peter was at the Tafts

School. By ten o'clock the next morning, we had gathered at the family home.

Strange tufts of memories tug on your heartstrings for years after events like this. We boys all needed haircuts. So we all went down to Mr. Perta's barbershop where Dad had taken us for years. He was so loved in that neighborhood, people gathered all around us, in shock, offering heartfelt condolences. Dad was only fifty-three. After cutting our hair, Mr. Perta refused to accept any payment. We were so touched at this gesture. It reflected the feeling of the whole community. Everyone shared in our mourning.

The Evening Times in Little Falls, New York, announced Dad's death on December 14, 1939, with this headline:

Dwight Baum, One of Nation's Greatest Architects, Dead

A memorial service was held at Hendricks Chapel at Syracuse University. Ironically, Dad had designed the chapel in earlier years. A colleague, Professor A.E. Johnson wrote a poem from which the following is excerpted:

"If ever there were sermon writ in stone,
How eloquently here his praise is sung."

We made arrangements at the Riverdale Presbyterian Church for Dad's funeral. The church was heavily supported financially by the Dodge family. Dad had redesigned this church.

After our formal good-byes, we took our last family trip together. We boarded the train with the casket bearing the stilled body of the man who had been the center of our family to attend another service at Aunt Margaret's on West Tennessee Street in Syracuse.

On the train from Yonkers to Syracuse, Mom said, "This may sound terribly irreverent, but you know, boys, I can't help remembering that old sad song, 'In the baggage coach ahead, there lies a coffin.'" I'm sure she never thought she would be burying her husband at such a young age.

Years earlier, Dad had bought a small cemetery plot for his parents overlooking the Crouse plot where the eighty-ton boulder stood and at the time the family had joked that this was the only time the Baums had ever been able to look down on the Crouses. Dwight's final internment was in Oakwood Cemetery in the Crouse plot by the huge boulder.

I returned to MSA at Pittsburgh to work for a few days then made a hurried trip back to New York to be with Mother and my brothers for Christmas and New Year's.

The effects of the depression on the architecture business had impacted Dad's modest estate. Despite the fact that he was a prominent architect, his office had never really made a lot of money. He had barely been able to keep the office together during the depression. My brothers, Mother and I decided to give the business to the employees, to the office manager, designers, all of them, with a percentage of the profits to be paid to the family.

Unfortunately, after only eight months, without Dad's guidance and drive, the employees had dried up the business. One of the many newspaper editors who wrote about Dad said, "The driving force of that brain made him a dynamo of activity." He was right. Without that spark, his creative genius and energy, the company wasn't getting any new business. The firm closed down and the office was evacuated. Long after Dad's death, Mother sold the building and today, multiple renovations later, it still stands - across the street from Manhattan College.

After Dad's death, I started toying with the decision to leave MSA in Pittsburgh and go back to New York to be closer to Mother. And it just so happened there was an incredible opportunity waiting in the wings.

The BAC - Doing My Duty for King and Country

In August of 1940, eight months after my father's death, I took a vacation and flew my plane to New York. The plant always closed down in August and it was a perfect time to regroup mentally and focus on the future.

Halfway there, I hit a headwind. The plane was using too much gas bouncing around. The gas tank gauge was a cork with a wire on it that indicated when fuel was low. I had to land in a cornfield close to the Pennsylvania Turnpike, which was under construction at the time. I taxied to a gas station, bought five gallons of gas, put it in the tank and flew on to Harrisburg, then to Bethlehem, Pennsylvania where I spent the night before heading to New York.

The next morning, airborne once again, I headed straight toward Fieldston, circled Mother's house at one thousand feet, gunning the engine to signal her and watched as she ran outside to wave. Pointing toward Flushing Airport, slightly to the east of La Guardia, I flew on to the airport, maneuvering to avoid a big DC-3's flight path into LaGuardia. Mom arrived at the airport to pick me up as I was taxiing in from a smooth landing. I had wanted my car in New York during my two-week hiatus and Chuck Mayhan, my roommate, drove it from Pittsburgh because he wanted a reason to visit the city.

While on vacation, a friend introduced me to a very distinguished British gentleman. Conrad H. Biddlecombe had served as a major in the Royal Flying Corps during World War I. Biddlecombe had immigrated to the U.S. He had held various jobs in the States and at the outbreak of WWII, when the Germans overran Europe, was hired by the British Mission in New York. The British had lost everything on the continent. The British Mission, which had been very small, suddenly exploded in size and Biddy went to work for them in July 1940.

One month before, when a German invasion was imminent, Prime Minister Winston Churchill had given his famous speech before the House of Commons, pledging, "We shall go on to the end; we shall fight in France; we shall fight on the seas and oceans; we shall fight with growing confidence and growing strength in the air; we shall defend our Island whatever the cost may be; we shall fight on the beaches; we shall fight on the landing grounds; we shall fight in the fields and in the streets. We shall fight in the hills; we shall never surrender…"

I met Biddy at the offices of Eastman Dillon. We talked for a while and Biddy was pleased to learn about my engineering background, and that I knew how to fly. My business degree from Harvard carried some weight, also. It was evident after the first few minutes that Biddy had plans for me. He was desperate for help. After talking a while longer, he looked straight into my eyes and said, "Young man, I want you to come work for me."

Naively I told him what I had been making at MSA, which after two years had been boosted only by fifty dollars. Biddy offered me the same, a full two hundred dollars a month. That was August 13, 1940, and all I could think of was that I had another week of vacation left. I truly was interested but I wanted to negotiate some time off. I told Biddy that I would have to give two weeks notice, plus take my extra week's vacation.

Biddy said, "Goddamnit, Son - there's a war on! We need you now!" Biddy picked up the phone and called the plant. Even though the plant was closed for vacation, Jack Ryan was found in his office. It took only moments and a lot of patriotic talk for Biddy to talk Jack into releasing me, permitting me to take "a leave of absence." I think we all knew it would amount to more than a leave of absence.

I returned home to Fieldston, packed, took the night train to Pittsburgh, spent two days dictating unfinished business into the old Ediphone dictating cylinder machine. I packed as much as I could and boarded the night train back to New York. When I arrived in Manhattan, I checked my suitcase at Penn Station, took the subway down to Wall Street and turned up at 37 Wall Street. It was eight a.m.

In four days, my life had taken a one hundred-eighty-degree turn, and I was totally focused on my new future. I would spend the next five years with the British Air Commission.

Biddy was my superior. His office was on the eighteenth floor of an old building and there was a tremendous amount of work to be done. Biddy was preparing to become director of Armament and Equipment Supply for the Royal Air Force in America. I was intrigued with our task. We were responsible for figuring out armament supplies and designing the how-toss for affixing guns and bombs onto airplanes. The engineering skills and business acumen my job entailed was vitally important and the work incredibly challenging. And for the present, at least, we would work out of the office in New York.

On my first day, I found myself searching the building for furniture. I found a vacant, beat-up desk. The whole building had been closed for years. It had the old elevators with open mesh, grill doors and they still operated by an ancient hydraulic system.

By this time, all of continental Europe had been overrun. British had lost virtually everything on the ground in their retreat to Dunkirk. Most of the RAF had been based in England and about a third of them had been lost over France.

The French, Dutch, Belgium and Norwegians, in fact most of the small European countries, had ordered P 40 Fighters and other small planes, Martin and Douglas light bombers, all from the U.S, as well as the Lockheed Lode Star passenger airplanes which the British used for reconnaissance purposes. Deliveries had just started. The deal in this operation was that the British would take over all the contracts. All contracts were written in English except for the French contracts. My rudimentary French taken at boarding school helped me through the required basic interpretation, and we were soon in business.

Biddy's job was to oversee everything equipment related to navigation including compasses. I took over the armament portion: bombsights, guns, bombs, everything but ammunition. There was a file cabinet with a drawer full of contracts. First off, I had to see exactly what airplanes were on order then determine what we needed regarding armament.

Many of the airplanes that were sold to Europe were designed to use European guns. It was my job to figure out what the differences were. I had to determine the number of guns needed and the modifications needed for the mounts in the airplanes so they would accept the American-made guns. I was to figure out which manufacturers could do the job, then follow through from the order through production and delivery, plus take care of any other challenges that might pop up in the overall supply of armament.

The British, by neutrality laws, were prohibited from borrowing money from the United States for military purposes, so they were forced to pay for armament out of their own pocket. They were rapidly running out of money, even after seizing all the British-owned American securities and liquidating them. Plus, there was a fair amount of British owned real estate in this country. The British treasury sold it as quickly as they could.

Roosevelt and Churchill were willing to collaborate in a Lend-Lease program. Roosevelt was able to talk a Democratic Congress into the program. This permitted the U.S. to buy military goods and lend or lease them to the British for eventual return or payment. Everybody but the extreme right knew this arrangement was nothing but fiction. The Chicago Tribune was violently opposed to this program, quoting George Washington who had said "No foreign entanglements."

I started working with Uncle Sam to get the government to buy the guns and bombs needed for Britain. I would write the requisitions and all supporting documents, then submit the paperwork to the War Department for the equipment that needed to be manufactured.

Communications with Great Britain were by cable and always encoded. The cables that came to us from London were called MAPS: Ministry of Aircraft Production; and cables from us to them were called "BRINY" – meaning British in New York. Because of cable charges, wording was sometimes too sparse. And I would receive them marked according to the eyes that were permitted to view them: Normal, Confidential, Secret or Most Secret (the latter replaced by Top Secret, the US Army designation which was later adopted by the Brits as well).

In the early days, all the British groups operated out of New York. They stayed away from Washington, DC, fearing that Republicans might use their presence in DC to encourage people to vote against Roosevelt. I had worn a Wilkie button on my coat lapel to the office one morning and Biddy pulled me aside saying, "Bill, I really wish you wouldn't wear that. I can't say anything against Wilkie, but we desperately need Roosevelt to be re-elected." I never wore the button to the office again.

Simultaneously with my going to work for the BAC, the historic air battle had started. I anxiously awaited every edition of every daily newspaper, especially concerned because there was a five-hour time difference between London and New York and the day's news was already old when I got it.

By September and October, the Germans had shifted to Luftwaffe night bombing raids on London. I knew it was extremely serious when I arrived at the office one morning in October to see the cable, "Most Secret, Most Immediate," the cover said. I opened it. It was from Lord Beaverbrook, an ex-Canadian who was now under Churchill and in charge of all the BAC's air production. It said:

> We Require Immediate doubling of all aircraft machine gun production orders and an acceleration of delivery by a minimum of six months. Please rely urgently—Beaverbrook.

Right after the presidential election in November 1940, the BAC secured space at 1785 Massachusetts Avenue in Washington and our entire office prepared to relocate. Franklin Roosevelt had just been elected for a third term as President of the United States.

My colleagues and I found a rooming house. The landlady's name was Mrs. Slaughter. I packed up the Buick in November and headed for my new quarters, leaving my two New York girlfriends behind. After only one night at The Slaughter House, I decided to go apartment hunting. I found a nice one-room apartment with a kitchenette on the third floor of a relatively new building. It was at the top of a hill on Sixteenth Street and had no parking facilities but it was near a couple of embassies and that seemed like a good trade-off.

The British weren't short of clothing, yet two competing women's groups organized ongoing clothing drives that nearly drove me crazy. One was called *National Bundles for Britain*, and the other, *Bundles for America*. It was a massive drive that turned into huge fund-raisers. The British charity was co-founded by Lucy Drage, a wealthy artist and interior decorator. She had married an Englishman who was a Colonel in the Royal Horse Guards and they resided in England for ten years before returning to live in a mansion in Kansas City.

Not to be outdone, Adelaide Frost Durant, a Michigan woman and daughter-in-law of the founder of General Motors and Chevrolet (who later married Captain Eddie Rickenbacker) learned about the British effort and was incensed that America did not have an equal relief effort. Known to have a volcanic personality, she spearheaded the counter fund, *Bundles for America,* and raised four million dollars to help families of U.S. servicemen overseas.

The groups were half-social and half-charity. Somehow, my office got caught in the middle and that was a distraction I certainly didn't need at the time. During the Battle of Britain, German airplanes were sometimes shot down over England and in some cases the wreckage was recognizable. England had shipped over to the U.S. the wreckage of a Messerschmitt to promote one of the charities and when it arrived, the women's groups battled viciously as to which one could use the wreckage for their fundraising efforts.

I received a cable from the Ministry in late 1940, briefly describing the competition among the women and pleading, "For God's sake, sort out this fight and get these women off my back!" It was a lose-lose situation but I eventually sorted it out and my real work resumed.

The commission was divided into two distinct areas: the Supply (paperwork) Department and a Technical Department that worked on issues with the United States such as how to fill the bombs, aircraft design and joint development on how to adapt aircraft so the U.S. and Brits could both use the armament. The thinking was that in case Germany totally overran Britain and Britain collapsed, the U.S. would still be able to use their planes and bombs. Everyone expected Britain to be invaded at any minute by German paratroopers and infantry. The public had caught on to Nazi Germany by now and people were petrified.

The RAF was vastly outnumbered but the British made Spitfire was better than the Messerschmitt 109. German bombers would drop bombs during night raids, having given up on day raids after suffering heavy losses in the daylight. Late in 1940-41, as aerial bombing was intensified, the devastating raids on London occurred.

The first bombs had to be made in Canada because of the 1930s Neutrality Act, which prohibited their being manufactured in the United States. Early on, the British and the Americans began to work together through the Royal Air Force (RAF) and the U.S. Air Corps. The Air Corps, originally a division of the U.S. Army, was created as a separate division after World War II to become the U.S. Air Force.

The British had recognized that their bombs were inefficient, made with cast steel and because of an obsolete design, with a poor ratio of explosive-to-steel content. The U.S. had designed bombs fabricated from sheet steel, obviously cheaper to make with a more efficient ratio. So both sides began to work together to modify the bombs. Thus occurred a time-consuming controversy over bomb lugs.

To hold the bombs in place in the planes, the British preferred to use only one lug where the Americans thought there had to be two lugs to hold them securely. The British argued that two lugs would hold the bombs too securely, possibly preventing them from releasing. The Americans thought only one lug wouldn't hold them securely enough and the bombs would release prematurely. They both decided to make bombs that would adapt to either aircraft, American or British. They adopted the standard operating procedure of placing two lugs on the American side of the bomb and one lug on the British side of the bomb. The loaders could use whichever they wanted, depending on which side was flying which aircraft.

Bomb casings were made in Milwaukee. I flew to the manufacturing plant to oversee operations a number of times. I also had occasion to visit a plant in Canada to watch their manufacturing process. On a side trip, once in 1941, I had some business to attend to in Canada at Canadian Westinghouse. En route home, back across the border, I had smuggled back some Canadian wool for Mother. I don't know to this day why I was worried about it. More importantly, on the back seat lay a roll of blueprints of bombsights. This was before we were actually at war. I was going across Niagara Falls.

The border guards looked into the car, paid no attention to the wool, but saw the blueprints. Of course they noticed the big type: BOMBSIGHT! They were very upset. Asked about it, I explained, "Look, I'm bringing the blueprints *into* the United States. Whatever secrets the U.S. has, have you ever heard of the U.S. smuggling blueprints of a bomb sight device *into* your country? They started laughing and let me go. Mother was delighted with the wool and I was delighted not to be detained in a foreign country.

I think my most exciting trip was to the Hercules plant in Pennsylvania where they filled bombs for the British.

There was a shortage of TNT at the time, so they had to mix TNT in huge vats with ammonium nitrate. You had a bomb eighty-five percent as potent as if it had been all TNT. I remember watching a man mix it once, watching the big paddles go around the vat, watching him stir it. The operator had just finished filling it when the huge copper lid slammed shut. I nearly died from fear! But it didn't explode. Of course, the operator laughed for quite some time. I was not thrilled with his morbid sense of humor.

Hartford Connecticut Colt was a machine gun maker and I visited that plant as well. They were having a problem with the Grumann F4F Wildcat airplane mounts. Guns tended to jump out of the mounts when fired. The Brits had designed the mounts for quick removal from an airplane. But when the gun jumped out of the mount, it would jam. They finally figured out that with a certain vibration, the rings would loosen, releasing the gun, causing it to jam.

The plant was rather archaic in operation. In the basement where they did the testing, they had sandbags to stop the bullets, but when testing the .50 caliber machine gun bullets, the sandbags were useless and during my visit, as I watched the testing, they started getting frantic phone calls at the plant - it seems that bullets were dropping from the skies over downtown Hartford.

Early on, I had become my own man and even among the bureaucratic nightmares that sometimes threatened to thwart my efficiency and ability to make decisions and carry them out, I stood my ground. The BAC was charged with conducting their business as precisely, efficiently and appropriately as did the RAF in England. Office procedures were no exception. In their office correspondence file, all papers were kept in order. Correspondence was to have holes punched in the upper left corner and was kept in manila folders secured by strings. I filed all cables and correspondence accordingly and thought nothing more about it.

One day I was summoned to the office of J.C. Ordd, a self-important Canadian who was temporarily Biddy's boss. Ordd proceeded to lecture me blisteringly up one side and down the other. He had reviewed the correspondence file and was furious. *The very effrontery of this young man doing correspondence with the ministry in England without passing it through him! All correspondence was to be approved by Ordd and prepared for his signature!* He raved on and on. I stood quietly, raging inside as I tried to keep myself from picking up an office chair and throwing it at the blustering old fool.

I waited until he was finished, then said simply, "Sir, I left a good job to come here. I don't expect to be talked to like that." Turning on my heels, I left the office and went straight into Biddy's office to report the incident. I told my superior that when I was asked to do a job, I would seek help if I needed it. I said if I made a mistake, I would correct it once it was called to my attention. But I told him that I would not tolerate being spoken to in this manner. Biddy said, "He's an S.O.B. and we're getting rid of him." A week later, I went to work to find Ordd gone. We proceeded with our work without interruption.

In 1940, when the British were desperately seeking aircraft from the U.S., even though they were unhappy with the performance of the Curtis P40 fighters, they were dissuaded from attempting to acquire one particular, projected U.S. Air Corps plane that had a huge, new air-cooled engine. This plane was the P47. On hearing of the British needs for a highly maneuverable fast fighter, the North American Aviation Company made a proposal to design a new fighter they thought they could deliver quickly.

The Air Corps was opposed to North American taking on the contract but reluctantly agreed so long as the fighter contained a U.S. manufactured liquid-cooled engine rather than the Rolls Royce engine, which was not being produced in the U.S. The Rolls Royce engine had been successful in empowering the Hurricanes and Spitfires. The Air Corps rationale was that if Britain should collapse and the U.S. Air Corps suddenly needed these new airplanes, that they would be useless without the proposed Rolls Royce-supplied engines.

The Air Corps then permitted the North American Aviation Company to accept the rush design and delivery contract for three hundred twenty of the P51 airplanes so long as they were designed to use the Allison liquid-cooled engines. This engine was an American attempt to make an engine comparable to the Rolls Royce. The British Air Commission reluctantly agreed to the use of the Allison engine and the tests of the first of the three hundred twenty airplanes were successful.

The British had bought those planes with their own money but had no funds with which to buy more. The Air Corps reluctantly agreed to the production of three hundred more P51s for the RAF alone, under the Lend-Lease agreement. These fighter airplanes were highly maneuverable and carried three .50 caliber machine guns in each wing.

The RAF squadrons in North Africa used these airplanes with reasonable success against the comparable German fighters. However, some aggressive RAF officers who were obviously dedicated to the belief that the Rolls Royce engine had to be superior to the Allison engine, made some field modifications of several P51s to accept the Rolls Royce engine. The performance was significantly improved. In the field, the concept that had demanded use of the Allison engine was of no consequence to U.S. Air Corps operations. The ongoing close cooperation in the field between RAF and U.S. Air Corps personnel led some American pilots to fly the British-modified P51s. They raved about the performance improvement, demanding that the Air Corps adopt the P51 equipped with Rolls Royce engines.

For once, the Air Corps production staff did not reject this request. The P51 production line, which was about to be closed down, was maintained through the Air Corps' order for vast numbers of P51s. Simultaneously, the Packard Motor Car Company was given an order to build the Rolls Royce engines, and production began with amazing speed.

As the performance of the Rolls-Royce engines was improved, the RAF and U.S. Air Corps discovered that the P51 was amazingly adaptable. Long-range releasable fuel tanks could be attached to their wings, enabling long-range protection of bomber squadrons. It was found that medium-sized bombs also could be attached to the wings to assist the P51s in providing ground support.

The RAF believed that the two American bombsights earlier described were useless under actual conditions. This was particularly true when the RAF's bombing of German facilities was largely confined to nighttime, carpet-bombing air raids where area targets did not require a super-accurate bombsight.

However, the British were certain that a useful bombsight could be developed. Their research and development finally produced one where the optics device was simply a projected target-cross drawn onto a sheet of plate glass. The positioning of the target indicator on the plate glass was very complex, but the British had developed the actual equipment in the form of a box, approximately eighteen by twenty-four inches. This was filled with pneumo-electromechanical actuators. The aircraft's absolute height, air speed and direction were automatically inserted.

The bombardier had to insert ground height and bomb characteristics and then take control of the airplane, directing it until the projected raster on the gyro-stabilized glass plate coincided with the target. Then he would push the bomb release. Since so much of the work was now automatically controlled and the bombardier had the simplest of optics, the accuracy of the British Mark 14 bombsight, in the real world, surpassed that of either the Sperry or Norden sights that were both American made, quite complex and rather useless because of their complicated optics.

One day I received an urgent cable that design drawings and a prototype were en route. I was asked to "urgently press for manufacture" in the U.S. When the material came, I presented it to the Air Corps who shook their heads but agreed that the relative simplicity of the targeting indicator should be very advantageous. They recommended that the AC Sparkplug division of General Motors in Flint, Michigan be given the contract to produce this bombsight.

An Air Corps officer and I took the drawings and prototype to Flint. The manufacturers in Flint were primary producers of carburetors and fell all over themselves with the prospect of making these bombsights. They did, however, express concern about the way the prototype had been made. They said it looked as if it had been made in a tool room by people who were all using different complicated mountings for the various components. They offered to produce a bombsight based on the British design but altered to be actually workable, and one that would be physically interchangeable with those produced in England.

When I got the first unit, I quickly shipped it off to England. Upon receipt, the Brits analyzed the American-made product and immediately cabled me, asking, "What have you done to our bombsight?" AC in Flint had redesigned the bombsight physically for production purposes without changing the operational characteristics. Because of this, the American-produced bombsight cost substantially less to produce than the British version without sacrificing quality. The British had to admit the final product was superior to their own in terms of reliability and maintenance. AC successfully produced some ten thousand of these bombsights.

Another interesting British development was a gyro-stabilized gun sight, originally designed for installation in aircraft gun turrets. This had always been a problem because shots from a gun turret were rapidly deflected by the air stream, which was always at an angle to the direction of the target.

In addition, if the aircraft were maneuvering, other elements of direction or deviation would be introduced. The only answer to this problem had been the use of tracer ammunition, which allowed the gunner to redirect the guns in an effort to offset these deviations. The gyroscopically controlled gun sight largely minimized wind and aircraft maneuvering dislocations. I placed an order for a large number of these gun sights, which for some reason the U.S. Navy insisted on handling. It was not long before various tests conducted by the RAF found that this gun sight, the Mark VII, increased the firing accuracy of fighter airplanes engaged in dogfight maneuvers.

When the first of these gun sights came off the production line, the U.S. Navy quietly pocketed the order. From certain sources, I learned that the Navy did not yet have any program to install and use these sights on currently active naval aircraft.

I made application to the Munitions Assignments Committee that the production of the bombsights should be diverted and delivered according to the original requisition, since there was aircraft in use waiting for those bombsights.

My experiences with the Munitions Assignments Committee and the Air Corps had thus far been very favorable and I had a wonderfully constructive working relationship with them all. My sole experience with the Navy allocation was something different, however. My application was routinely denied without explanation. Not to be outdone by bureaucrats, I appealed directly to a committee called the Munitions Assignments Committee-Navy.

I showed up at a meeting to be confronted by the actual committee, with Admiral Joseph Mason Reeves at the helm. I stood face to face with this full-fledged admiral from World War I, in a uniform that displayed one broad stripe and four lesser stripes. I was armed only with my integrity, my commitment to do what was right, and my rationale.

Upon listening to my verbal application, Admiral Reeves responded sourly, "I don't know why the British think they own everything. Churchill has a round of martinis with the President and walks away with anything he damn well wishes. This bombsight is not a British development because it is called the Mark VII and we all know the use of the identification MARK is a Navy identification. We're going to be able to use these gun sights and I don't want them diverted to the British. Request denied."

I stood firm. I said, "With all due respect, Sir, I believe these are of British design with unique advantages and we have aircraft in use whose performance can be significantly improved with the use of these gun sights. I respectfully request that this be referred to a sub-committee for further discussion."

The admiral became red-faced and looked straight into my eyes, "The Munitions Assignments Committee-Navy *has* no sub committees. I *am* the Munitions Subcommittee-NAVY…request denied!"

I solicited help from my superior. Biddy and I quietly made some comments via other channels. In short order, the gun sights were diverted back to the BAC for immediate use. I never heard another word from Admiral Reeves.

Early in 1941, Italy, already in Albania, attacked Greece and had their heads handed to them by the Greeks. Germany came to Italy's aid and rapidly advanced into Greece. The British responded by sending reinforcements from Egypt to Greece. The aid proved too little too late, and the Brits were overrun and pushed out of Greece and Crete, having suffered heavy losses. Egypt had been a British protectorate, almost a colony, and the British forces there moved west into Libya, an Italian colony. The Italians were pushed back and the British were making great progress until Hitler again came to the rescue of Italy.

The Germans heavily reinforced the Italians, pushing the British back. This was made easier because of the losses in Greece and because the Germans could readily supply their North-African forces across the Mediterranean from Italy, and with little British naval opposition since the central Mediterranean could readily be defended from land air bases. The British held out on Malta. But this was no help against the German supply convoys to North Africa. Because of the heavy British losses of aircraft, there was a panic call for re-supply of Egypt, but the request could not be met through the Mediterranean.

With tremendous effort, the BAC crated up one hundred P40 fighters and twenty or more Douglas and Martin bombers. Under maximum secrecy, they were placed on a fast freighter and shipped from the East Coast, virtually unescorted to Takoradi, a port in Ghana, West Africa. On arrival, the planes were assembled and flown across Africa up to Egypt where they helped hold the German's thrust into Egypt.

The Germans reached as far as a hundred or so miles from Cairo until they were held at the passes going down into the Nile Delta. Some of the British had been cut off in northern Libya and one of the earliest British disasters was the overrunning of this enclave. It was this effort that made German General Erwin Rommel famous. Gradually the British forces were re-supplied through the Indian Ocean while the Germans were held at the pass. Meanwhile, the British and Americans had together organized the invasion of Morocco and Algeria.

In the fall of 1942, after heavy fighting against the Germans on the east in Egypt and on the west in Algeria, the Allies gradually wore the Germans down. They were assisted by British code breakers who learned of the critical German shortages by reading Rommel's messages. In the east, with the breakthrough and retreat of the Germans, under British pressure, the RAF was critical in attacking German and Italian ground supply efforts.

While I was not involved directly in any of the spy efforts other than the normal British diversion of supplies of bombs to various theatres, I did have one rather unique urgent cable request from the RAF in Egypt.

After reading the cable several times, I wondered how to word the requisition. I knew the request would go through the normal channels to U.S. Army Ordinance, my source of guns and bombs.

The request from Britain was for the supply of a large quantity of rubber prophylactics. I was astounded to see that this seemingly out of place request was in the neighborhood of a hundred thousand condoms. In the early '40s, those items were rarely mentioned.

With some embarrassment, my secretary typed up the requisite forms but meanwhile, I had cabled Egypt requesting an explanation for the need. I knew I might be called upon to justify the order. The request would, I was sure, fascinate the receivers of the order. Another more logistical problem may have been an issue as well. Should these *units* have been ordered through the medical division? This was certainly outside the realm of normal armament supply.

The answer came quickly. It was no joke. The condoms were needed to cover the muzzles of aircraft machine guns. The guns normally had their breechblocks retracted when the gun was not firing so that after firing, air could flow through the barrel to assist in the cooling process. Under normal conditions, this process posed no problems. However, with the RAF operating from makeshift dirt and sand airstrips during the advance, when a squadron took off, only the lead airplane would be flying through clean air. In subsequent take-offs, airplanes were sent through dust, dirt and all the whirling sand the first plane had stirred up and left in its trail.

This debris, flowing through the open gun barrels, frequently compromised or jammed the sensitive breechblock mechanism causing unacceptable firing failure. They had solved the problem - with condoms. After enjoying a few laughs, my friends in U.S. Army Ordinance passed the requisition along to the appropriate army medical authorities.

Washington D.C. was an exciting place to be during the early 1940s and events were not all war related. The National Gallery of Art - Smithsonian Institution had slated a dedication of the new A. W. Mellon Art Gallery for the evening of March 17, 1941. Because of Dad's stature in the arts community, Mother had received an invitation. I knew President Roosevelt was to be there and I was aware of the protocol, so I called the Secret Service and asked if I could use Dad's invitation. I was approved to go.

The event was memorable. I sat quietly with the others, watching presidential aides assist the lame president to the rear of the podium. People knew about his challenge with polio but it wasn't spoken about in polite society. I stood twenty feet from President Roosevelt when he made his speech and dedicated the gallery.

My friendship with Jim Wyld continued to flourish. Jim's fascination with rockets, airplanes, anything related to physics or flying, never waned. Early on, he had become a member of the American Interplanetary Society, predecessor to the American Rocket Society.

In 1941, Jim and Bill Harry shared an apartment in Greenwich Village. Jim built a small rocket motor on the roof of his apartment house. He had summarily decided to run a test. This experiment was only attempted once. The sound caused such a commotion that further tests were out of the question. The neighbors certainly took notice but luckily, everything was put away before the fire department arrived.

Jim held several jobs, but inevitably was terminated when his interest in rocketry invariably exceeded the needs of his employers. It was difficult for a genius to concentrate on mundane topics like fluid heat transfer units. Jim and I kept in close contact throughout this period and visited each other whenever we could find a spare weekend or holiday.

On June 8, 1941, a hot Sunday afternoon, I drove with Jim out to the wilds of New Jersey to watch a motor test. I took the camera, ready to shoot the exact moment of lift-off.

The motor cut off a few seconds after firing and I jumped up out of the safety of the slit trench to photograph the spiral of vapor curling up from the nozzle. At that precise moment, the motor exploded and I snapped the shutter. The photograph shows a blur in the air but fortunately the debris was directed in the opposite direction. The witnesses, stunned, remained unscathed. I sent the photo to a publication called "Astronautics" and it made the front cover of the August 1941 issue. I got a photo credit and the film was retained by mutual agreement by the American Rocket Society.

Jim was especially interested in liquid fuel rockets and had already designed several rockets and their guidance systems. Jim later invented a number of complex rocket mechanisms, including a theory of counter-cooling.

His graduating class at Princeton had earlier voted him not only *the most non-collegiate member* of his class but *the least likely to succeed,* as well. Jim Wyld would have the last laugh. He became the first self-made millionaire of his class, in the prestigious science of rocketry. He was indeed a real rocket scientist.

Shortly after the article was published, a representative of the navy contacted Jim and three colleagues. They were asked to stop publicizing their results. They were offered a development contract for rockets to assist aircraft in water takeoffs. This was the genesis of Reaction Motors, Inc.

The company was founded by Jim and his three buddies and literally started on a shoestring. It was grossly under-funded. The four owners of RMI were inexperienced and rather naïve in the laborious and painstaking process of trying to get paid from government contracts lathered in bureaucratic red tape. On at least two occasions, Jim went to Washington and stayed with me while trying to get payment for work done from the Navy.

At one time, the sheriff was literally on the doorstep of Reaction Motors. When Jim discovered the problem, he dipped into his savings account and used money left him by a relative. The four colleagues trudged to the bank to withdraw the funds and save RMI. Jim's father, an astute businessman saw that Jim was properly compensated for the rescue.

Years later, the Rockefellers were brought in as venture capitalists and funded RMI, bringing it into the financial world.

As busy as I was at work, things finally began to perk up on the home front. Early in 1941, I learned from Mother that Hilda's husband had died several months before. They had been married only six months. Her stepdaughters had gone to Syracuse to live with relatives. I decided to give her a call and was pleased to find out that she was delighted to hear from me. It was just as easy to visit her in New York from Washington DC as it had been from Pittsburgh, and we began dating again.

On a weekend in the spring of 1941, Hilda was en route to Norfolk to see a friend in the Navy and missed her airplane connection in DC. She called me and I immediately invited her to dinner. That evening the flame took hold. It would burn for more than half a century. I believe still that love is a strange phenomenon. How do you know you're in love? Who knows—about the voice or physical attraction or interests? It's the chemistry. Who can say what attracts the fancy of one person to another?

Our courtship continued. I sent her flowers after she had a wisdom tooth removed and recalled how very impressed she was by my gesture.

In September 1941, I sold my airplane to a milk truck driver for five hundred and fifty dollars. After a year with the BAC, I decided it was time for a vacation. I invited mother to ride to D.C. by train, and then drive with me to Florida. I had bought a new Buick in January 1941 for the costly sum of one thousand, one hundred and ninety-six dollars and fifty cents.

Meanwhile, back in New York, although my father was gone, Mother continued to play bridge with her long time neighbors, Hilda's parents. It seemed there would be no interference from her parents, unlike my own parents' marriage. It was important to Hilda that everything be done right. Although a widow in her mid-twenties, she made me take her home one night to ask her father for her hand in marriage. I certainly had no objection.

Thanksgiving, November 21, 1941 was my birthday. And that was the day she said a definite *yes* to my earlier proposal.

A few days later, I heard the most wonderful story. It was days before the attack on Pearl Harbor. The German Embassy in Washington was still operating, that is until Germany declared war on the United States a few days after Pearl. A British officer had dropped by my office to chat. We were on very good terms. He said the British Embassy was having a terrible time with the telephone switchboard. They were expanding and they were unable to keep up with the rate of expansion. They were always getting crossed wires and things of that sort. He had become involved with the logistics of the project and had become very frustrated indeed. Prior to Thanksgiving weekend, he had been working out some communications problems, and he kept getting disconnects and crossed wires. Finally he became fed up when someone got on the line just as he was trying to make a connection.

He had been trying to get some help, but the embassy people had been very lax to offer assistance. So he decided to give the embassy a good scare. The next time he was hooking up some wires and someone extra came on the line who shouldn't have been there, he hollered, "Achtung!" in the best German accent he could muster, adding, "Zis is der Cherman Embassy! Heil Hitler!" Then he hung up.

He didn't know what happened until a few days later. He met a friend on the embassy staff who was also working on communications. He asked his friend if he enjoyed a good American Thanksgiving and his friend replied, "Oh, God, it was terrible! I spent the whole goddamn day down a manhole trying to find where the crossed wire was. We believe we found a wiretap of some sort the German embassy had on one of our lines. Somebody came on the line speaking in German and ending up with Heil Hitler. My God! I checked every line there was and I couldn't find a tap anywhere, but there must be something wrong!"

Well, my friend kept very quiet about his little game after that. Needless to say, he swore me to absolute secrecy.

On the weekend of December 7, Hilda and I heard about Pearl Harbor on the car radio. We had chosen that day to hunt for an apartment in Washington DC. As we went by the Japanese Embassy, we saw the embassy staff burning papers in the courtyard. It was surreal. The country was at war thousands of miles away and the Japanese were burning documents in the nation's capitol in plain view.

The next day at the office, I discovered that the BAC had changed faces. British officers who had all been wearing civilian clothes prior to the attack on Pearl Harbor suddenly showed up in full RAF uniform. Biddy looked up from his desk and growled, "There are more damn Brits here than when they burned the city!"

But an apartment still had to be found and we continued our search. Hilda and I had come across the Marlin Apartments near the cathedral. I negotiated a ten-dollar-a-month increase from Biddy so we could afford the ninety-two-dollar-a-month apartment. Apartments were scarce because of the war. When we arrived at the apartment, ready to sign the lease, we found out it had been taken that morning. Everything else we had seen was terrible. But the landlady of the apartment we wanted said she really preferred to rent to young people. She promised to let us know if anything became available.

As luck would have it, at least for us, five days later Italy and Germany declared war on the United States and the Secretary of the Italian embassy was picked up by federal agents and incarcerated in

White Sulphur Springs. The Secretary's apartment was in the Marlin. It was a corner apartment and suddenly became available. It was even a better apartment than the one we had looked at, and all for the same rent. I signed the lease New Year's Day and we were married January 17, 1942.

The wedding took place at Hilda's home in New York. We were surrounded by family and friends. Minutes before the wedding, there I was, dressed to the nines in my tuxedo, sitting on the sun porch engrossed in an article in Time Magazine. The U.S. had evacuated Manila. I was so focused on reading that I failed to notice the minister who had come to speak with me. He had sought me out, hoping he could help me feel less nervous. But the only thing I was interested in was finishing the article without being interrupted.

We planned to drive to Florida for our honeymoon. I had driven my car from DC to Richmond and left it in a hangar. I flew to New York for the wedding. After the wedding, a chauffeur drove us to Newark, New Jersey, with rice falling out of the car all over the road. We flew to Richmond and found the car nestled in an airplane hangar under a beam where a multitude of doves had built a nest. Doves might have been a lovely wedding gift but their residue certainly wasn't appreciated.

We began the drive to Florida and I suddenly realized I had left my glasses at the home of Hilda's parents. Love was indeed blind. A quick call to New York got them on their way and they were delivered by mail to us in Florida. Four hours outside of Richmond, we also realized we'd left a piece of our wedding cake under our pillow at the airport motel. We had a good laugh, wondering what the hotel maid would think of her find. After two luxurious weeks honeymooning, we returned to DC, happy and relaxed, to our new apartment. I lifted my bride into my arms and carried her over the threshold. But we both knew what was in store. The war was heating up and I was needed at the office.

Japan was overrunning the Philippines. German submarines were attacking the U.S. shipping industry on the eastern seaboard. People were ordered to keep lights off along the coastline so Germans couldn't see lights on the shore and use the lights for target practice.

I worked incredibly long hours with only Sundays off and Hilda settled into housekeeping. Our apartment was up on the hill, right across from Massachusetts Avenue. A real estate developer by the name of Cafritz owned several apartment buildings in the DC area, including ours.

We were on the second floor of the Marlin, but it was a short flight of stairs up to the second floor. We didn't even have to take the elevator. The building was L-shaped, and down the corridor from us on the east side of the building were two apartments which were joined together. They were owned by Joe Kressman and his wife. Joe was one of the leading anesthesiologists in the country. He had been in the military for some time and then gone into private practice. He had invented a number of devices for use in his field.

Now semi-retired, he and his wife had joined two apartments together. They had a daughter, also named Jo, who was about eleven at the time. The Kressmans went out a fair amount, and I would baby-sit Jo and help her do her homework. They had a fine radio phonograph that I could listen to. In return, I'd ask them to baby-sit for young Jim when we went out occasionally, and we counted on him to give us expert medical advice. It was a helluva good tradeoff.

Down the corridor the other way were the Fletchers. They were British. He was a wing commander on the BAC technical staff. His wife and Hilda became great good friends.

The apartment house had a very sophisticated radio antenna system with an all-wave radio on the roof that fed to all the apartments through coaxial cable. Since everyone had all wave or short wave radio there, I regularly listened to the BBC and German stations as they broadcast propaganda. One day I went up on the roof, found a problem to be a dead tube, I replaced the tube, told the apartment manager what I had done, she wanted to know what it had cost, I said "about $1.25. Forget it."

After Pearl Harbor, Washington went through blackouts for quite some time, which of course was nonsense. There was no way in the world the Germans or the Japanese could have gotten an airplane all the way over to Washington. But we still had air raid drills and blackout curtains.

Hilda became an air raid warden. She was convinced of the futility of much of what was going on, but it was something that a lot of the women of the apartment enjoyed. One day they were talking about bombs and asking me what I do. They asked what they should do if they were to find any incendiary bombs at the building, and I told Hilda, the thing to do would be to pick it up by the dead end, throw it out a window, and that they would be perfectly safe. I explained that only ten percent of them had explosives in them, and the explosives didn't go off until the very end, so they were perfectly safe to pick the thing up and quickly throw it out.

Well, the ladies wouldn't believe her, so as I had ordered seventy-five million of the four pound incendiary bombs and had a couple in the office unfilled and marked *inert*, I brought one home and handed it to Hilda. She took it down to one of the air raid meetings.

She held it up and they took one look at it and they all scattered. She said, "It's inert!" But they wanted no part of it. The next day, an FBI agent came around. He said, "Mrs. Baum, I understand you've got an incendiary bomb in the apartment." She produced it, the man looked at it, saw the marking and said tenuously, "Please don't ever show that again. These ladies were scared out of their wits!"

There was rationing, of course. When we first got back to the apartment after our honeymoon, we didn't have much in the way of canned goods. Shortly thereafter, we were given coupons for canned goods and other supplies. I remember going to the store right after we got back to Washington. Sugar was in short supply—I couldn't believe it. Finally they had coupons for shoes, even clothing. Women were taking the cuffs off trousers to save cloth. Butter was going to the troops, so margarine became available to the general public and because of the laws against colored margarine, there were plastic packs of margarine with a little bubble of color in it. People would break the bubble and knead the pack to move the color through the margarine so it looked like butter. From time to time, eggs were in short supply, as was beef, but there always seemed to be loads of chicken. From time to time, cigarettes became in short supply, but since I went over to the military exchange regularly, we had an unlimited supply of cigarettes.

~

Another important item my outfit produced was the British designed, four-pound incendiary bomb. Earlier, I had placed an order for seventy-five million of these cheap nasty bombs. The bomb

103

consisted merely of a cast iron hexagonal nose followed by a magnesium hexagonal tube and a lightweight, similarly shaped tail. The bombs were fused with the simplest of impact fuses and filled with thermite, which ignited the magnesium. Once lit, they were impossible to stop and the burning magnesium could ignite anything nearby that was combustible.

One out of ten of these bombs maintained a small explosive charge which would detonate after the bomb had burned a while and would discourage anyone from trying to pick up an ignited bomb to toss it away. They were packed in tin containers, which upon dropping would tear open, releasing the individual bombs. They would drop willy-nilly onto the target.

The only down side was that they required more magnesium than had been produced up until that time. A new plant was built in Henderson, Nevada that used power from the Hoover Dam to produce this magnesium. (The present industrial complex at Henderson is a direct result of this bomb order from World War II.)

Early into the manufacturing and production stage, I received a frantic telephone call from a junior officer engaged in a ship-loading operation in Philadelphia. He reported that a cargo sling had broken and several cases of these bombs had fallen between the ship and the pier.

He had moved the ship but what should he do, he asked. And could his diver safely approach this cargo? I politely responded, "Put the ship back. I can think of no safer place for these bombs than under forty feet of water." The bombs remain today where they were dropped on that day in 1942.

There was one problem with the incendiary bombs. They were of British design with only one strict specification: that of the metal star holding the actual detonator slug that would trigger the burning of the magnesium. This was designed to be critical because as the bomb safety was activated upon, the bombs were released from the tin case.

On impact, the detonator slug would pull the star loose and ignite the bomb. After several months of production, I received another frantic communique'. This time, it was a cable from England. Somehow a Lanchester that was being loaded had released a bomb tin. Upon hitting the ground, several of the individual bombs had ignited. They had started a fire before the aircraft could be moved and the plane was destroyed. It turned out that the supplier had not bothered to meet the specifications—*that one critical specification.* And the resulting softness of the metal caused some of the bombs to be activated with only a short drop from the bomb bay.

~

In 1943, while Hilda was pregnant with Jim, we decided to repeat our honeymoon trip and go to Florida again, but we couldn't drive because of gas rationing and the unavailability of tires, so we took the train. Of course the train schedules were always interrupted, so our train to Sarasota was a long, long trip indeed. I think we got in eighteen hours late. We stayed at the same place at the end of the causeway out to the keys. There was a RAF training station near Sarasota. We saw some young RAF fellows in Sarasota, and invited a bunch of them to have dinner with us one night at a restaurant. We had lots of fun. To get to Miami, we arranged to go by train. Unfortunately, train service was interrupted so we had to go part way by bus. Buses were very full, and of course Hilda, being pregnant, was not particularly comfortable. In those days, blacks had to sit in the back of the bus. It was hard to believe.

The hotel in Miami Beach where we had stayed on our honeymoon had been taken over by the military so we stayed at a hotel in downtown Miami. The RAF had an advanced training unit in the Bahamas. I'd been sending bombs there, not bombs to explode, but rather demonstration practice bombs. I wanted to go to the Bahamas to see what they were doing over there, how they were being used, so I arranged transport in a military airplane from Miami over to the islands. Transport to Nassau was in a C46, twin-engine plane, not much bigger than a DC-3. It was rough aluminum with seats on the side where you could sit in a parachute, if you had a parachute.

I flew to Nassau and immediately was engaged in a big hassle with the local people. They wanted to charge me a ten-dollar tourist tax. I informed them that I was going over on British government business. In those days the Bahamas were a possession of the British government and I kept asking, "Why should I pay ten dollars when I'm on British business in a British possession?" A big, long argument ensued and they finally let me in without my paying the ten dollars, which I'd fought so hard for because I knew I'd never get it back from the BAC administration as a reimbursable expense.

I spent one night there at a fancy hotel because the rates weren't terrifically high. I was all set to go back the next day and found out the C46 airplane had blown a tire on landing. They couldn't get another tire till the next day, so I was stranded there for another night. I made due at the bar. As I recall, I believe I knocked off two big bottles of fine British beer of some sort made to the pre-war standards, before they reduced the alcoholic content.

There were two movie theaters in Nassau. I thought I'd go see a movie to kill time that evening and as it turned out, the movie theatres were terribly segregated. One theater had a picture I wasn't interested in that was for whites. The other theatre had a picture that looked interesting, but that was for local blacks only. I hadn't realized the level and breadth of segregation in the area. Telephone service between the Bahamas and Miami, even though it was only one hundred miles or so was very expensive, so I decided to send a telegram. I worded the telegram very briefly because then telegrams were very expensive though the thought of the cost is laughable today. I think I said, "Stranded in Nassau. Blown tire. Be back tomorrow." Some bureaucrat didn't like the wording, so they never sent the telegram. Poor Hilda was sitting in Miami in the hotel wondering what ever happened to me. I complained about the non-receipt of my cable and about nine months later, got a letter from the cable authorities in Nassau apologizing for the censorship. They included a check for one pound ten shillings.

While in Miami, we took a bus out to the Jai-Alai pavilion and watched some games. It was really very exciting. We also went to the dog track once but didn't enjoy that as much. We took the train back to Washington without any further event.

~

That same year, I received a top secret cable stating that a special package of diagrams and blueprints were coming by way of the embassy and instructing us that all assistance would be given to put this product into earliest production in America. An embassy messenger soon brought the package to me. My British counterpart at the BAC opened it to find the plans for huge, special-purpose bombs.

One bomb weighed twelve thousand pounds. It was called Tall Boy Medium. The other weighed twenty-two thousand pounds, with a code name: Tall Boy Large. These were to be made of cast armor steel and would be capable of deep penetration without breaking up before detonation. It was explained that they were urgently needed to attack "mysterious works" which the Germans were known to be building in France and Belgium.

The designer, Barnes Wallis, had also been responsible for designing the bouncing bombs used by the 617th Squadron in the attack on the Mohne and Eder dams in the Ruhr Valley in western Germany. The Dam Busters raid took place on May 16, 1943 and the result was heavy flooding. German production was badly damaged. Seven of the nineteen airplanes used by the RAF in the raid were shot down. The RAF had incurred such heavy losses that they chose to use the bouncing bombs only rarely during the remainder of the war. The raid was so successful and so dramatic a story, Hollywood made a movie about it. Entitled simply "The Dam Busters," it became a morale booster among several other true stories during World War II.

After reading the cable, I grabbed the phone and made an appointment with General Copeland of the U.S. Army Ordinance Department. I quickly caught a taxi and went straight to the Pentagon. A colleague and I unrolled the plans for the general who had already been alerted via the White House by the British Embassy. This project was indeed to receive the highest priority. The three of us booked a reservation to St. Louis on the night train. General Copeland had already determined that a St. Louis firm, Scullin Steel Co., a producer of tank turrets, would be the ideal manufacturer.

The Scullin people took one look at the plans and fell all over themselves with excitement. The challenge was incredible. The bomb was designed to be perfectly streamlined in order to attain supersonic speed and to withstand enormous impact as it penetrated before exploding. The armor steel on the nose was ten or so inches thick and the actual pointed nose was a tungsten steel insert. The fusing was a delayed action fuse in the rear of the bomb, designed to ensure detonation after deep penetration.

The British had made several prototypes of the bomb for testing but did not have the facilities to make a substantial quantity. The U.S. Air Corps could not believe that a bomb of this size or magnitude could be carried and launched, primarily because the conceptual design of U.S. Aircraft was so different from that of the Lanchester, the British heavy bomber.

The British Mission had given us assurance that there were at least two Lanchester squadrons that were capable of deploying the bomb. The first production was for a larger number of the twelve thousand pound bomb, which was successfully cast and finished. We shipped them disguised in a covering entitled "pressure vessel" to Yorktown, Virginia. There they were loaded with a special explosive comprised of RDX, the latest British development. This was blended with aluminum powder to change the character of the blast. The same explosive was being used for the latest U.S. Navy torpedoes. I then shipped the completed bombs off to England by the usual means.

I prided myself on the fact that I was able to get bombs over to England faster than the Air Corps could get their bombs to England. My team had developed a highly efficient ship-loading arrangement that worked quite smoothly. However, we only had one destination and the U.S. Air Corps had to ship to both Europe and Asia destinations, so I was forced to concede that our shipping procedures might have been a bit easier in that respect.

The bombs were first used prior to D-Day to strike huge submarine pens in France. The heavy structures had been built with concrete roofs, twelve to fourteen feet thick. Several direct hits were made. One penetrated so deeply, the ensuing wave destroyed the ships in the pen. The bombs were also used to destroy high-speed, German E boats used in the straits of Dover, which took refuge in those pens.

The RAF also got a direct hit underneath a critical rail tunnel in France on the line from Bordeaux. This precluded the German's further use of the rail line to re-deploy troops during the battle of Normandy.

The bombs were also successfully used to breach dikes in Holland, flooding out the Germans, and to destroy locks on the canal system, also critically important to the Germans. As a result of some inadvertent publicity, the code name Tall Boy was disclosed, and they renamed the twenty-two thousand pound bomb Grand Slam. There was only one squadron that could carry these massive, heavy bombs. A limited number of Grand Slams were made and used. One outstanding victory using these bombs was a direct hit on the BattleshipTurpitz, which had holed up in a fjord on the northern tip of Norway. The Turpitz was the largest German battleship ever built and had managed to remain relatively unscathed through other British attacks as well as an attack from the Russians. The RAF 617 "Dam Busters" and nine squadrons finally did her in.

Years later, I visited the war museum in Oslo and on display was a piece of the Grand Slam bomb that destroyed the Turpitz. The U.S. typically used five hundred-pound bombs to thousand pound bombs. The British typically used thousand pound bombs to four thousand pound blockbuster bombs.

~

In the meantime, Hilda and I were about to become parents. Doctors Hospital was our designated hospital. At the time new mothers were expected to be in the hospital for ten days or so. Hilda's obstetrician was located in downtown DC. For many years afterwards, she talked about one of her favorite memories. She was in the elevator on the way to the doctor's office for a check-up when four fully armed U.S. soldiers joined her in the elevator en route to their assignment, an anti-aircraft gun on the rooftop. It was only a few blocks from the White House.

On October 6, 1943, I took a photograph of her outside the Marlin Apartments. She always hated it. It showed a very pregnant woman who was to give birth less than twenty-four hours later. That evening was a time of considerable discomfort to Hilda and around three-thirty a.m., I was awakened by a strong suggestion that it was about time to drive her to the hospital.

After settling into her room, I was advised by the doctor to go home, that the birth process would take several hours. I followed his advice and went back home to bed, routinely proceeding the next morning to the office as usual.

Around two-thirty that afternoon, I received a telephone call from the doctor who said, "Why don't you come on down and meet your new son?"

I snapped to attention and headed down the hall, telling my secretary where I was going. I was walking down the stairs when I heard her yell out, "Mr. Baum's a new father!"

When I saw Jim, I noticed he had hair on his ears, which was a good sign because engineers, of course, always have hairy ears. Our one-bedroom apartment soon had a crib in it and we had the usual problems of babies wanting to sleep during the day. Jim spent his first two years in the apartment.

We lived on the regular minimum gas rations, until early in 1945, when things seemed to be letting up, and everybody and their brother seemed to be getting C coupons, which meant almost unlimited gasoline. So I applied for some, claiming I had to get over to Baltimore to the Martin plant from time to time. I had no problem getting coupons. I never truly used them, because we didn't drive all that much. Of course you had to make your tires last. All the tires being produced were going to the military. The old Buick seemed to hold up very well. We didn't have a garage, but there was a vacant space across from the building on 39th Street.

We parked there until one time when we looked out the window and saw some kids trying to steal gas out of our gas tank. I yelled at them, went down and they went away. I got the license number of one of their cars, and forwarded it to the police. Their mother claimed they'd never been out that night at all. The trick then was to find a lock to put on the gas tank. This was fine, except that no two gas tanks had the same kind of opening. We never did find a proper lock.

Early in 1944, my draft exemption ran out again and this time, the local draft board was reluctant to defer me. They reclassified me 1-A. Now they were drafting young men with families, and Biddy wasn't about to lose me. To help emphasize my importance to the war effort, the BAC decided to ship me to England to tie up some loose ends there and to meet the recipients of some of the guns and bombs I was sending over. I had no passport at the time. Issuance of passports was extremely restricted because of the draft. Those who were classified 1-A were ineligible for a passport for obvious reasons. I couldn't see how I would be permitted to leave the country.

With Biddy's guidance, application was made to the top draft officials for special approval for passport issuance. Some bureaucrat decided that the application couldn't be accepted until I undertook a physical exam to determine whether or not I could even be drafted.

Washington D.C. was segregated at the time, even during the draft process. In the first two weeks of the month, white potential draftees were given physicals, and the last two weeks of the month, physicals were given to blacks. Due to time constraints, arrangements were made for me to have my physical during the second two weeks of the month.

So there I stood, one fine day, at a not-so-stout one hundred thirty-eight pounds, stark naked in the middle of a room filled with two hundred big, strong black men, also naked. The exam proceeded without incident, but the looks I got from the other draftees made me laugh every time I thought of that experience. The last part of my physical was an interview with a psychiatrist. "What's your reaction to going into the army?" I was asked.

"I think it's the craziest thing in the world, because I've been trying to win this war for the last three and a half years," I responded. I was dubbed "sane" and my classification remained 1-A.

The BAC pleaded with the draft board to issue a passport to me. The British ambassador issued a special certificate of insurance confirming that I would definitely return to the U.S. Finally the passport was issued.

The trip was as unique as the passport process. One of the early British B-24 bombers had been reverse lend-leased back to the Americans. It had been damaged from a hard landing. They had repaired it in San Diego and the Air Corps had turned it back to the British. It was to be converted into a cargo airplane and the British would give it British markings and fuel it. The plane, ID #AL610, had ten seats. This plane would fly my colleagues and me to England.

We assembled together at the Washington airport. At first we couldn't get the engine started but eventually boarded. We flew first to Bermuda. After spending a day in Bermuda at an American air base, we flew that night to Terra Sierra in the Azores. We took off again the next evening after dark and flew over Ireland, which was a neutral country. We were flying at low altitude when suddenly we looked down to see men rushing out of their tents, aiming anti-aircraft guns toward the sky –toward our plane! It was illegal to fly over a neutral zone, but we were soon long gone and luckily were not hit.

We landed at the airport near Glasgow to refuel, then flew on to an airport near London. A driver took us into the city and we were shocked to learn that there had been a ferocious air raid the night before. We had missed it by hours. I was saddened to see the devastation in this beautiful city.

Arrangements for my lodging had been made at the Strand Palace Hotel. My colleague Charlie Miller had been registered at another hotel across the street. Both hotels were down the street from Trafalgar Square, providing a convenient bus ride to the Ministry of Aircraft Production, which was located west of the House of Parliament along the Thames. I was issued a ration book for two rather unique necessities, tea and a gas mask. I was to remain in London seven weeks. I knew I would need tea but hoped I would not need a gas mask.

During the course of my stay, I made numerous trips to aircraft factories, bomb storage facilities and specialized bomb-loading plants. In one plant I was invited to help workers load a four thousand-bomb blockbuster with explosives. It was similar to one I was having made in the U.S. I got to witness a test of some new fusing for the bomb.

Shewberryness had been the site of an ancient fort that guarded the north entrance to the Thames. On the wall of the fort, an armored turret from a warship had been mounted. The new fuse they were testing, the BR, was hush-hush. As a special favor related to my VIP status, I was allowed to screw the fuse into the bomb—of course *without* the electronic operating mechanism. Then I connected the detonator to the wires that would be used to explode the bomb. As I watched, I saw someone standing on the edge of the fort, holding the ends of the wire together to show me they were short-circuited. As I walked back to the fort, a mere three hundred feet away, I did everything I could to control my ability to run like hell. Quickly taking refuge behind the turret, I followed the countdown and watched the explosion through the viewing slit.

I couldn't believe what I had just witnessed! The realization that those very bombs were being dropped en masse on Germany...on anyone—gave me chills. Suddenly war had become very, very real.

Simultaneously with the explosion, there was a *PING* as a piece of shrapnel from the bomb casing hit the brick wall beside my shelter. A huge cloud of brick dust erupted. Everyone ran out to see the huge crater the bomb had caused. The hole was thirty-to-forty feet in diameter and at least ten feet deep, even though the bomb had been ten feet above the ground upon ignition.

I realized that as devastating as the damage was to London, it was relatively nothing compared to the mass destruction being done to German cities. It was sad to see that St. Paul's beautiful old architecture had been so badly damaged. The House of Parliament had taken a direct hit. Barrage balloons had been scattered around the city of London and between London and the English Channel. They were designed to discourage low-flying German airplanes. Balloons were attached to a cable then raised ten thousand feet or so above the city so the German planes would run into the cables.

Even though I was working with the British, I was required to register as an alien while in London. I hadn't had time, as my immediate instructions were to make a quick trip to Edinburgh. I arrived minutes before the hotel dining room was closing for the night, quickly checked into the hotel and dashed into the restaurant just in time to order.

As I was enjoying my dinner, a man in plain clothes rudely approached my table. He identified himself as the Scottish police and brusquely asked if I were Mr. Baum. He demanded to know why I had not registered as an alien. The bureaucrat was not impressed when I explained I had had no time for paperwork. The officer insisted that we go to my room to retrieve my passport. He then proceeded to read me the riot act. When the fool finished his tirade, I said calmly, "You forgot one thing. This passport clearly states that aliens must register within forty-eight hours of their arrival in a community. Since I have just arrived and have absolutely no intentions of staying forty-hours in Edinburgh, I do not feel compelled to do so."

Trying to appear nonplused, the Scot collected as much dignity as he could muster, then turned and walked away, harrumphing and mumbling something like, "Well all right, but don't do it again."

While in London, I had experienced two air raid alerts but no bombings. The eerie sound of the sirens at night, echoing off empty bombed-out buildings, was a sound I would never forget. It was spring 1944. During my visit, a representative of the Minister of the Mission inquired as to whether I would accept an award. The BAC wanted to propose that I receive the Order of the British Empire for my work with the Mission. I was completely taken by surprise and visited the American Embassy in London to inquire whether I would be permitted to accept it as an American.

They said, "Of course!" and I prepared myself to accept the honor. It would be awarded in Washington DC in August and I had to wait until I returned home to the States to tell Hilda, since all my homebound correspondence was officially censored.

During the country's preparations for D-DAY - the invasion of Normandy - scheduled to take place in early June 1944, I had begun to notice highly visible markings on the roads indicating respective locations for invasion vehicles. This signage was part of the intensive misinformation campaign. The British were in hopes that German over-flights would lead the enemy to believe the invasion would be north of the Calais Channel opening and in northern France and Belgium. It turned out that Hitler bought the idea that much of the invasion would be north, so during the weeks prior to D-Day, everyone was prohibited to leave England.

This mandate posed a problem for me since I was scheduled to return to DC. In addition, the Ministry was reluctant to have me return on Pan Am by the circuitous route through West Africa to Brazil, then back up to the States because the Luftwaffe was still intercepting flights to discourage air traffic.

I was re-scheduled to return to the States by special permit by sea on the brand new Moratania. The ship had been introduced into service at the outbreak of the war. The Moratania had replaced the original ship of that name. It had been converted to a troopship and was retrofitted to carry nearly ten thousand troops, packed shoulder to shoulder, from America to England.

Going westbound, however, the ship held a much smaller human cargo: Three British specialists and me - all crammed into one small cabin. We were instructed to wear our life jackets at all times.

The ship left Liverpool unescorted, traveled north of Ireland and zigzagged at high speed throughout the entire voyage. No one was allowed on deck at night for fear that he might inadvertently light a cigarette and be spotted from the air or from a submarine. The trip would have taken five days had the ship proceeded via a straight course. As it was, it took seven days at high speed due to its required diversionary tactics.

We arrived in New York a few days before D-Day. The ship anchored off New York harbor until dawn, then docked. Despite the fact there were only four of us, there was still the nuisance of dealing with immigration and customs. Providing me with yet another bureaucratic irritation, officials immediately confiscated my passport and a map with important notes I had taken in England. My papers were never returned.

I rushed home to Washington DC to Hilda and young Jim who was only seven months old. He had grown so much in those few weeks that I could hardly recognize him. News came shortly after my return that the first V-1 buzz bomb attack was made on London. The buzz bombs were unmanned, flying bombs named for the sound they made.

Still concerned about my draft status, I was relieved when through British appeal, I was re-classified by the draft board to 2-B. The British ambassador had made yet another appeal and this time it was approved.

On June 6, 1944, D-Day came to pass. Our office was literally thrown into mourning to learn that Biddy's son, a fighter pilot with the RAF, had lost his life in the battle. The war had suddenly struck too close to home. We no longer felt protected by the span of an ocean.

There was always an undercurrent of *not invented here* between the British and American Air Forces. The bomb lug controversy was not the only turf war to be handled. A similar controversy arose about incendiary bombs. The Americans had designed the N 69 bomb, a heavier incendiary bomb filled with napalm. Napalm was invented by the Standard Oil Company of New Jersey. The U.S. Chemical Warfare Service had successfully claimed sponsorship of the U.S. designed bomb. I have said often that turf battles are not interrupted by minor events such as war.

It was decided to test the effectiveness of these bomb designs. The Chemical Warfare Service had a huge facility in the desert southwest of Salt Lake City. On this site they had built four blocks of buildings representing a typical German city. Then they built four blocks of buildings representing a typical Japanese city. The sites were unbelievably authentic.

Buildings representing the German mini-city were constructed with brick and slate roofs. There was installation between the floors and the buildings were decorated with furniture, a prototype of a typical German house. The Japanese buildings were constructed just as carefully, although of light walls and thin roofs, with traditional tatami mats covering the floors. Structures were made with wood and paper partitions made of the same spruce wood typically used in Japan.

When all was ready at the site, I flew out to Salt Lake City with Stanley Curtis, my British colleague. We were driven to the area near Dugway, Utah and quartered at the base's BOQ.

Bomb shelters had been built adjacent to the demonstration construction. The next day, an incredibly beautiful day, several American bombers flew over and dropped bombs on the international project, first on the German village, then on the Japanese village. Both British and American incendiary bomb types were used. Having no opposition, the bombers were able to fly low and accurately. The bomb patterns were as regular as could be expected for those bomb types. Stanley and I stood outside the bomb shelters until we heard "Bombs Away!" then ducked for cover. After the fire trucks arrived and did their work, we observed the relative damage of hits by the two types of bombs.

What had transpired, most probably, was predictable. The British bombs did their job against the German construction, piercing the roofs and coming to rest inside the houses to ignite, then setting everything on fire. The American bombs, of lighter construction, tended to glance off the tile roofs, fall into the streets and harmlessly cough out their ignited napalm against the brick walls. On the other hand, the British bombs penetrated the Japanese houses and tended to bury themselves harmlessly in the earth whereas the American bombs would similarly penetrate, and either set the interior on fire, or if they fell outside, set the building on fire. It was a fascinating exercise and both sides retired feeling victorious.

While in Salt Lake City, I decided I wanted to hear the Mormon Tabernacle choir. Taking Stan with me, I flashed my Pentagon access badge and was given admission to the tabernacle, which was at the time closed to the public. We heard a very moving private concert. It was an incredible experience.

Back in DC once again, in August 1944, Hilda and I drove to the British Embassy on Massachusetts Avenue for a brief formal ceremony. The British ambassador, Lord Halifax, greeted us. After being presented with my award, I attended a brief reception with Hilda then we went out to celebrate privately.

The citation read:

> *To Dwight C. Baum, Honorary member of the Civil Division*
> *of the Most Excellent Order of the British Empire*
> *For displaying outstanding ability.*
> *His zeal and loyalty have been exceptional.*

At war's end in 1945, Biddy left the BAC before I did. I still had some things to wrap up. I became director by default as well as the last employee of the BAC. I received a bonus of a thousand dollars for "exceptional service," but the icing on the cake was that I got to write my own dismissal notice. The memo was short and sweet, and I took pleasure in signing it to myself:

> *The services of Dwight C. Baum,*
> *Director of the Department of Armament*
> *and Equipment Supply Services,*
> *British Air Commission, are no longer needed.*

During the last several months of service, as the war had been nearing its end, I no longer had to work through weekends. I chose to spend Sundays at the Library of Congress searching for financial information about utility companies. I visited the Federal Power Commission and rifled through their public files. I still yearned to find a small utility company I might be able to buy. I wanted to learn all I could. The SEC had relocated from DC to Philadelphia and now occupied the premises of what had been the Philadelphia Athletic Club. I went up there a couple of times. Their file room was in the area that had been a huge swimming pool. Whenever I took a trip near Philly, I would stop off at the SEC to rummage through their files.

The Federal Power Commission was still in Washington. I enjoyed looking at some of their records as well. At first they were really dubious about making some of them available to me. I don't know why, although they claimed "war secrecy," but that went away pretty early on. And I copied quite a bit of records from their files on power companies and power plants.

Through my searches, I identified several potential targets and put together a possible means of financing for an attempt to purchase. By today's standards, the amounts would not have been taken seriously, but the investment dollars I was looking at were huge at the time, especially for a young man starting from a point of virtual zero-based capital.

I had continued investing through Eastman Dillon with modest success. In my spare time, I mapped out all the small holding, company-owned electric and gas utilities in an endeavor to identify one I might be able to purchase. The holding companies were beginning to be broken up and small isolated properties were considered orphans. Among those I examined were County Gas Company of Red Hook, New Jersey; East Missouri Power Company and Missouri Edison Company, operating north of St. Louis. I also evaluated Rockland Gas Company, located across the Hudson River from Yonkers and Wisconsin Southern Gas Company, which served the Lake Geneva area.

With nominal capital available, I concentrated on focusing on how I might leverage myself into position to buy the equity control. In today's vernacular, that strategy would be called a leveraged buy out or LBO. As I put these potential deals together, I would run them by a friend, a stockbroker at Eastman Dillon, to see if my financing and acquisition concepts made sense.

The final plan, for which I developed a four hundred, ten thousand dollar deal, was the Wisconsin Southern Gas Company. Superficially, it seemed to be a manufactured gas property with no future.

There was no natural gas at that time in Wisconsin. However, the pipeline from the gulf into northern Illinois terminated a few miles south of the state line. My bid was contingent upon the Federal Power Commission's allowing the line to be extended a few miles into Wisconsin to serve Lake Geneva and Burlington, two of the company's principal towns. The other bid for the property was four hundred thousand dollars. On the last day of the period during which the pipeline extension into Wisconsin could be protested, an unholy alliance of the American Association of Railroads, the United Mine Works of America and the Wisconsin Coal Dealers Association appealed the FPC's order. I was aware that such an appeal could take eighteen months or more and that this property would not survive as a manufactured gas property without conversion to natural gas.

I had my deposit refunded, and almost simultaneously received a call from a Washington law firm power broker. The law firm offered to take on my case and obtain clearance by pulling political strings to get the pipeline through the FPC. I knew their legal fees would be hefty and the process both bureaucratic and time consuming. I declined.

As I wrapped up my responsibilities with the BAC, I received tentative job offers, one from American Cyanamid, a chemical company, and one from Magnavox. But my passion, I had learned, was in corporate finance and I didn't seriously consider either of them.

Biddy had moved to California, closing a chapter of camaraderie and mutual respect we had shared during our work together. Contact between us was rare and Biddy died shortly thereafter. In December 1945, Hilda and I went house hunting for our first home. We found a small colonial in a beautiful neighborhood in Westchester County at the extreme northern tip of Yonkers. The house was lovely and had a small brook in the back yard.

With gasoline rationing ended, we drove to New York several times with young Jim. This was before safety belts and baby seats, and Jim would stand between us all day long. And it always happened that minutes prior to our arriving at our destination, he would collapse as dead weight and sleep for hours. But he refused to miss a minute during our travels.

Our wedding day

Hilda and I sharing cocktails and some laughs
after an Eastman Dillon meeting

Investment 101: Eastman Dillon

Out of the blue came an offer to work for Eastman Dillon and Company in the Buying Department. The job encompassed a challenging combination of corporate underwriting and securities research, typical of the industry in those days. I accepted without hesitation and once again, forgot to ask about salary. Eastman Dillon started me at four hundred fifty dollars a month, the identical and rather inadequate salary I was paid by the British. But I was so thrilled to be in on the ground floor of what I considered to be the most stimulating and challenging profession in the country, I was like a kid on a hot August afternoon. I had accepted an ice cream cone without asking the flavor.

I celebrated New Year's Eve by preparing for my new professional life. That eventful day was January 3, 1946. I scurried off to E. D.'s Wall Street office to fill out my employment papers and to meet with Bob Evans, my new employer. Ironically, it was the very same office where Biddy had recruited me five short years before.

My new job involved analyzing and developing underwriting memoranda. In addition, I was responsible for identifying potential investment opportunities. My days of visiting with Jim Wyld and reading his dad's Wall Street Journal had been well spent. I knew now that I had been destined to become a financial expert. Over time, I had taught myself to read balance sheets and to interpret profit and loss statements.

I had always been intrigued by corporate finance. The investment world was fascinating to me. Upon inheriting four thousand dollars on my twenty-first birthday while a student at Cornell, I had started a brokerage account with Eastman Dillon. After graduation from

Harvard in the summer of 1938, Mother advanced ten thousand dollars to me. She said, "Invest it, and ultimately half is yours and the other half you can split among your brothers."

By the time of her death in 1972, I had built that initial sum into the grand amount of four hundred seventy-five thousand dollars, *after* taxes! During the war, I earned an extra thousand dollars a year from a small job and in addition to that sum, invested every spare cent I could get my hands on.

In 1941, I had learned about what may have been the first capital firm and invested two thousand dollars in a start-up company called Photomat, which was working on the development of the first paper-offset printing plate.

They had begun manufacturing the successful product upon the U.S. entering World War II; priorities prohibited the use of valuable chrome chemicals to be used for this process. The country needed the chrome for strengthening steel and other wartime uses. Photomat nearly went bankrupt and I was pressed to make a small additional investment in a valiant endeavor to save it. I learned early on that this was a classic example of how start-up companies always seem to need more money and more time than originally planned in order to survive.

Initially, substitute chemicals turned out to have a short shelf life and the company nearly expired a second time. Suddenly the government discovered that the product they were making was the solution to the requirement for multiple copies of all kinds of shipping documents using the paper plate. And those documents could be produced on an ordinary typewriter, quite an inexpensive and easy solution. The priority problem vanished with government need and Photomat took off vertically. Now the company had a new problem. Since previous profits had been non-existent, earnings were taxed more than ninety-percent as *wartime excess profits.*

During the early 1940s, the Wall St. Journal published a weekly investment portfolio submitted by investors. The column ran on the editorial page. I sent in my portfolio for analysis and to my surprise, they ran it. Due to its length, they had to run it over two days and the editor added the comment that the writer had been an "American member of a foreign government mission." The financial editor mentioned that my portfolio was certainly unusual in its complex makeup of frequently obscure securities, but he thought the results were nevertheless more than impressive.

My strategy for investing never wavered from the beginning. I was never a speculator, nor a stock trader. I always concentrated on trying to buy value stocks for a long-term hold, so I was never worried about liquidity. I would study the company's profit and loss report, read the balance statement, and find ways to pick up stocks for less than what I believed to be their value. Some were quite obscure stocks that other investors wouldn't touch. I would simply hold on to them. As any other investor, even with a solid strategy, I made my share of mistakes.

One of my first assignments with Eastman Dillon was to analyze companies in the plywood and the textile-converting industries. I happily buried myself in securities manuals, prospectuses, spreadsheets and annual reports. The work was like a breath of fresh air and the hours long, but I never complained. How lucky could a guy get to be able to work at his hobby, I asked myself many times. I never tired of corporate finance.

I was invited to the company dinner at the Pierre Hotel on the twelfth of February, Lincoln's birthday. Although the most junior member of the firm, I was introduced all around and once again met E.D.'s newest partner and my boss, E.J. "Bob" Evans.

Bob grew up in the Midwest. In the early 1920s, he moved to California to become a securities salesman for Blyth Witter in Long Beach, and rapidly became their most successful individual producer. He rose up through the ranks, going with Blyth when the firm split, and was transferred to head sales in New York only weeks prior to the 1929 market crash. The Blyth organization survived, but had to cut back heavily and Bob returned to California. He used to say he preferred to starve in the sun than in the cold.

In the depths of the depression, he gradually built up his clientele until he became one of the seniors at a local Los Angeles firm called Nelson Douglas and Company. He remained very friendly with both Lloyd Gilmour and Charlie Blyth as well as with all the Witters of the Dean Witter organization.

Nelson Douglas and Company was a correspondent firm with E.D. and when Bob Evans developed a potential underwriting for Thrifty Drug Stores, he took the business to E.D. That move resulted in his being asked by Gilmour in late 1945 to become a partner and open an Eastman Dillon office in Los Angeles. At the time, the company had no operations west of Chicago. Bob started business in Los Angeles with one secretary in a two-room office at Fifth and Spring Streets. It was then that the stark realization hit him. He no longer had even the minimal staff that the Nelson Douglas organization had offered.

Lloyd Gilmour, a co-founder of Blyth Dean Witter (1914) went with the Blyth organization when the firm split apart in the 1920s. He left Blyth in the mid-1930s and acquired control of Eastman Dillon, founded in 1907 by Tom Eastman and Herb Dillon. Successful during the 1920s, even surviving the crash, E.D. had powered down to a few offices as both Eastman and Dillon were reaching retirement age. Gilmour's initial ownership of the firm was massive. Early on he put into effect his rather unique ideas by permitting up-and-coming younger partners to earn substantial partnership interests at a give-away price of twenty thousand dollars for a one percent interest, depending upon their performance.

The day after our company dinner, I was called into the office of senior partner Lloyd Gilmour where I shook hands again with Bob Evans. Bob and I went into the conference room where he invited me to talk about my interest in securities research and corporate investment. Of course I complied without hesitation. Fifteen minutes later, Bob said, "I want you to come to work for me in California."

Stunned, I informed him that Hilda and I had just bought a home in Scarsdale and that I would need to discuss the opportunity with her.

The master salesman responded with confidence, assuring me that this was a great opportunity as I would be working directly with him; that there was no way in the world I wouldn't love the west coast; and so far as housing was concerned, there was *no place like southern California!*

My head was reeling with the thrill of working in this field in such an agreeable climate. I went home from work that night with a special evening planned. Hilda and I were staying temporarily with her parents. I asked her mother and father if they would feed little Jim so I could take my wife out to dinner. And sitting in a lovely Italian restaurant on Riverdale Avenue in Yonkers, daiquiri in hand, I *innocently* inquired, "Honey, how would you like to live in California?"

"When do I pack?" was her response.

The next morning, I reported back to Bob that subject to finding adequate housing, I would be delighted to accept the position.

It seemed that presidential birthdays marked very special occasions for me that year, as I caught the night flight to Los Angeles on Washington's birthday. Hotel accommodations were tight. Through a fellow named McDowell, a friend of Bob's, I rented a room at the Elks Club off Wilshire Boulevard by the newly named MacArthur Park. McDowell and I drove around the Pasadena area and I found a possible purchase, a colonial home on Virginia Road. The asking price was thirty-five thousand dollars. In hindsight, I should have taken it, but knowing nothing about the area, and having committed to pay around thirty thousand for the house in Scarsdale, which thankfully had not yet closed escrow, I decided to pass up the opportunity.

Six weeks later, after we had searched high and low and been subjected to all the usual real estate scam artists, Muriel Barnum found an ideal place for us at 1308 East California. The house was a white Monterey and was listed at thirty-two thousand. I made an offer that was accepted. In the meantime, Hilda had sold the purchase contract for the New York house to a friend for a thousand dollars so we got out of that deal.

I flew back to New York to organize the shipping of our household furniture. We had left some things in storage in DC and some other things in New York. Hilda decided to stay in New York with our son while I drove to California, so I asked Mother to drive out with me. It was April, and that spring seemed particularly beautiful, with the war over and a bright future ahead. The trip across country was enjoyable, although it was difficult to find a hotel, and we ended up with rather primitive motel accommodations at best.

Naturally, our new house was bare when we arrived. Mother and I gathered together some necessities for our temporary comfort. We borrowed a couple of cots and made trips to the Five and Dime store for rudimentary items. For the first few days, we shared one cocktail glass and one coffee cup between us. Once the furniture was due to arrive, Mother took the train back to New York and I waited for Hilda and Jim, then two and a half years old. They arrived at the Glendale airport in a DC-4.

I remember that at the time, little Jim was fascinated with the wires used in electronic equipment and I had secured three feet of multi-colored cable, which I presented to him as he got off the plane. He jumped up and down, saying, "Bire! Bire!" He seemed to be more excited about the colored wire than he was at flying or at seeing his dad. For years, Jim kept that wire and called it "*my* bire!"

As I drove my family into the driveway of our new home, I realized how strange it must have been for Hilda to be arriving at a home she had never seen. But an architect whom Dad had known had designed the house, so I knew she would like it. Plus, it was surrounded by all the lush landscape California had to offer.

Early on, Jim showed an interest in building things—anything! He always had a project underway. Upon the boy's arrival in Pasadena, since our furniture had already been delivered, he quickly proceeded to make use of the packing crate materials to build an airplane. Perhaps we should have known then that he would grow up to become a pilot.

Hilda and I Discover Palm Trees and Paradise

Hilda and I settled comfortably into our new home in Pasadena. Bob Evans and his wife Hope immediately took us into their hearts and we all became very close. They had two children, Bob Jr. and Tom. In the fall of 1946, a few months after my arrival in California, Tom, then a student at UC Berkeley, died quite suddenly and unexpectedly. We were all utterly devastated.

I quickly settled into my office with Bob Evans. I was thrilled to go to work every day. Since Hilda and I had only one car, I would sometimes drive downtown; other times I took the Pacific Electric. The inter-urban trolley stop was located on Lake Street, a short distance from the house. Occasionally I even hitched a ride to work. It was a different time and a safer world.

On the lower floors of our office building were the offices of the FBI and Nelson Douglas Company. Bob and I worked on several pieces of corporate finance, which resulted in private placement of debt securities. We were looking at a company called Southwest Lumber Mills - which was barely public and which had leases on timber in the White Mountains of Arizona from the Navajo and Apache Indian tribes. I thought it was worth exploring.

My brother Peter, formerly a second lieutenant in the Signal Corps in Japan, was released from the army at the end of August. Mother, Mrs. Case, still a loyal companion, and Peter's wife Virginia drove out to California to spend some time with us and planned to meet Peter in San Francisco upon his return to the States.

In the beginning of September, when the family headed back east, I caught a ride with them as far as McNary, Arizona where Southwest

Lumber was headquartered. I wanted to spend several days checking out the company. But it was September 1946 and while I was there, the stock market crashed once again. McNary was isolated at the end of a long rural telephone line operated by the Navapache Telephone Company.

During a thunderstorm I could see static electricity flashing all around the lightning arresters on the line. I tried to call Los Angeles from the pay phone at the local gas station and the Native American operator of the station taunted me, "White man damn fool! Smoke signals much better!"

I returned to Los Angeles by train to find a brand new securities industry. What had happened was a junior version of overpriced stocks following the end of the war boom. This was the fourth stock market crash I had experienced: 1920, 1929, 1937 and 1946.

~

Although intriguing and completely fulfilling, my professional financial world was joyfully interrupted a year after our move to California. On March 5, 1947, Hilda and I celebrated the birth of our second son, John Edward Baum. This time, Hilda experienced a shorter hospital stay and Jim allowed us to placed a crib in his room on the second floor of our little house at 1308 E. California Street.

With John newly born, we decided not to take a trip that year. A year later, however, Hilda found a wonderful babysitter-quasi-nursemaid. Mrs. Howell was quite trustworthy and we felt we could leave the children safely at home in her care. On a warm summer's day, she and I took off in my new red Studebaker Land Cruiser and drove to the Bar Lazy J Ranch. The Bar lazy J opened in 1912 and to this day is the oldest continuously operating guest ranch in Colorado. Located in a valley near the Colorado River, it is fairly close to Denver. After spending several days there, we drove on to Denver, then made our way to Pike's Peak.

We had been trying to get Jim into a very special pre-school. Polytechnic School was located on California Boulevard only three blocks from the house. We had left our itinerary with Mrs. Howell and when we arrived at Pike's Peak, somehow she had managed to have a letter forwarded to us from the school. We were delighted to read that Jim had indeed been accepted. We found a telegraph office on Pike's Peak and sent a wire to the school confirming Jim's placement. The fellow who operated the station used Morse code with the old-style clicker. That was the last time I ever saw that system in operation.

But it was three years later that we found paradise! Hilda's parents had taken several trips to Hawaii in the late 1940s. Her dad, an educator, was required to conduct surveys for the Punaho School in Honolulu. The stories that we heard from her parents intrigued us so much that we decided to take a luxurious three-week vacation to Hawaii. It was with this trip planned and reservations secured that we found and purchased our new house at 1011 Oak Grove Avenue. On Memorial Day, May 30, 1950, I signed the papers. We had managed little more than a walk-through after making our snap decision to buy it when we left for Hawaii in early June.

We planned to stay at the Halekulani Hotel, which was one of the three quality hotels in Waikiki. At that time, Waikiki was a village. We planned to tour all the islands then stay the last week at a resort called The Hotel Hana-Maui at Hana Ranch. The remote resort was located on five thousand acres near the peaceful village of Hana on the island of Maui.

Arriving at the Hana Ranch for our last week of vacation, we did indeed discover paradise. The hotel had been converted from a sugar mill and was quaint, lovely and remote. It overlooked a beautiful small bay. Charles and Anne Morrow Lindbergh, seeking privacy, had established their home in the area. It was fairly primitive and the roads were quite rough. We could drive from a tropical rain forest to desert floors laced with cacti in less than four miles. We loved the resort so much that we returned the next two years as well.

Time and again, while on vacation that first year, Hilda and I sat quietly over cocktails sketching our recollections of the layout of our new home. The house had been built around 1924 and was quite spacious for a growing family. It was located just on the border of Pasadena in San Marino. We knew instinctively that we had made a wonderful purchase for long-term occupancy. This was our dream house, the home in which we would spend the rest of our married life. It cost all of twenty-seven thousand, five hundred dollars.

By this time, though it was still early in my career, I was able to pay cash for all but ten thousand dollars. I got a mortgage from Bank of America for a ten-year term at four and a half percent. I've laughed through the years as mortgage lenders have telemarketed me, time and again, offering me a lower interest rate. Of course, my house has been paid for more than forty years, but even so, when I ask them if they can beat my initial interest rate of four and a half percent, I get the last laugh.

By the time we returned home from Hawaii and were ready to move, Jim, now six, and John, three, were heavily involved in building projects under the watchful eye of Mrs. Howell. They had completed a structure at the old house that was supposed to be some sort of cabin, but looked more like an outhouse. Of course, we had to bring it with us to the new home! I still have a mental picture of it being towed the half mile on a wagon from California Street to Oak Grove Avenue in San Marino.

The boys created so many happy memories for us in that house. One year Jim, who was interested in science at Poly, decided to build a solar energy project. He used the cellar as his construction site and it turned out to be quite a project. Who was it that said, "The best laid plans of mice and men...?" It turned out that there was one small problem. When Jim tried to move the project upstairs so he could transport it to school, he discovered that it was too big to fit into the stairwell. He had to cut it into pieces and reassemble it. But he got a prize for his project and that made the struggle all worthwhile. For another science project, Jim developed a demonstration of an ultra-sound machine. The project earned him an entry into the L.A. Science Fair.

Jim joined scouts and Hilda became the den mother. She was a good one. Like me, Jim was never much interested in athletics, but John was fascinated by one sport in particular – baseball. I bought him the very first Philco transistor portable radio on the market so he could listen to the games. Hilda and I would be inside the house and hear a rhythmic "Thud...Thud...Thud." Upon investigation, we would find John outside intensely listening to a game in the back yard while tossing the ball against the house. At one time there was about a six-inch-deep, mini-trench in the yard where he had stood a determined pitcher's stance while concentrating on the game and throwing his baseball against the house.

Our one-car garage was constructed in a manner that made the floor a bit lower than the driveway. When it rained, water would seep into the garage. For our fireplace, we used sawdust logs that we stored in the garage. One day after a heavy rain, we decided we wanted to light a fire in the fireplace. We went into the garage only to discover that the logs had become soaked and had totally disintegrated. Hilda and I stood there staring helplessly at a huge mound of wet sawdust.

In 1949, our family grew by one. Bob and Hope Evans presented us with a puppy we named Timber. The empty maid's room off the kitchen had a linoleum floor and that became Timber's room. He discovered that he liked to chew linoleum and in short order, literally destroyed it.

We all loved Timber, the boys especially. I built a mesh fence so we could close in the property for his safety. There was a huge fig tree in the yard that bore massive figs. When they ripened and fell onto the ground, bees would swarm the figs. Timber and the bees feasted on the figs, co-existing without a problem, although Timber sometimes got sick from eating too many figs.

Later, as the boys grew up and John followed Jim into Polytechnic School, they entered Timber in the school's annual pet show. There were twenty different classes of dogs and exactly twenty dogs, so every child and dog could come home with a prize. Timber always came home so proud of his prize. Hilda often volunteered as class mother. She had a good sense of humor and was well liked by the students. She was instrumental in fund-raising for the schools and working on whatever project they were doing at the time.

Once he learned to behave, Timber was allowed the run of the house. He used to sit on the hearth in the evenings, warmed by the fire. One Saturday night Hilda and I had a party and the next day, John and I took Timber for a walk. He was fourteen at the time. Halfway home, the poor thing collapsed on the sidewalk. We had to carry him back to the house. That afternoon the veterinarian made a house call and we put him down. He had lived a good life, but it was time to say goodbye. We didn't want him to be in agony while we were waiting for the office to open on Monday.

The family album

The family in Acapulco and
John looking quite mischievous

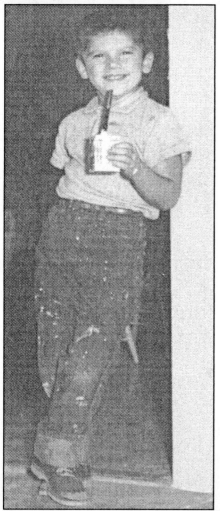

Timber

A Walk Through Our San Marino Neighborhood

When we bought our house on Oak Grove Avenue in 1950, the city was already almost built out. There was a vacant lot next to ours that was sold a couple years later. The buyer was a speculator who built a one story, California style house. The Loud family...their real name...bought the house. They owned the Ford and Lincoln dealership in Pasadena. They were very good, quiet neighbors and we got along just fine.

Across the street from us there was a large, white wood house on a two-and-a-half acre lot. It was finally torn down and the lot divided. Two houses were built there, big nice houses. Next to that, down the street was a very large interior property with a huge house on it and a driveway going up to Oak Grove Avenue. Somebody bought the place, sold off the lot on the south side of the driveway and later on built a street, Oak Grove Lane, into the property in a T formation, so in all, about eight lots were built there.

A couple owned a huge house in that mini-development. The woman always seemed to be mad at her husband. She tried to spend as much of his money as she could, collecting rooms and rooms full of artifacts and furniture. When they finally sold the place off, they held a two- or three-day auction. Somehow, even with all the stuff still there, the Harvard Business School Club was able to secure the place for a reunion. The grounds were quite nice and we had a fine party there.

The next house down the street was a huge white mansion, probably built around 1913. At the time we moved in, it was owned by Doc Strube, a local dentist who had gotten into the promotion business. In the early 1930s, he convinced California legislators to amend the state law to once again allow horse betting. He then promoted the Santa Anita racetrack very successfully.

Our neighbors to the south were the Kestors, a retired advertising man who invented the name Palmolive. Next to that was the Robins house. They owned the Quality Department store in downtown Los Angeles on Seventh Street. Next to their house, on the corner of Virginia Avenue, was the Braun house. Braun had developed a very successful high-tech engineering design and construction company. They made their riches in the petrochemical and oil industries, and conducted major engineering and construction projects, as well.

By the end of the 1950s, there were only one or two undeveloped lots here in San Marino. There has been of course a fair amount of *mansionization*. People would buy houses, tear down everything but the front door, and build a larger house on the property. However, the city always, thankfully, had the foresight to adopt some reasonably decent restrictions, so we were able to hold houses down to size, for example, like the people who bought the Loud's house next door. Some Chinese people bought it, tore it down and fought to build a huge mansion. We managed to get that cut down to an appropriate size that matched the rest of the neighborhood.

Over the years, the wealthy Chinese moved quite heavily into San Marino. The only fault I had with them was their continual determination to *mansionize* their houses then enclose them with huge iron fences. Many of them reside in the area only infrequently, so while I understood their wish for security, the garish iron fences and gates with huge bolt holes just weren't appropriate because of the openness of the neighborhood. The population of San Marino, based on the most recent census, was fifty-one percent Oriental. We never had any problems with anyone other than the mansionization problems.

A man named Lee is the present owner of the Robins house two doors down from us. We met with him after he bought the house. He was working on plans to expand it and Jim gave him some ideas as to how he could better his design. Mr. Lee is a Cal Tech graduate, a Chinese-American who speaks perfect English. He was a major player in the syndicate that promoted and built the Global Crossing Sub-Sea Cable System. He eventually resigned as an executive of the company so he could sell his stock. This spring, I read that he sold his stock in Global Crossing, obviously before the collapse, for one hundred twenty-four million dollars. That's how he could buy the Robins house for four and a quarter million and add another million into additions and improvements.

One day in the late 1950s, I saw an advertisement in the newspaper for a sale of land in the county on the east side of the San Fernando Valley. I went to the auction, where they were selling off these little lots. I knew they weren't very big. The bidding started at ten dollars. I bid fifteen, bought a lot, and proceeded to buy the three adjacent lots for fifteen dollars each. Mind you, the lots were only about twenty by sixty feet.

These obviously had been part of a promotion of some sort. People probably received a free lot with a magazine subscription or something of that nature. They were out by Keyhole Canyon. I bought the lots sight unseen, had one registered in my name, one in Hilda's name, and one in each of the boys' names. We referred to our lots sometimes as our rich *branch* properties.

Every few years, we would go for a drive and try to find the lots. We eventually found approximately where they were and it turned out that somebody was developing a big cemetery down the hill below our lots. Who knows what they were worth—all I know is that we had to pay, among other things, flood assessment danger insurance. But I still have one registered in each of our names. The one in my name and the one in Hilda's name we should have transferred over to young Jim. We never did, unfortunately. The last time we were up there, a couple of years ago, there was a sign bordering on some adjacent property offering lots for sale. I never got around to checking out what they were asking.

Just a Ham at Heart

Throughout my adolescence and all the way through university, I had worked hard to acquire the knowledge and skill required to build radio sets. I had always wanted to become licensed as a ham radio operator. Unfortunately, I had never been able to get my Morse code speed up enough to meet that challenge and pass the test.

I had never lost my interest in electronics. I would never forget my *investment* purchase at Macy's while home from school. In addition to that special record changer, there was another one that was far superior, a changer that turned records over to play both sides. I remembered a young math teach, Stu Summerfield, at Berkshire School who had one. I had always wanted one.

In 1943, while still in DC, I saw a changer for sale in the New York Times. It was owned by a funeral home in the Bronx. I had successfully negotiated for it and hired a mover to bring it to DC. It arrived in a big mahogany box and was to my surprise a dual changer with the conventional 78 RPM plus a 33 RPM conversion. RCA had introduced the 33 RPM briefly in the early '30s and recorded a handful of classical and pop pieces but the Depression prohibited further production.

When I shipped the player to California, after our move, I placed it in the cellar and ran wires up the steps so I could push buttons on the stairway and operate it from there. Sometimes records would get stuck, other times even break. We frequently had guests over for dinner and Canasta and would entertain them incessantly with one of our favorite records, "Manhattan Towers."

139

I wanted music in the bedroom so I managed to run wires up through the wall and on up to the center of the ceiling. I mounted a fifteen-inch loud speaker up there and made a square cloth cover to hide the speaker. It worked out great. Then I got a couple of war surplus aircraft radio receivers that broadcast in Shortwave and FM, installed those in the bedroom, and used them for music sources.

By the end of 1947, a number of TV stations had become established in Los Angeles, so I bought my first TV Motorola ten-inch television, which I installed in the den on the first floor. It cost four hundred twenty-five dollars, a lot of money at the time. But it had twelve channels and I tuned it off of a rabbit ear.

I saw what we would now call the first reality TV show at that time. Kathy Fiscus, the daughter of the manager of San Marino's water system, fell down a well. Rescue workers tried to get her out for nearly seven days. When they finally did, she was already dead. But Channel 5 covered the scene all day long for nearly a week. That broadcast was revolutionary for that time.

Also, at Yucca Flats the government was running an experiment outside Las Vegas with early atomic testing. Channel 5 again managed to rig up a microwave relay system to bring the signal down to Los Angeles to rebroadcast the event.

I became absolutely fascinated while messing around with short-wave radio stations. I read about the Teletype in QST Magazine and found out I could listen to Teletype stations. I was so intrigued, I finally ordered a Teletype converter and machine. The old United Press International was getting rid of their equipment so I went down and picked one up from the newspaper office for ten dollars. It was a Model 10 – what a machine!

The downside was that it was very noisy electronically. The noise level was as loud as the loudest talk I could find on it. Although it wasn't worth it for listening quality, it got me interested again in amateur radio and I decided, once and for all, to get my license.

Finally in 1952, two years after we moved into our San Marino home, I succeeded in getting my Morse code speed up to par. Hilda would do the dishes after dinner and I would retire upstairs to practice my code so I could pass the test. When I got my license, I immediately set up a radio room. The call letters assigned to me were at random, but I thought it unique that my call letters became *W6FRB,* which could have stood for the Federal Reserve Bank. I thought those letters appropriate since I was in the process of developing a lifelong career in finance.

Nearly every evening after dinner, I would hide away in my radio room. In just one evening, I might speak with someone from Ozark, Alabama, then someone else in South Africa, and later on, perhaps, a ham operator in Norway.

Until personal computers made it possible for every household in America to type-talk to people throughout the world, in real time, ham radio operators had a great advantage. I had a multitude of experiences throughout the next fifty years with my hobby. Once in 1960, I heard a "CQ...CQ...CQ" was lingo for "seek you" or "I want to talk." I responded to find that the operator was stationed in Greenland in the U.S. Army. He was engaged to a woman in the States. I wanted to help them talk to each other so I ran a phone patch by hooking up my transceiver to the telephone line. The young man from Greenland spoke with his fiancee' in Arizona for an hour and a half. By the end of that time, they had worked out their wedding arrangements.

Another time, I had contact with someone from a remote island in the South Pacific and again ran a phone patch between him and his family in the States. Two months later, a large box arrived at the house. The islander had sent me quite a thank you, a replica of a native outrigger canoe.

I was on the radio one night when I located a man who lived on Pitcairn Island. He claimed to be a descendant of the real Fletcher Christian, made famous by the movie "Mutiny on the Bounty." The only communication on the islands in the South Pacific was by ham radio. Fletcher and I communicated for years, eventually becoming friends. In the early 1990s, as I was planning a cruise, I discovered there was a small tourist ship that would stop on Pitcairn Island. I immediately signed up for the adventure.

We landed on the island in a storm. The boat captain waited for just the right wave, and when a very large one came, we rode right into the "Bounty" cove. I had taken with me some radio equipment he wanted. Nine of the fifty-seven inhabitants on the island were ham radio operators. Three times a year, the supply boat would come by, but other than that and an occasional small tourist boat, their only communication with the outside world was through their radio system. Armed with a video camera, I sat with Fletcher for several hours, taping the story of his life on Pitcairn Island. After visiting for a day, our small tourist group traveled onward on a small cruise ship to visit Easter Island where I was able to visit with another ham I had met on the airwaves. Through the years, I met other ham operators I was later able to visit - one in St. Petersburg, Russia, another in New Zealand.

~

I am sure Hilda was happy I had chosen that avocation rather than cooking or trying to manage other household chores. I wasn't very good at those things.

One night, friends of ours, the Gertmenians, came over for dinner. Hilda and Doris, Con's wife, gave us an easy job to help them with dinner. Con and I were charged with preparing some Chinese pea pods. Simple enough. Committed to doing our job well, we meticulously took the time to carefully wash all the pods, break them open and remove every single pea. We worked tirelessly and after ending up with about a teaspoonful of peas, threw the pods away. We didn't know they were to be cooked whole. It was a family joke for years. We were never asked to help with the meal again.

The Gertmenians had children the same age as ours. One summer when they all were in the crawling stage, we discovered a lovely private beach down at Laguna Niguel. In the summer we would pay a one-dollar fee to use the beach for the day. We would cook hot dogs and the kids would play on the beach. But it was a long drive down and traffic was quite heavy because there were no freeways.

My Years with First California Company
...and an Intriguing Brush with the Mob

During the boom of the 1920s, the banks were heavily involved in the securities business. They performed highly questionable acts including bailing themselves out of bad deals by foisting those deals on public investors. As a result of various scandals, Roosevelt passed a law mandating the divorcing of banks from the securities industry. The domino effect was that many local securities firms were created from the securities divisions that had split from the banks.

In 1904, A.P.Gianini founded the Bank of America. The first bank, named the Bank of Italy, opened in San Francisco. Having survived the earthquake of April 18, 1906, the bank soon made a name for itself among the Italian-American community by offering services primarily, and heretofore, ignored by the larger banks.

On that foundation, the Gianinis built the Bank of America - first into a statewide powerhouse - then through a holding company called Transamerica Corporation, finally working their way into controlling numerous other banks in the west plus a major bank in New York. The Gianinis relinquished control to New Yorkers during the boom of the late 1920s, but after the crash fought to gain back control of the Transamerica group. The fight was bitter but there was enough stock held in the west, together with additional purchases, to permit the Gianinis once again to push out the New Yorkers. Of course, the Italian-Americans from California were of tremendous help.

One of the assets of the group was an investment banking organization named BancAmerica Blair. Upon passage of Roosevelt's

143

legislation, BancAmerica Blair was spun off as an independent company and the securities department of Bank of America was spun off into two financial firms. One of these was called Walston, Hoffman and Goodwin and the other one was subsequently named First California Company. The Walston organization became members of the New York Stock Exchange.

A.P. Gianini and his son L. M. Gianini secretly controlled First California Company until they sold their stock to some San Francisco contacts. The Gianinis hired two inexperienced managers to run First California. They certainly took good care of their family. Claire Gianini Hoffman was A.P. Gianini's daughter and she became the recipient of Bank of America referrals for listed stocks.

During the battle for Transamerica Corp, a San Francisco North Beach man by the name of Virgil Dardi helped the Gianinis enormously. Dardi was under the Gianini wing and relied upon Gianini for advice and judgment much of the time. As a reward for Dardi's help, when a management position opened up in Blair Holdings Corporation, Dardi was rewarded with the presidency.

BancAmerica Blair had barely survived the crash of 1929. But by the mid-1940s, the firm had a securities subsidiary called Blair and Company, Inc; a shipyard, which was being liquidated; and the Pepsi Bottling Company of Los Angeles.

Blair Holdings was a public company whose shares were of little interest to anyone. There were three Blairs: William Blair and Company, still a highly respected Chicago-based investment banking firm; D.H. Blair of New York, who had a third- or fourth-rate securities house and later was put out of business for violations; and Blair and Company, Inc.

~

When Bob Evans left the Nelson Douglas Company to join E.D., his interest was not paid out. He negotiated the merger of Nelson Douglas into First California Company. First California suffered severe losses following the market crash of 1946. Whatever form Gianini control may have taken, that control was sufficient to force a change in management of First California. The president and chairman were fired and in early 1947, the former sales manager, Ted

Burr, was installed as president. Bob Evans was well known to the Gianinis, having negotiated the acquisition of a number of smaller banks in the west for Transamerica Corporation.

The Gianinis approached Lloyd Gilmour, requesting that he permit Bob Evans to leave E.D. to become chairman of First California Company. The three of them had developed a solid relationship and because of that, Evans and Gilmour agreed. On May 1, 1947, the deal was signed. After only a year and a half with Eastman Dillon, I found myself accompanying Bob to our new offices - along with Steffan, our secretary. The Los Angeles office of Eastman Dillon was now closed.

Ted Burr was in the main office in San Francisco and Bob Evans and I took over in Los Angeles. First California had approximately fifteen offices scattered throughout California and Nevada and the company benefited enormously from the Bank of America relationship.

~

With the assistance of Bank of America, First California Company did a great deal of successful underwriting during 1945-46, including California Pacific Utilities Company, the spin-off of the Portland Transit Company and the first and second Kaiser Frasier offerings.

The Kaiser Frasier Company was a startup engineered by Henry Kaiser, the dam and ship builder, and Frasier, a former officer with Chrysler. Together they saw the opportunity to meet the post-war needs for automobiles, with a new company. They started with inadequate capital, no plant, and an obsolete automobile design. The initial stock offering was very successful and with the shares at a big premium to the offering, a second offering was made which promptly crashed in price with the September 1946 market crash.

By mid-1947, the Kaiser Frasier Company had produced relatively few cars and was running out of money. It was decided that a third stock offering must be made and First California Company, Allen and Company and Otis and Company were to be the sole underwriters. At the time, the Kaiser Frasier stock, which had been in the twenties and thirties, was selling for less than ten dollars.

The whole tone of the investment market had become quite negative and as the registration statement was about to become effective, Kaiser Frasier stock was subject to heavy short selling on the American Stock Exchange.

As the registration statement became effective, the underwriters placed a stabilizing bid. To the horror of all of us at First California Company, they began to buy stock faster than it could be sold by our own organization. As with all underwriting situations, there is a provision in the contract with the issuer that the deal need not be completed if certain events take place. These events can be things such as outbreak of war, a banking crisis, or material adverse litigation being filed prior to closing. Thanks to Bank of America, First California Company attended the proposed closing with a check on the table for the full amount of our participation. The Allen representative was there with a check in his pocket.

The Otis representative turned up and immediately started raising questions as to whether or not there was any pending litigation. Stalling for time, he made numerous phone calls and finally announced with glee that there had been suits filed against Kaiser Frasier in two states. Therefore, they had no obligation to go through with the closing. This of course killed the deal. The incident caused a great scandal leading to a full SEC investigation, which clearly identified Otis as having maneuvered and promoted the lawsuits. Cyrus Eaton, the owner of Otis, had a devious record of looting investment trusts to save his own firm and in the 1930s was ultimately thrown out of the business.

At the low point following this fiasco, First California's capital was less than four hundred thousand dollars. From this point on, through Herculean efforts, Bob Evans and Ted Burr began to rebuild the firm with the assistance of Jack Mackie, a new sales manager. In the next year, 1948, the firm broke even and in 1949, began to make money. By 1950 and '51, First California Company had fully recovered and had become quite profitable.

However, at this time, the Korean War had broken out and the U.S. government re-imposed the Wartime Excess Profits tax law to sop up the monies being made on military contracts. While First California Company had no such contracts; it was caught in the excess profits tax net. There were several ways to ameliorate this tax, however. One way was that they were allowed a reasonable return on capital, but even at this time, First California's capital was still nominal. Another way was based upon the excess of earnings averaged over the preceding four years. This was again a nominal amount. The final exemption was based upon historic capital, still again a nominal amount.

Due to oddities of the tax regulations, Blair Holdings Corporation had a very large paper capital, far in excess of their cash capital. The Gianinis took the necessary steps to enable First California to merge into Blair Holdings Corporation and into a tax-free merger, which protected our earnings from the excess profits tax. I converted my options into Blair Holdings stock. And the Preferred stock was rapidly retired at a premium of twenty-five percent.

There was no interruption in my business operations and we had no problems cooperating with the New York Blair organization. However, two new problems arose. The Pepsi Cola Bottling Company, a subsidiary of Blair Holdings, was operated by a Scotsman who did his job to maximize operating profits. Rather than concentrating on case sales, they concentrated on the bottom line, choosing to ignore unprofitable business. This type of operation was anathema to the parent Pepsi Cola Company which made its money from concentrate sales and which held that all bottlers should focus on maximizing case sales rather than profits.

As a result, Pepsi Cola Company organized a shareholder raid on Blair Holdings Corporation, causing the Los Angeles bottling operation to be sold off to a new operator, one who was more inclined to dance to Pepsi's tune.

For years, the Los Angeles bottling operation made little money, while vastly increasing sales volume. Virgil Dardi remained head of Blair Holdings and did not interfere with the securities operations. Bob Evans used to say, "Dardi wouldn't draw a breath without first checking with either A.P. Gianini or his son Mario."

In the mid-1950s, A.P. Gianini suddenly died and his demise was soon followed by the death of Mario, heir apparent in the bank's hierarchy. Without guidance, Dardi fell into the hands of some devious Mafia securities operators. Simultaneously, there was a vast boom in Canadian Oil stocks ranging from real companies to fraudulent shells. The Mafia types secured control of Stanwood, a pseudo-Canadian Oil company. Its stock was low-priced and there was little or no information available.

Not long after, Bob was urged to become a director of Stanwood. Returning from that meeting, he came back to our office with a few apparently promising *facts* and minimal balance sheet figures. He handed them to me with a request to look them over. He had qualms about the situation and the company. It took me no time at all to check with a reputable Eastman Dillon-sponsored Canadian Oil Company to confirm that the material furnished to Bob was primarily nothing but hot air. Plus, I discovered that the company had little relation to even potentially valuable holdings.

Late one afternoon, after I had spent a day or so confirming my strong, adverse opinion on Stanwood, I received a phone call from someone who identified himself as being a friend of Virgil Dardi. The man said he understood that I had a favorable opinion on the attractiveness of Stanwood stock. I replied with my usual candor. "Quite frankly, I think the company is a rip off and I wouldn't touch it with a ten-foot pole."

The next morning, at six o'clock, my phone rang at the house. Dardi was screaming, "Do you want to get me *killed*? What ever did you say about Stanwood?" he demanded.

When the man calmed down enough to listen, I told him that in my honest opinion, it was a rip off and that my advice to Bob Evans was to immediately resign from the board.

Later on, I came to believe that Dardi had become a patsy for the Mafia. I also believed that the New York Blair also rejected any attempt to make them push the shares.

~

I was still with First California Company in January 1955 when, with the flurry of a big family Christmas behind us, Hilda and I decided to mix business with pleasure and take a trip to Central America.

When we arrived in Tegucigalpa, Honduras, we met Charlie Avery, head of the Costa Rica railroad. Charlie had heard that Costa Rica militants were threatening to attack Nicaragua, and there was imminent danger to his railroad. We rode with him in his private rail car down to Puerto Libon where, despite the impending doom, we all had a wonderful time. But among those in his private car was an American about my age, probably in his early forties. I will use the pseudonym *Fred Armour* because he was the son of a famous Chicago meatpacking family who had lost all their money. Fred was born with the proverbial silver spoon in his mouth, had been sent to all the right schools in the east, and even though his family had lost its money, it was Fred's intention to live in splendor regardless of how he obtained the funds to provide him with that lifestyle.

We did not know at the time that he was traveling through Central America trying to sell lubricating oil; he had targeted the Costa Rica railroad an obvious prospect. Once he met Charlie Avery, poor Charlie had no chance. Fred had locked onto him, somehow managing to get himself invited on this trip and here he was, in Charlie Avery's private car, traveling down the coast in style. Fred was a name-dropper. He knew all the right names and enough about the people he mentioned to have everyone believe that he really did know them. He was well spoken and appeared to be of some means. Charlie had been completely taken in by him.

We discovered shortly thereafter that Fred was one hundred percent con man and quite qualified at his pseudo-profession. After meeting with him and listening to his arrogance and vulgar exploitations for more boring hours than I care to recall, I completely forgot about the man until a few weeks after my return from our trip.

One afternoon I received a call at the office and the caller identified himself as Fred Armour. He had recently returned from Central America and was so excited. He said he had run into an unbelievable opportunity and asked if he could come by and discuss it with me. As an investment banker, of course I was intrigued. I should have known better. Nevertheless, I set up a time for him to come by.

When we met in my office, he explained that he had been representing the Cetro Oil Company, a rather small, outdated firm. Cetro made small quantities of gasoline and lubricating oil. Fred said he had been representing them *alfresco* in Central America and South America, but now he had additionally obtained the right to represent them in the Caribbean as well. Plus, he said he had gotten a contract for the sale of lubricating oil. Of course he needed *a little capital* to get the company started and asked if I might be willing to put a little money in with him. Naturally, he assured me that "we'd make nothing but money!"

They were organizing a company down in Panama and operating as such, there would be no taxes to pay. *This guy was good!* He had a quasi-business plan that made some sense, so I agreed to put ten or fifteen thousand dollars in. Doug Fletcher, who was working at that time with Blyth and Company, also agreed to put some money in, so altogether we raised about forty thousand to put into this private company from which we would get a percentage. Fred would run the company as its president, but we would have a board here in Los Angeles, and we were to control the checkbook. We renamed it the Sensa International Victorian Corporation.

We gave Fred a ten thousand dollar advance and the credit card he was to use only to send us messages via the Tropical Wire Company, which was primarily the communications company that had to be used. We wished him *Godspeed* and told him to keep those orders rolling in.

Every week or so we would get a report from him telling us that he had called on so-and-so and prospects were excellent. Then we would receive another letter saying he had moved on to Brazil and there were even greater potentials there, but we never got any actual orders. He kept promising that they were about to come in. This game went on for some time, and by the time we had gone through twenty-seven thousand dollars, we had become a little concerned. Still no orders. Finally, we got a report that he was going to Havana where the prospects were tremendous due to all the sugar mills. By this time, our patience was running very thin indeed. We had not yet received as much as one order from him.

In addition, we were also getting big communications bills from the Tropical Wireless Company. Fred wrote to say he urgently needed more money - he was about to close some big contracts. We wrote him back saying 1: We were canceling the Tropical Wireless account, 2: He would not get another dime from us, and 3: Where were the expense account reports he was supposed to have sent?

We had never received one report for all the money we had advanced to him. We heard nothing further from Fred, but later on, we received a collect telephone call from him, which Doug very wisely rejected.

We certainly learned something from that episode. We paid off Tropical Wireless and basically forgot about the Sensa International Victorian Corporation. We only had five hundred dollars on the books for a charter. The few remaining dollars we had remaining in the till were distributed equally to the investors.

Everybody got conned in that one, but we wrote it off to experience earned. We realized that Fred was an ideal con man and unbelievably good at what he did. He really opened our eyes.

Seven years later, our family was vacationing at the Getty resort, south of Acapulco. Jim and John were out doing something, but Hilda and I were relaxing at the bar having drinks before dinner. All of a sudden, Hilda looked up and said, "Oh, my God! Isn't that Fred Armour at the bar?"

I looked over and there he was. He was talking to someone at the bar, but turned around toward us when he felt someone looking at him. He recognized us and immediately got off the bar stool, walked over to our table, introduced himself, pulled up a chair and sat down at our table. Imperiously, he commanded our waiter to bring his drink over.

Completely ignoring the oil company fiasco, he launched into this story about all the wonderful things he had been doing since that time. Then he mentioned that his wife and children were in the car, that he had come in to check out the hotel to see if it was adequate for their needs. What arrogance! I just looked at Hilda and Hilda looked at me.

Needless to say, we didn't offer him a drink, and as the temperature got cooler, he finally stood up and walked away. I think he may have gone back to the bar for another drink, but the minute he exited the room, I took it upon myself to round up the hotel manager, told him the story and said, "If this man tries to get a room with you, get his money in advance. If he uses my name as a reference, completely ignore it." I told him that Fred was just no good, and was the worst kind of American.

The manager was very appreciative and promised to keep his guard up. He said he would refuse to even rent him a room under any circumstances. Whether Fred actually had his wife and kids outside in the car remained to be seen, but he completely disappeared from sight.

Several years later I was talking with a friend who had a winter place near Mexico City. In the course of the conversation, he happened to mention he had run into an American, Fred Armour, and that they had become pretty good friends. When the man went home to the states, he had offered Fred the use of his hacienda. A month later, he went back to Mexico and discovered that all his shirts were gone, all his personal effects were missing from the hacienda, and there was no sign anywhere of Fred. I couldn't help myself. I couldn't stop laughing.

He said, "What are you laughing at?"

I replied, "Well, I've had some experiences with that con man. But he picked me clean, too, so you're among good company."

Not long after that, Charlie Avery of the Costa Rica Railroad was in town. We mentioned Fred and we all had a good laugh. As I told him our stories, he said, "My God, if you'd given me even the slightest hint you were going to do any business with him, I would have warned you off."

I just shrugged my shoulders and said, "Live and learn!"

My Directorial Debut - a String of Directorships

Capital requirements of the securities business in the early days were relatively nominal, but First California Company's capital of less than five hundred thousand dollars was truly minimal. With the losses in trading and the slow state of the securities industry at the time, it was touch and go. We didn't know whether First California could survive. One problem was that six percent preferred stock had been sold to Italian-Americans in San Francisco with the implied warranty that it could be sold back to the company with no loss at any time. The total issue was only a little over two hundred thousand dollars, but this was money that even in those days could not be withdrawn without placing the company in capital deficiency.

Bob Evans and Ted Burr came to me and said, "Bill, we need help." They pressed me to step up and buy some of this preferred stock. I agreed to do so in exchange for receiving options on First California common stock at the current book value, plus my election to the board of directors. This was actually my first of many board appointments. For the purchase, I used the base of the ten thousand dollars Mother had given me to buy the stock. It had grown into eighty-six thousand dollars.

I made another interesting investment in the early years with First California. I had bought a few shares of a very small gas company operating in Oregon and Washington. These were propane-air systems, operating in difficulty against the competition of very cheap electricity. I had briefly been a director of Northwest Cities Gas Company as a result of my having the deciding votes in a stupid proxy fight over a nothing company. To my surprise, one day I received a notice that Northwest Cities Gas was to be acquired by a newly created gas company headquartered in Seattle. The owners had expressed the hope that someday they would have access to natural gas.

Northwest Cities Gas Company became a huge stepping-stone in my career.

My first directorship was hardly a real one. It seems that in the late 1920s, somebody promoted small gas companies in Clackamas, Walla Walla and other Washington cities up and down the Columbia River, plus Astoria down at the mouth of the Columbia - as well as Eugene, Oregon.

The local gas source was down along the Columbia. There was no attempt to evaluate the size of the gas deposit. It turned out to be shallow gas, a very limited amount, but still - a number of the towns were piped. A gas company in Texas had for some reason bought control of the Northwest Cities Gas Company. They had earlier floated a small bond issue when they were taken over by the larger Texas company. A bond indenture by the Texas firm required them to keep all subsidiaries solvent.

Northwest Cities Gas Company had never made any money despite the fact that it had been bought by the Texas Gas Company. In the 1930s, the SEC broke up the Texas holding company; the new company refinanced their existing bond issue and got rid of the bad indenture provision. They probably let Northwest Cities Gas Company bonds go under default.

Northwest Cities went into receivership. It was reorganized and each thousand dollar bond got ten shares of new stock. In browsing the utilities securities manuals, I found this company, discovered that occasional shares showed up in the over-the-counter market and

started buying some myself. I think it was a twelve or fourteen dollar stock at the time. Earning no dividends, the balance sheet looked terrible, but the company had survived for several years, and I figured it might survive longer. I thought that ultimately, natural gas would come to the Pacific Northwest and this company could be an eventual winner. Of course, the fundamental problem was that electricity was so cheap in the Pacific Northwest (at that time, three-fourths of a cent) and there was really no way a gas company could make any money in competition with electricity.

I received notice of an upcoming annual meeting and dumb me; I called the president of the company who turned out to be a lawyer. He urged me to attend the annual meeting at the company's headquarters in Walla Walla. I arrived the day before the meeting, the president picked me up at the airport, we had dinner together and he filled me in on some facts. He was a lawyer who spent most of his time *lawyering* and only part of the time managing the company. Most of the managing was done by the town managers, but according to him, the company was barely hanging on by its fingernails. He owned very little stock himself. He told me that the largest individual stockholder was an automobile dealer from upstate New York who had been buying the stock for years with the belief, like mine, that natural gas would also eventually come there. The rest of the stock was pretty widely scattered.

He said he had proxies in for fewer than fifty percent of the stock and that he would not have a quorum. He was very concerned that the automotive dealer from New York would buy up a few more shares, force him out and take control of the company. It turned out the number of shares I had was enough to swing the vote. On the morning of the stockholder meeting, I met with the lawyer-president prior to the meeting. He recounted the proxy votes he had which were just short of the necessary number to have a quorum.

That meant that the automotive dealer from New York could not have a quorum either unless I threw my votes to him. By this time, the president had convinced me that I should not throw my lot in with the guy, so I did not go into the meeting room. The quorum was not present and the meeting was adjourned. As part and parcel of the discussion between the lawyer and the auto dealer outside the meeting room, it was finally agreed that they would have a subsequent meeting and that I would be elected a swing director to the board; the auto dealer could then have three board members and the lawyer would have three board members. The board was reconstituted and I was elected by proxy to the board of directors of the Northwest Cities Gas Company.

I took the late afternoon plane back to Los Angeles. For a year my name appeared as a director of the Northwest Cities Gas Company, but we never had a formal meeting, at least not to my recollection. They said the company was, for all practical purposes, broke! At the next shareholders meeting, I was not re-elected and I don't think the auto dealer ever took over. Regardless, the stock languished. I left my stock in the safe deposit box and didn't much worry about it.

Then suddenly, probably three or four years after my *non-directorship* adventure, I heard that a new firm in Seattle called the Cascade Natural Gas Company was proposing to roll up a number of small, natural gas companies in the state of Washington, none of which was truly profitable. Northwest Cities Gas Company was one of these. C. Spencer Clark, the promoter, had enjoyed a good reputation as an entrepreneur in the Seattle area for some time. Clark's intention was to get these companies together because natural gas would soon be coming to the Pacific Northwest. Of course, I agreed. I knew something about this because in 1952, I had organized a junket for Los Angeles securities dealers. We had visited Alberta, Canada to look at some oil and gas properties.

Plus, Eastman Dillon had an underwriting client called Pacific Petroleum, a major Canadian oil company, which had discovered substantial quantities of natural gas in the northwest corner of the province of Alberta. There was no need for this gas in Canada because there were vast supplies of natural gas further south.

However, the stuff up at the northwest corner of Alberta most likely would be brought down through the mountains into the province of British Columbia, then on down through the states of Washington and Oregon. Such a pipeline would require the permission of both Canada and the United States. Pacific Petroleum Limited was already trying to get permits to export this gas from Canada as well as Federal Power Commission permits to build a pipeline into the northwest.

Meanwhile there were substantial quantities of natural gas in northwest Texas and Utah, for which there was no adequate market. So a bunch of American promoters were trying to sell the idea of a pipeline from that area up through the state of Idaho into Oregon and Washington and ultimately into British Columbia. This provided an imbroglio that tied things up for several years.

Clark was attempting to do initial public financing through a small Seattle brokerage firm, which had only been able to find buyers for a little more than half the stock.

When I inquired about the deal and Clark found out that I was in charge of corporate finance for First California Company, he and Harry Jones, the small dealer in Seattle caught the first plane to Los Angeles and fell over me like a blanket! It turned out that Harry had been interested in selling securities to get the prospective company, Cascade Natural Gas, up and running.

When they showed up at my office, I immediately invited Bob Evans into the meeting. Within a couple of hours, we had agreed that the First California Company would underwrite and sell the balance of the unsold security issue of the prospective Cascade Natural Gas Company. It was not a huge amount, probably four or five hundred thousand dollars at the most. I wrote up a brief memorandum.

The issue was, of course, approved and we turned it over to the First California Company sales force. Within three days, we had sold the stock. The concept was correct, but little did I know it was going to take four years before the pipelines would ever be built and therefore able to lure natural gas into the state of Washington.

With a strong distribution capability, the First California Company, upon my recommendation, made it possible for us to easily clean up the offering of Cascade shares and I went on Cascade's board.

With the completion of the west coast pipeline bringing gas from Alberta in northern British Columbia down to the Vancouver-Seattle area, there remained one market nearby that did not have natural gas. This was Vancouver Island, but this area also had some rather important paper mills. The mills could provide a substantial load for natural gas if the resource could be made available. The problem was that Vancouver Island was separated from the main land by deep waters, and Puget Sound - with its rapid currents - had many islands and a great deal of ship traffic. It was not practical to build a bridge across to Vancouver Island, a bridge over which a pipeline could be carried.

Various feasibility studies had been conducted to address building a conventional steel pipeline to Vancouver Island, but the results always came up negative.

A long established, highly regarded company from the UK called British Insulated Callender's Cables (BICC) made the Atlantic cable. This prestigious company was formed in 1945 via the merger of two of the largest cable manufacturers, British Insulated Cables, Ltd. and Callender's Cables and Construction Company, Ltd.

BICC had recently developed a method of making a flexible, high-pressure pipe that could be used in places up to eight hundred to a thousand pounds per square inch, the kind of pressure that would be required in the gas pipeline. This pipe could not be made in large diameters, which is twelve to twenty-inch sizes frequently used in gas pipeline construction. It could, however, be made in a four to six-inch size. And at eight hundred pounds per square inch, a fair amount of gas could be passed through the pipe. BICC assured us that they could make pipe that could carry gas from the mainland to Vancouver Island and we accepted their guaranteed contract.

Based on that contract and additional engineering studies, Eastman Dillon and a Seattle investment firm, both of whom were involved in the Cascade financing, together raised around five million dollars to finance the project. Unbelievable though it seems, BICC suddenly discovered they could only make this pipe in one thousand to twelve hundred foot lengths. Plus, they had not yet developed the means for connecting these lengths for the kind of pressure that would be involved. After a tremendous amount of experimentation, they threw up their hands, paid us their penalty fee and voided the contract.

Meanwhile, with natural gas now available, Cascade was rapidly expanding its cities. This was a must for capital requirements and Cascade was definitely short of capital. With the Vancouver Island project dead for technical reasons, and the company having spent its cash on hand – coupled with Cascade's financial needs for further expansion and the similarity in management in some of the companies, we finally put together a deal to merge the Vancouver gas pipeline into Cascade.

Believe it or not, everyone came out ahead. Cascade kept the gas, which it desperately needed. The investors had found a way out. We collapsed the two companies into Cascade and got into the company just as it was expanding. Everyone was happy.

In retrospect, it still seems amazing to me that BICC could get so far along as to enter into a contract without knowing if they could manufacture their pipes to the required specifications and be able to connect them appropriately.

As I have said many times before, projects always take longer and cost more than initially anticipated. Cascade rattled along and was grossly short of capital until four or five years later. We hadn't counted on that delay.

Both pipelines were eventually built: The Pacific Petroleum line and the line from north Texas. In addition to the Northwest Cities Gas Company properties, Cascade also picked up Wenatchee, Washington plus cities north of Seattle - on up to the Canadian border and several other towns. We were finally able to profitably convert our towns to natural gas.

Even though propane liquid was relatively cheap in those days, for gasification, there was still murderous competition for cheap electricity. For some years it was touch and go as to whether the company could survive. Sadly, we were forced to sell off the city of Eugene, Oregon. At the time, we desperately needed the cash to keep us alive for a few more months.

Several times, Spencer Clark went to the bank and borrowed money on his own personal note to provide Cascade Natural Gas with money to meet the current payroll or another shipment of propane.

Meanwhile, a large New York investment banking firm had been promoting the Pacific Northwest line from Texas up into the state of Washington. We knew we had to vastly expand the distribution systems in our towns and take advantage of natural gas when it arrived. The money required was too much to be raised by First California Company, so the New York investment banking firm that wanted the pipeline agreed to join with First California Company to provide Cascade with the money to pipe the towns further on.

The original agreement was for the New York firm and First California to share the underwriting, but when the deal finally came through and we got the money to pipe our towns, the New York firm formed a syndicate and took the majority of the management fee for themselves. They had a tremendous battle with Bob Evans. I think eventually we received forty percent of the fee—we should have gotten half.

When the gas finally came down from Canada, we had gas simultaneously coming in from both sides of our system, so we had no further worry about supply. The original Northwest Cities gas system in Astoria, Oregon had been abandoned because it was in bad shape due to the nature of the terrain. However, Cascade proceeded to get franchises to the other cities in Oregon down in the Hoquiam area.

Spencer Clark was very ambitious. At one time he wanted to try to merge the United Cities Gas Company into Mountain Gas Company, which served Idaho - and Cascade Natural Gas, although I assured him the SEC would never permit those three companies to be merged. My thought was that United Cities would have had to be incorporated in Illinois.

Early on I had been elected to the Cascade Natural Gas Company Board of Directors and we had our quarterly meetings in Seattle. Typically, I would fly to Seattle on a Thursday afternoon and get a room at the Olympic hotel. We would have our board meetings all day Friday, after which I would take a late flight back to Los Angeles.

Cascade was not as profitable as we had hoped it would be because of the severe competition over electricity. Then Clark found a small company in Colorado that was building a pipeline into Utah. They ran out of money and were desperate, so Spencer acquired the company. Of course, they put Cascade under the Federal Power Act (now the Federal Energy Regulatory Commission). These laws authorize FERC to license hydropower development proposed by federal agencies. They had a rule about investment bankers being on the board of directors. It was definitely a *no-no!* I had to choose between staying on the board of directors and resign from Eastman Dillon or the alternative. Naturally, I resigned from the board of directors. Cascade has struggled to make money over the years but they never made a tremendous amount. Recently, however, I read where they crossed the *one hundred thousandth customer* mark.

Over the years I paid my dues to the oil industry. I'd been *picked* a couple of times. I guess I'm an optimist but some of these promoters are pretty damn good. Over the years I had more faith in geologists than I should have had. Always it seemed that when we finally got down to the level where the oil was supposed to be, there was a fault that was on the wrong side of the oil-water interface or something of that nature. But I never dropped much money into any of them, except for two.

One of these was in an area northeast of Wheeling, West Virginia, an area where the wells were *absolutely guaranteed* to strike gas. The outfit had been in the area for quite some time and had a pretty good track record. I think we put around three hundred thousand dollars for a twenty-five percent interest in these three that were *certain* to hit wells. The wells were drilled. I was assured that all three hit and that they were waiting on the ability to connect to either the Columbia gas system or one of the other gas-buying pipelines in the area. Then communications stopped, and Lloyd and I decided to check things out in person.

We flew into Wheeling, rented a car and drove up to see the wells. Without too much trouble we found the company office, which was for the most part abandoned. It turned out that the company had had a bunch of bum wells and was virtually bankrupt. One of the people there got in the car with us and we went out looking for my three wells.

We found them in short order. All three had valves on them. We cracked the valves open, and from the sound they made, we determined that all three wells certainly had a lot of high-pressure gas. We couldn't tell anything about the volume, however. But there was no pipeline anywhere near them. We learned that in one case, a local landowner absolutely refused to allow any pipelines to be constructed anywhere on his property. I received a couple of notices from a bankruptcy court that everything had disappeared into the sand. I presume some local lawyers set things up and made off with the wells.

The next venture I went into was with a company that had been set up to buy a bunch of shut-in distributor wells east of Wichita. The wells were owned by a company that had defaulted; so the bank that had originally loaned out eighteen million dollars had taken the wells back. They negotiated to sell the wells to this new company that had approached me. They were going to take back two or three million in paper on the wells and get a few million dollars in cash out. The company was to be headquartered down in San Diego and was expected to expand into a good-sized company.

I had the good sense to get a second lien on the wells. (The bank was first lien.) Even though the price of oil was down, I thought that properly managed, the wells should eventually pay out handsomely. But the people running the company really had no knowledge of how to manage it. They had been in the business solely to be able to buy fancy furniture and other perks for their San Diego office. They didn't really care about the business end of it. The oil produced enough to pay the interest and usually the principal on the bank loan, although they got behind a couple of times. I had to fly to Fort Worth once to meet with a banker. Needless to say, he was quite unhappy.

He said, "You know, I'm really teed off with this property."

I responded, "*You're* teed off? *You're* getting *your* money! I've got the equity in this thing. I'm the one who should be teed off!"

He laughed. Later on, his bank was taken over by the government.

The Kansas wells were finally sold to an operator who presumably knew how to operate them. I did all right. I got most of my money back, but meanwhile, I'd been suckered into buying a couple other wells with the company. Fortunately, it turned out that they were legitimate. And finally, everything was in the hands of an operator who knew what he was doing and I was consistently getting checks. When oil went up to thirty-six dollars, they were wonderful checks, when it went down to ten dollars and the wells were operating in the red, they were still paying out. But I always learned something from those experiences.

The other venture I went into was in southern Alabama. A fellow with a solid reputation and good business background told me there was shallow gas down there. At the time, the cheap gas at Mobile Bay was being developed. But he said there was shallow gas—only a thousand to twelve hundred feet deep, and that he had a really active drill. It was a meteorological device that allowed us to pick up radiation of the shallow gas almost without fail. The instrument was even capable of identifying whether or not there was gas in an anti-climb. The amount of money required was not much because it was pretty cheap to drill a twelve hundred foot well.

After a couple of wells had been drilled unsuccessfully, I flew down to Alabama, went out to the property with one of the drillers and a woman who worked the machine with him, and found that there was gas there all right, the small gas wells were indeed producing.

We drove all around the wells. The machine showed there was gas present. Then we went around some other places where we had drilled and it showed there was gas present, although we knew there wasn't. I went to a well they were drilling at the time, and the well started flowing with salt water. Of course, it turned out there was no gas present. So I wrote the matter off. I only lost thirty-five thousand dollars.

I spent the rest of my visit driving around the countryside. I drove down to the eastern entrance to Mobile Bay where I found an old fort. There was a well right there on the beach. Silver-colored salt water was spritzing out of it. I put a match to the bubbles and they burned. There must have been a leak from some of the gas way down deep because that area is a very prolific oil and gas producer—offshore and also in Mobile Bay. (Now, let's leave on the crest of a wave—as Kay Fletcher once said when she walked out of my Washington apartment one afternoon after having one too many cocktails with Hilda.)

~

There is a massive gas field called the Yucatan. It is spread over a wide area that covers part of western Kansas and Oklahoma. It is relatively shallow with relatively low pressure, but very long-lived. It has been producing now for fifty years. Big operators expanded it by drilling in large blocks. The property was always managed well. It was never raped by small operators who were often quite prone to drilling smaller wells. Their goal was to get the gas out rapidly so they could run off with quick profits.

For years it had produced at the rate of one well per section or square mile. At this level of drainage, all the gas could be reduced, and ultimately more wells would have to be drilled. The landowners who held the royalty interests were not happy but still, the low level production over the long run would earn them the money they would ultimately get from the royalty.

They petitioned Kansas Commission on Oil and Gas to require additional wells to be drilled so that production could be stepped up. After several hearings, the commission required one well to be drilled for every quarter section, rather than one well per section. The oil and gas business was in the doldrums at the time when the Kansas order came out.

A friend of Joe King's held a quarter interest in a large area. He was overextended with some other properties and he could not come up with his twenty-five percent of the money required to drill the additional wells. We negotiated that Eastman Dillon would put up the money to drill his interest in these additional wells, thereby owning half his interest. Since this was a known producing gas field, we knew the gas was there. It would be like shooting fish in a rain barrel, we thought.

Eastman Dillon formed an organization called Udoga. We put up the money to pay for this fellow's interest in the additional wells, and, "Ping! Ping! Ping!" -- They hit well after well! There were hardly any dry holes.

In addition to the rights he already had, a few areas had some rights of potential production from lower horizons. Those had been drilled with various stages of success included a few failures. Operating costs for a gas well are normally very low, so extra money is used from time to time for some exploratory work, but he had some successes there, too.

Basically, however, our payments were tied to the price of natural gas, and when gas dropped down to a dollar ten, things weren't so good. When gas hit over seven dollars, a year and a half ago – brother, were we in hog heaven! At the present time (spring 2002), I believe we are getting around a dollar eighty to two dollars for our gas. Now when some promoter calls me to go into an oil well or a gas well venture, I say, "Look, there's only one I've ever been in that's been okay, and that was with friends. Every gas and oil venture that I've ever put money into with a stranger has been a dog. Thank you, but I don't need any more dogs!"

~

My next directorship was with a company called Walker Scott, headquartered in San Diego. Walker Scott's main department store was an old multi-storied building downtown. They had a branch in La Jolla and were looking for money to build another in Escondido. The store was run by George Scott who had been in business for many years. He was well known in the community for wanting things run his way. He wasn't a bad operator, just fiercely opinionated. We did some financing for him. It was a very small market, and I served on the board of directors for a number of years.

And then once in a meeting, I made a comment about some employees that may have been inappropriate. I don't recall exactly what I said. Nevertheless, my opinion irritated Scott tremendously and at the next annual meeting, I was promptly removed from the board. The Escondido store had been built, but it was only moderately successful. I had no animosity towards Scott at all. We just didn't think the same way. Finally, the company got into some financial difficulty and was liquidated, although it was not forced into bankruptcy. The stockholders got paid off and that was the end of that.

Another company for which I was a one-time director was the Buffums Department Store Company. Buffums was a fine, small, very upscale, family-owned department store. The headquarters was located in Long Beach. Eastman Dillon, of course, had a Long Beach office, and through our manager, Bob Evans and I got in touch with the owner. I don't recall the exact reason I was asked to go on the board, but they were opening a new store in the Santa Anita Mall. We got a twenty-percent employee discount and Hilda loved that. But the family was older, tired of the business and surely lacking in management expertise.

Suddenly, out of nowhere came an Australian company that was itching to get into the U.S. market. They made a friendly tender offer for Buffums stock that we all agreed was a good deal. The family and all the public stockholders sold out to the Australians and I left the board. The Australians had asked me to stay on but I had a full kettle of fish at the time and didn't want to remain on any more boards if I couldn't find a public purpose, so I resigned. The Aussies ran the store for several years, but weren't able to keep it afloat and the store was finally closed down.

Soon thereafter, I became involved with the Southern California Petroleum Corporation. Oil had been discovered in the Gulf of Suez on the west side of the Sinai Peninsula. This small company had a drilling subsidiary called the Camay Drilling Company. The subsidiary had a number of rotary shell rigs - four to six thousand foot quality rigs. They had successfully arranged a drilling contract to drill in very shallow water off the coast of the Sinai Peninsula, which lay between Sinai and the main body of Egypt. They had gotten some big ideas from a contact they had met while drilling in that area. One of the investors in the company with the oil concession was the Italian Government Oil and Gas Company, IGOGC.

Several wells had been successfully completed when the 7-Day War broke out between Israel and Egypt in October 1973. The Egyptians threatened Israel from the Sinai-Israeli border, a big mistake on their part. The Israelis attacked and overran the Egyptians who fled in great disorder. In fact, they retreated up the west coast of the Sinai toward Suez. They went through the Camay drilling site so fast, our manager said, "Those guys were so scared they didn't even stop to loot! I've never known an Egyptian who wouldn't loot anything he could lay his hands on."

Then there was a naval gunboat battle in the Gulf of Suez between a couple of the Israeli and Egyptian speedboats. When our people saw the battle going on there, they shut down the rig and pulled out, abandoning the site. Somehow, through one of my connections, I had acquired a few shares of stock in the outfit that had the concession for oil drilling in the Gulf of Suez. The Italians made peace of a sort with the Israelis and made an agreement to obtain oil from the wells. Israel was taking most of that oil because they owned the Suez by that time. But they could track it up the Suez because it got to the east bank of the Suez Canal. The Egyptians wanted to get the rest of the stock, so I offered mine. After some initial confusion in the wording of the telegram, I sent my stock off to a bank in Italy and promptly received my money.

Not long afterward, oil was discovered in Libya, which was at that time a kingdom. Camay got the contract to drill some of the first wells in Libya. All of a sudden, the King of Libya was overthrown by Libyan dictator Moammar Gadhafi. Again, we lost our contract. We sold the oil well equipment. I had a few shares of stock in that company, sold that concession, and that became nothing more than a write off.

Southern California Petroleum had bought some gas production in eastern New Mexico. They also had some oil and gas production in California. After the company became solvent, a Beverly Hills stockbroker started bringing his clients into Southern Cal stock, and he finally had so much of it, he effectively gained control of the company. The president resigned and I stayed on the board for a short time until there was really no reason for me to be there. Once all our customers were out of the stock, I resigned. But the fellow who had bought control of the company gradually turned it into an investment vehicle.

He always kept enough production going so that he wouldn't be a personal holding company, but he started investing in personal stocks and did pretty well. I finally sold out. He made an offer to buy out the stock from the small stockholders and although I wasn't particularly small, I guess I had five or six hundred shares, he paid me a quarter over the market and I was out.

~

My next oil and gas experience might be construed as if I were an involved onlooker. This was an exceptionally interesting experience. Bob Evans somehow had come into contact with a man called Charles Gus Glasscock who owned Glasscock Tidelands Drilling Company. Gus had a number of drilling rigs located on barges he was using to drill in shallow bayou waters in east Texas and Louisiana. He had seven or so of these barges and occasionally accepted drilling deals, taking a participation in the project as part of his remuneration. He was able to build up a modest amount of actual oil and gas production.

However, his real desire was to enter into a new contract type of drilling, putting into offshore water - not bayou water, but deeper water. Somebody had already designed a drilling rig that was a barge on *legs*. They would push the legs down into the bottom of the ocean, hoist the barge out of the water so it floated above the waves, then drill from the barge.

He was building these barges and was actually drilling in deep water. The barges worked well in water up to one hundred feet deep. The barge would be towed out to position over the drilling location and the legs would be pushed down through the holes in the barge to the floor of the ocean, as deep as they could go. Then the barge would be jacked up on the legs until it stood well above the highest waves expected. The drilling rig would push its drill shaft down into the ocean floor and drill a short distance whereupon a service pipe would be sent down and cemented into place. Cut-off valves and other safety measures were put in place, then the rig would drill to the required depth.

Gus successfully drilled a number of wells. The barge rig was named "Mr. Gus the First," but now, Gus wanted to go further. He wanted to build a modified barge rig that would drill a fifteen thousand foot well. It would cost more than a million dollars. Eastman Dillon financed that project and "Mr. Gus the Second" was built.

Since these rigs were actual marine vehicles and they could go in the open ocean, they had to be licensed by the U.S. Coast Guard. They also had to have a marine mortgage on them. At the closing of escrow for "Mr. Gus the Second," the mortgagor said that under marine law, there had to be a plaque on the barge saying that it was the property of so-and-so with the name of the mortgage company included.

Gus said he would be damned if he was going to have his friends come onto his boat and think it belonged to some damn insurance company back on the east coast. He almost refused to sign the closing papers until they all agreed they would put the mortgage notice up in the drill pusher's cabin—that would make everybody happy and Gus would be *legal.*

Unfortunately, happiness was short-lived. In the second drilling job, one of the legs of the rig partly gave way, and instead of simply turning the rig over to the insurance company, Mr. Gus decided to cure the fall himself. Unfortunately, it got worse and worse until the rig was lost in the sea. That stunt got him into some deep difficulty. Finally the company was taken over by somebody else and Mr. Gus was out.

Bob Evans served on that board. The C.G. Glasscock Tidewaters Oil Drilling Company was located in Corpus Christi, Texas. I often went to Corpus Christi with Bob to attend board meetings. There was always a roaring gale coming in off the gulf. I once asked, "Doesn't the hot air off the gulf bother you?"

Bob replied, "You should be here whenever that wind stops. It's so much worse."

We would fly down to San Antonio and take a flight on an airline called Air Texas. It was predecessor to Trans Texas, the airline run by the guy who ruined Continental and Eastern. They flew DC-3s from San Antonio down to Corpus Christi. The planes were almost always empty. They would stop over at Beeville and other small towns, drop off a bag of mail and go *bumpity-bump* all the way down to Corpus Christi. The flight attendants all wore cowgirl outfits.

Gus had a son who was also in the oil and gas business. Gus Jr. proposed a formal company with a great name, the Great Basins Oil Company. At that time, there was more and more discussion of the oil bearing bases of the west, which hadn't even been drilled, so young Glasscock formed this company. They secured leases on various tracts of land in basins in Utah and Nevada. There are, believe it or not, a few barrels of oil in Nevada - and the First California Company did the financing. We did a couple million shares of stock at three or four dollars a share. I was elected a director of the Great Basins Oil Company.

We had a very broad syndicate, not only of the underwriters, but group members as well. I think there were forty-three members of the underwriting group who were selling group stock. I went to the closing for First California Company in Denver. I think there were about ten copies of every damn document I had to sign. By the time I got through signing all those duplicates of duplicates, my signature was no longer legible the way it used to be, and it has never been legible since.

Great Basins never really found oil or gas of any great quantity. They did drilling partnerships a number of times but never really came up with anything. We still had some money left, so Bob Evans negotiated the purchase of an oil well drilling servicing company located in Odessa, Texas. I went down there for a couple of meetings with the company we had bought. They made equipment for fishing stuff that was dropped down drill holes and things of that sort. I was always a relatively minor player in that field. We paid too much for it, the business didn't turn around, and the guy who was running it retired, leaving a successor who wasn't a good manager.

The Denver underwriter of the Great Basins project, Charlie Peters, was on the board of directors with me. Once I was at a meeting in Denver at the height of the uranium boom, which was located in northeast New Mexico. I asked him (mind you, I took a dim view of the numerous uranium ventures being promoted) if there were such a thing as an *honest* uranium company.

He said, "Yes, there is one, but you won't believe the name."

My curiosity piqued, I asked, "What is it?"

"The Lucky Mack Uranium Company," he replied. "They're in Wyoming. They really are producing uranium."

I asked him what the stock was and learned that it was around three or four dollars a share, so I bought about a thousand shares. They had contracted with an old-line Salt Lake City company called the Utah Construction and Mining Company, which had iron mines. It was a big construction company. I had known about it for some time.

I knew it was a very thinly traded over-the-counter stock, but it turned out that relating to the prices in the pink sheets, there was a *BID* and an *ASK*. Whenever I hit the *ASK*, it disappeared. That was a subject ask, the only stock that they'd show me if any ever turned up, but none ever turned up. The bid was very good because the Utah family, an old Mormon family, wanted to give back the few shares they had to the public.

Separately, it turned out that the Yucca Mining Company wanted to go public and decided the best way to do it was to merge with the existing public company. Since the Lucky Mack Uranium Company was an honest-to-god operating mine, they merged into that company and I wound up with stock in the Utah Construction and Mining Company.

That was a great company in its own right. They had a large iron mine in Peru as well as in some other places. They had three special ore ships built to carry the iron ore up to the United States and over to Japan. They ran coal in southern Utah and did all kinds of things in addition to construction work.

At that time, the uranium utility business was booming. General Electric was in the business, too, of course. GE decided they should tie up a supply of uranium for some of the power plants they were building, so they proposed a merger-acquisition of Utah Construction and Mining Company. I ultimately ended up with a slug of General Electric stock. My cost-per-share was so ridiculously low that it was absurd.

Firms below the top rank of established companies are especially notorious for the way they handle their shareholders. What goes for secondary industrial companies is tripled in spades for mining companies. You could list anything on the Vancouver stock exchange and the promoters would run it up and down and issue false press releases. So when my friends in Vancouver, the Ontario boys, called me up one day to tell me they ran across a mining prospect that looked very interesting indeed, and asked if I would like to put a little money into it, knowing who they were, I said, "Yes, of course."

I put five or ten thousand dollars into it. It was a prospect. They said it was very rich at the surface and they were putting money into it to see if there might be a depth. And the name of the company—they laughed when they told me—was Roche DeBull Mountain Mines, and it was going to be a British Columbian corporation, not a public corporation.

When I received the paperwork, it said right on the certificate, 'An Especially Limited Company,' which meant that it could not be transferred to just anybody without special permission, and that no public market could be developed on it until the British Columbian authorities gave the okay.

A professional team was sent in to check out the prospect. I soon discovered that while it was indeed very rich on the surface, this was a perfect example of surface enrichment. In fact the prospect was worthless. Now, for an ordinary Canadian mining prospect, that wouldn't be too much of a problem. They would find another prospect, issue some fancy press releases, run the stock up, sell some more stock, and play the game again. But no, this was an especially limited company *run by my friends*!

What did they do when they found the prospect was worthless? They put the company into liquidation. And over a period of a number of months, all the unspent money came back to us. Each time we took the certificate in, they stamped it, and another distribution of capital was made and bingo!—like the cook joint in Ishmir was honest. When I mentioned this to a Canadian friend one time, he laughed and said, "Well, it's probably the only time in history that a mining prospect has given money back to the investors. There should be a law against that—it breaks with tradition!"

~

Back when Bob and I were still with First California Company, somebody brought us an oil and gas deal from east Texas-west Louisiana. Naturally, their engineers were saying there were substantial quantities of oil and gas on the property. Although they did some drilling for participation, primarily they were an exploration outfit and looked money-good on the basis of their reports regarding reserves. We agreed to do the financing.

This deal turned out to be a great disappointment. But the worst disappointment of all was that a few weeks after we agreed to complete that deal, a young fellow came in to the office saying he heard about us because of our Glasscock involvement, and he had a great deal he wanted to finance. He was collecting natural gas from various wells around the state of Texas and delivering the gas to the pipeline companies. He said he was exempt from FERC regulations, that he had all kinds of contacts for the purchase of gas, that he knew where he could sell the gas, but he needed money to expand his systems.

Unfortunately, we were already tied up with the Lecuneo Oil and Gas Company, the Louisiana-Texas venture, so we had to pass on the deal. We were very impressed with this fellow so we referred him to our affiliate firm Blair and Company, Inc. back in New York. They did his financing.

He was so sure of himself. He said, "I'll tell you what I'll do. You sell *XYZ* shares of the Class A stock to the public. I'll take a Class B stock until I make my earnings. I'll take no value for my stock, but when I deliver those earnings to you, I'll convert my class B stock into Class A stock. It'll then be one class of stock."

That sounded like a great deal. Blair did the deal and Bob Evans and I got a small finder's fee. This guy took the gas company and entered into a long-term contract to deliver natural gas to the municipal power plant of the city of San Antonio. The price of gas suddenly went up and he was caught short, but he worked his way out of that and moved on. This became one of the great success stories in the oil and gas business. He made vast amounts of money for himself and many of his shareholders.

~

In 1952, while still with First California, and still searching for small, cheap, utilities stock investments, I would continually peruse Moody's Utilities Stock Manual. I frequently ran across a company known as the United Cities Utilities Company. The firm owned several small gas companies scattered from Minnesota to Georgia. Although the Public Utilities Holding Company Act had broken up the old widely scattered properties of holding companies, a provision of the act permitted the SEC to exempt very small holding companies. As United Cities was exempt, it had not been broken up. The sparse figures in the Moody's Manual indicated that the company had around a hundred ten thousand shares of class A common stock, callable at two dollars a share and held by a hundred or so shareholders.

The sole voting rights applied to the hundred thousand or so shares of Class B common stock, held by eighteen to twenty shareholders. I had never seen a quotation for United Cities shares. However, one day, while skimming through the over-the-counter pink sheets, I glimpsed an offering of a hundred sixty-eight shares of Class A common stock at a dollar fifty a share. I wrote up a ticket and gave it to our trading department who promptly hit the offer and bought the shares. No further offerings showed in the pink sheets. I wrote to the company headquarters in Chicago, requesting an annual report and such additional information as they could send. To my surprise, I received a lengthy letter from Arthur K. Lee, chairman and president of the company, enclosing the sparse annual reports and answering in detail some questions I had posed in my letter. In those days, over-the-counter companies were not required to make filings on 10 Ks and 10 Qs as they are today.

Subsequently, I called Art Lee in Chicago and we had a very friendly conversation. Of course he was curious as to why I had bought the shares and when I explained my ongoing interest in utilities, Art became very outgoing. Several weeks later, I received a phone call from a small securities dealer in Chicago who said he had additional shares of United Cities and asked if I were interested. He had five thousand shares of Class A which I could have for a dollar fifty a share. I knew the shares were callable at two dollars a share, but the call privilege expired in less than a year and the company's balance sheet was such that there was no way they could afford to buy in those shares.

I called a few friends in the Los Angeles Society of Securities Analysts and together we bought the block. I took down twenty-five hundred shares for myself. In subsequent conversations with Art Lee,

I invited him to California. Art and his wife came to Los Angeles and the four of us had dinner together at the Bel Air Hotel.

When Hilda and I walked across the lobby of the Bel Air, the only other people present were an older couple. Our meeting was a classic example of the magnetism that draws people together. Despite the disparity in our ages, we hit it off immediately, as did Hilda and Sylvia Lee. In no time, we were on a genuine, first name basis and I was treated to the fascinating story of United Cities.

The company had been promoted at the end of the utility boom in 1929. The ability to gasify butane had been developed as a substitute for coal or oil to produce city gas. Some promoter had gone around the country finding the largest county-seat towns without gas where he could con the locals into giving him franchises to install a system to deliver butane-air gas mixture through distribution pipelines. During 1930, when there was still some life in the old utilities boom, he had secured bank financing and proceeded to install systems in towns from Hastings, Minnesota to Gainesville, Georgia, including several other towns in Wisconsin, Illinois, Tennessee, Georgia, and North and South Carolina.

The systems were completed and gas service offered by mid-1932. In the depths of the depression, the company started up service, then went hopelessly bankrupt. It was obviously impossible to refinance the bank loans. The company ended up owing everybody for meters, pipe and butane. The Skelly Oil Company was their butane supplier and the American Meter Company was another large creditor.

Art Lee had started out as a typewriter salesman in Wyoming in the early part of the Twentieth Century. He obviously was quite successful because he drifted into banking and during the 'teens, organized a number of country banks all over Wyoming. In those days, you could get a state bank charter for less than a hundred thousand dollars capital, and a national bank charter for not much more. This group of banks did very well despite the low economic status of Wyoming until the market crash and deflation of 1920. They were finished off by a collapse of the cattle market in 1921. His banks all went broke and he followed suit.

Under the rules of the time, bank stockholders were obligated to the par value of their shares in addition to losing their original cost of what they had paid for them. Cleaned out, Art started anew. There was an oil boom in Northern Wyoming and he found that most of the oil wells required pumping. Several companies started building electrical systems to run electric pumps and Art Lee promoted one such system. The period was the mid-1920s. The oil boom arena was unregulated and vicious. One of Art's company plants was burned down by a competitor. In any event, the company was successful enough that he sold it out to what later became Pacific Power and Light.

With that money and his increasing knowledge of the utility industry, he and some friends got together to build a pipeline through the newly discovered Oklahoma gas fields, then up through Colorado Springs and Denver. Unfortunately, at the same time, Standard Oil had the same idea and had much more clout.

Art, however, had already entered into a contract with the Colorado Springs Municipal Power Company, so Standard Oil had to buy him out.

With money in hand, Art and a friend began researching cities in Kansas and Nebraska that did not have natural gas and they obtained franchises. They formed their own company, ARGUS, named for Art and his partner, Gus...and began to pipe many of the towns using second hand pipe. The company was successful and Art finally sold out to retire comfortably to Chicago. Before long, some of the creditors of the formerly busted butane-air gas project asked Art to run the reorganized company, which was named United Cities Utilities Company. Operations in each state were separately incorporated out of the holding company.

Although the company had been reorganized, it was penniless and the mid-1930s was not a particularly prosperous time in the type of communities they served. Butane air had problems anyway, since butane is the heaviest of the readily liquifiable oil fractions. Plus, it is a by-product of gasoline manufacturing.

Although it was cheaper than propane by a couple of cents a gallon, its disadvantages were offset and Art converted all the towns to propane air. Finances were still questionable, however. Frequently he would give due bills in payment for propane, meters and pipe. He always met these notes on their due date and gradually built up a reputation as a good operator. He would squeeze every possible penny out of his business he could in order to meet his obligations. The company gradually grew and finally, the first natural gas became available in one of the towns, Hastings, Minnesota. The results were spectacular. Art was able to undercut fuel oil costs significantly and the coal available was all dirty bituminous coal.

When I first found United Cities, I believed that natural gas would become available to all the towns, as did Art Lee. Art desperately needed more money and I talked First California Company into doing a three hundred thousand dollar "Regulation A" offering of six-percent convertible Preferred stock.

This was a small issue even for First California. But as a Regulation A offering, expenses were substantially less than they would have been had a full registration statement been involved. The shares were sold solely through First California and shortly thereafter, I was asked to go on the United Cities Utilities Board. At that time, the United Cities head office was located in the merchandise mart in Chicago.

One day, I was about to leave to go to the airport for a meeting in Chicago, but complained to Hilda that I had had a bad night and an uncomfortable feeling in my stomach. After taking my temperature, Hilda suggested I stop off to see my physician before leaving town. Luckily, I took her advice. The doctor pressed on my stomach a couple of times and suddenly I was driving to Huntington Hospital where I blandly parked my car and walked into the Emergency Room. Three hours later, I woke up in the Recovery Room, sans my appendix. It had been ready to burst.

At that time, a new pipeline was built through southern Illinois and the company converted the towns in the area to natural gas. Shortly thereafter, someone built a pipeline across Tennessee, picking up gas from the lines along the Mississippi River. This permitted United Cities to convert all their Tennessee towns to natural gas. This was critical because all electric service in Tennessee came from Tennessee Valley Authority at what were essentially government-subsidized low rates, as low as half a cent per kilowatt-hour.

Several of our towns required relatively short pipelines to connect with the major gas transmission lines. With the growth of the towns' systems, through the availability of cheap natural gas, we were constantly short of capital. The Hastings, Minnesota property had been earning thirteen to fourteen percent on its capital.

At that time, Minnesota Utilities negotiated their rates individually with towns served. When the pipeline serving Hastings was permitted by the Federal Power Commission to substantially raise its rates, my colleagues and I knew there was no way the local authorities in Hastings would permit the gas company to recoup those costs through increasing theirs. They were already making far more than knowledgeable utility regulators would permit. Because Minnesota still was a cost-based state so far as utility rates were concerned, a utility operator out of Colorado made us a very generous offer for the Hastings property.

The buyer figured he could use his new cost basis to step up local rates. Though the United Cities Utilities Company hated losing Hastings, the money was manna from heaven, supplying our needs for other properties. Not long after that, we found that the gas company serving Bristol, Tennessee and Virginia could be bought from a local operator who was in way over his head.

We also found that Virginia had a "no-foreign utilities" rule. That meant that only Virginia incorporated utilities could operate inside the state of Virginia. At this time, the United Cities Utilities Company was under pressure from the SEC to be broken up because growth was such that it had far exceeded the exemption permission for small holding companies.

The reason why the SEC suddenly took an interest in our still relatively small utility company was that Art Lee had incurred the wrath of two of their major pipeline suppliers by insisting that they stop certain practices. The suppliers had used practices that were particularly costly to communities and they had gotten away with it for years.

Art had made his point with the Federal Power Commission and the two major pipeline companies took action to show their displeasure. Politically, they pressured the SEC to revoke the exemption from the utility holding company account.

This change required us to become an operating company, which would remove us from SEC holding company jurisdiction. All the states, with the exception of Illinois and Wisconsin, and now Virginia, permitted foreign utility companies to operate.

We decided to collapse United Cities Utilities Company into the Illinois subsidiary reincorporating it into the United Cities Gas Company. I had vaguely recalled that at one time, railroads could be incorporated in several states. Approaching our lawyers with that information, we were advised that it might be quite possible to secure dual incorporation in both Illinois and Virginia. We found that indeed it was possible and we became the only dually incorporated electrical-gas utility company.

Wisconsin, however, posed a problem. So Art and I got a one-year extension in time to dispose of those Wisconsin properties. Those were the least valuable properties, at any rate. We were fortunate in that almost simultaneously, several gas lines were built into central Wisconsin, permitting the sale of our properties for acceptable amounts to expanding local utility companies.

In the meantime, I had returned to Eastman Dillon as a partner and brought the United Cities business with me. I was successful in convincing E.D. to do the only "Regulation A" small offering they had ever done.

Subsequently, United Cities Gas deals with E.D. were increasing the large placements of long-term debt and full-dress common stock offerings of a million shares or more.

As I had anticipated, the call feature of the earlier common stock could not be exercised. The various convertible preferred stock offerings had increased the common share float and the shares had been split so that a reasonable over-the-counter market now existed. Art retired for the second time at age 70, and died soon afterwards.

His nephew, who at one time had been number two man in the company and would have eventually replaced Art, was unfortunately, a bit of a flake. He became involved in an operation called Mrs. America, which worked well for him, since his reputation was that of a womanizer. He spent an excessive amount of time on this program for which he had paid too much and which, under his management, was not successful. To his horror, Art had found out that at one time, his nephew had tapped the United Utilities Gas Company till to the tune of fifty thousand dollars or so, with, of course, a promise to repay. Art had fired him immediately upon discovery of that indiscretion.

Sometime before, I had identified a junior officer of Cascade Natural Gas as a potential leader. He had previously served on the staff of the State of Washington Public Utilities Commission. We were able to hire him to become number two man of United Cities. He immediately urged us to relocate the company headquarters from Chicago to Nashville. It only made sense.

Upon Art's retirement, this fellow was made president. Shortly thereafter, while visiting one of our towns, he accidentally ran into a Ku Klux Klan meeting in a small town in Tennessee. As a patriotic American, he was understandably quite upset and he promptly chose to move out of the territory, leaving United Cities.

His successor John Moxheim worked very hard to make several modest acquisitions for United Cities. These included a valiant attempt to acquire the Nashville Gas property. Unfortunately, Nashville Gas was controlled by a rather difficult individual. The owner made such demands that United Cities could not afford them. Moxheim was recruited by Piedmont Natural Gas to become its president. The company was twice our size and could offer him much more than United Cities could pay. With the power of a much larger company, he was subsequently able to acquire Nashville Gas Company for Piedmont Natural Gas, his own company.

Enter Benson Dushane. He had been vice president of the American Meter Company and for many years had supported Art Lee's efforts, accepting due bills as payment for meters when Art was having a difficult time. At this time, Dushane was retired from American Meter, so there was no conflict of interest. A director of United Cities for several years, he was made acting president while they searched for a permanent successor.

They finally hit a home run in finding Gene Koonce, number two man in the very efficient Knoxville Utility system. Unlike most municipal systems, this had been operated as though it were a shareholder owned company. Under Gene's leadership, United Cities was able to expand through acquisitions into western Virginia, to make a major acquisition of the Gas Light Company of Columbus, Georgia, several cities along the Mississippi, including Hannibal, Missouri, and a very substantial operation in eastern and southern Kansas.

By this time, I had succeeded Dushane as chairman of the board, serving in that capacity for nearly fifteen years with thirty-years as an active board member. The total market valuation of United Cities was now in excess of three hundred million dollars. At a utility conference in late 1996, the president of Atmos Energy Company approached Gene. Atmos Energy, a Texas corporation, was rapidly growing through acquisitions. United Cities negotiated a deal to be acquired by Atmos, which was three times their size. The deal negotiated more than maintained their dividend rate and represented a substantial step-up in market value.

A lawsuit came out of the blue from a company that could not possibly have even remotely approached the deal United Cities had already in hand. After throwing four and a half million dollars at attorneys and related legal costs, the Atmos deal was finally closed. Due to the merger, the board was disbanded.

~

Through a friend who handled the investment portfolio of the Pacific Mutual Insurance Company, which was modest sized at the time, I was introduced to the Dominguez Water Company. Two or three old California families controlled this company.

Juan Pedro Dominguez was a sergeant in charge of the Spanish Army. It was the army's charge to protect the Padres who came to California to open the missions. Dominguez petitioned the King of Spain for a land grant in exchange for his services. He was given a huge grant starting at Los Angeles, covering all land "south to the sea and west to the sea."

The company was having a problem. Since the ownership still controlled substantial quantities of land out of the original Spanish land grant, the California Public Utilities Commission took the attitude that the Dominguez Water Company didn't need to earn a normal rate of return because of the *presumed* benefits their ownership gave to their land values.

I suggested that Dominguez be converted into a public shareholder-owned utility through the offering of common stock. I talked Eastman Dillon into a relatively small offering of seventy thousand shares at eight dollars a share.

Of course the offering was sold in a flash. Not only because water company stocks are considered among the safest of investments but also because the common stock equity was so high. Additionally, Dominguez had a unique position in that some of its rights had been adjudicated as being senior to those of the local authorities.

Although the Dominguez territory was already fairly well developed, and growth possibilities were modest, the company managed, through consistently efficient operations to earn better than normal rates of return. As a member of the board of directors, I pushed for expansion and gradually, the company acquired numerous other small water utilities. Finally in the year 2000, the company was approached by the much larger California Water Service.

After a brief flurry of bidding from another California water utility, a superior deal was negotiated and Dominguez was acquired in the year 2000.

Again, there was no justification for my remaining on the board of the successor company and I relinquished my last directorship.

Back Home to Eastman Dillon

First California Company was so undercapitalized that it had basically become a disaster. Shortly after my brush with the mob, a South African group bid for Blair Holdings and by this time, Bob Evans, Ted Burr, Jack Mackie and I were all disenchanted with First California Company. Bob negotiated a return to Eastman Dillon. Jack Mackie and I were both included in his negotiations to become partners. Our focus was to open a major office again on the west coast. Ted Burr was not included in the offer, although he made several trips back to New York in an endeavor to convince Lloyd Gilmour to offer him a partnership as well.

The three of us started from scratch as Eastman Dillon partners on May 1, 1956, my nine-year anniversary of the day I had originally left E.D. We boned up on NYSE regulations and signed the partnership papers in New York. Returning to Los Angeles, we started from a zero base, but with all confidence and integrity intact. (By the time we finished building, we had seventeen offices in the West.)

In the 1950s, there were still many independent, modest-sized local and regional securities firms, most of whom enjoyed an easygoing camaraderie. If someone had a problem, it was common to talk to a colleague from a competitive firm to see how he would handle it. Out of the blue, we were offered the loan of two rooms on the balcony of the Lester Ryons and Company office in the old securities district in downtown Los Angeles. That would be our base from which to start operations. We had brought Lou Steffans, our secretary, with us and were eager to set up shop. This loan of space would be unthinkable today because of territorialism.

One of our first acts was to ward off the large number of First California people who wanted to come with us. One of our groups' last efforts with First California Company was to open a new office in Las Vegas. The man in charge, Dwight Gravitt (we called him *white wabbit*) was in the process of signing a lease for First California when he heard of the change, tore up the lease and dashed to Los Angeles to beg us to let him join the firm. He was so insistent and so adamant in refusing to stay with First California that we finally agreed, and a lease was written on the same space in Las Vegas while they were still looking around for a permanent home in Los Angeles.

We all decided that as the newcomers in town, we would break with tradition and establish our office out on Wilshire Boulevard, then an upscale retail district. Our office was virtually across the street from Bullock's Department store. In rapid succession, we opened offices in San Marino and San Diego.

First California brought a lawsuit against my partners and me. It carried on for a number of months, that is, until we let their attorney know of the desperate attempts of Ted Burr to leave First California in an effort to join us. When it was indicated that this fact would be reported to his board, the lawsuit was promptly dropped.

~

Eastman Dillon provided me with a challenge every day of my career. The world of venture capital was intriguing and constantly changing. For example, at the time Castro took over Cuba, on January 1, 1959, there happened to be a large, low-grade nickel depository under development in Guatemala. Castro seized the property. The ore was called laterite, and was quite different from the nickel ore mined in Canada. The nickel and cobalt recovery process from laterite had only recently been developed. The price of nickel had moved up.

Some creative thinker brought a project to Eastman Dillon because large deposits of laterite had been discovered in Guatemala. The deposit was really still a prospect, but someone came to us and convinced one of the partners that this would be attractive. A proposal was developed and the E. D. partners were given the opportunity to buy some stock. Without hesitation, I took my share. This venture turned out to be a classic example of the difference between a prospect and a mine.

First, definitive terms of the lease had not been agreed upon. Secondly, the size and quantity of the deposit had not been definitively decided. We knew there was laterite at the site, but no one knew the tonnage. Also, at the time, there was vicious guerrilla warfare going on in Guatemala. As it just so happened, the prospect was located on undeveloped territory, which was heavily infested by guerrillas. There was no infrastructure. No decent roads, no electricity nor water. We knew those services would have to be developed if the property were to be transitioned into a successful economic production.

After about a year and a half of messing around, my partners in New York threw up their hands and we wrote the whole thing off. The money involved wasn't a tremendous amount, but this was a classic example of the difference between a prospect and a mine.

Another challenging venture capital project was a steel finishing mill in Mexico. During the 1950s, the West German government paid reparations to Jewish survivors of the Nazi holocaust. One of the survivors who immigrated to Mexico came to Eastman Dillon with a very attractive project. Using reparation-related black Deutsch marcs, this individual could buy a specialty steel mill in Germany, take it to Mexico, install it there, using steel secured by the Mexican government owned steel mill, and make certain finished products for which the market was very good. He needed additional money, however, because he did not have sufficient funds to operate the mill.

After the Eastman Dillon partners agreed to put up some working capital, the mill was brought from Germany to Mexico, installed and put into operation. However, the operating figures did not look right; the money that the mill should have been making was not showing up. An investigation was made, and we discovered this guy from Germany was a thief. He had a sweetheart deal. He was stealing on the side. We quickly closed him down and negotiated a deal with the Mexican government. We sold the mill to the government and at least got some of our money back. We were amazed that this man, with his oppressing background would have been honest after all he'd been through, but he was basically a thief.

I soon learned that the business of venture capital is very risky. The ratio of value to success is high. Typically, the earlier you start looking for a greater reward you find that the ratio is commensurate with the potential for reward.

Another classic example of venture capitalism gone sour was a titanium dioxide project undertaken by the Eastman Dillon partners. Historically, white paint had been lead-pigment based. In the late 1950s and 1960s, there was increasing concern about the true poisons of some lead salts. The environmentalists and people in the medical profession concentrated on the lead in white paint, as well as the lead in gasoline.

Obviously, the lead ended up in the air, and there was tremendous concern about that. The solution to the lead-in-paint problem was found in using titanium dioxide as a whitener. Naturally, a substantial market for titanium dioxide developed. Titanium sources were readily available. Unfortunately, the quality ore, required for the whitest titanium dioxide, was not as readily available as was the lesser quality.

We were approached to finance a new plant with a new process, which could make fine white titanium dioxide out of lower-grade ore. The system properly checked out with laboratories and appeared to work fine. We headed up a group, which raised capital to build a large plant to make the titanium dioxide in quantities with the new process. From the laboratories to the small plant, the process worked fine, but from the small plant to a large plant, all kinds of new problems developed. Finally, we gave up and abandoned this project as well. However, someone else came along and bought us out. Again, we retrieved some of our investment.

In the late 1960s, we opened a second office on Wilshire by the Sheraton Hotel. I moved to the new office. One day Bob Evans called me and said some guys had come in with a project that was beyond him technologically. He wanted me to have a look to see what I thought of it. Two fellows came in my office, sat down, opened a briefcase and pulled out a piece of metal with some wires hooked to it. They took out some batteries, hooked them to the wires and asked me to hold the metal. They assured me I would not get an electric shock, though I was not worried about that—what can happen with six volts? Almost immediately, I felt one side of the metal getting cold and the other side getting hot.

"Hmmm, interesting!" I said. "What you're demonstrating to me is the Peltier effect. When two dissimilar metals make contact, current is passed through them and they get hot on one side and cold on the other. This is a cooling device, isn't it?"

They were actually surprised that I knew what it was. I had never really seen one before but I did know the theory of the phenomenon. They explained that an inventor in the Minneapolis area had developed a solid-state refrigerator. The refrigerator would be a polyurethane box specifically designed with their device to keep milk cold.

At the time, the milk delivery business was undergoing a revolution. Until then, all milk had been delivered in quart glass bottles. The dairy companies, Borden, National Dairy and the others all had milk routes. Two or three times a week, the milk truck would go through residential neighborhoods early in the morning to deliver glass, quart-sized bottles of milk. When the lady of the house would open the door, there would be milk, eggs, cream and butter, although their primary business was delivery of milk.

When I was growing up the milk had been delivered by horse-drawn vans. Small trucks eventually replaced the carts. Then as costs continued to rise, home delivery began to be less frequent. More and more people were going to supermarkets and buying milk in cardboard cartons. The inventors told me that studies indicated that properly produced and cooled milk would have a longer shelf life and the idea of the company was to make delivery of milk once a week directly to homes. What a time-saver for the housewife!

Each one of the homes would have one of these solid-state refrigerators which was inexpensive to produce and easy to operate, and the milkman would put a week's supply of milk into the refrigerator which would keep it at the proper temperature. Then as needed, it could be moved to the regular home refrigerator. Instead of two to three bottles per delivery, five or six bottles would be delivered each week, costs thereby would be substantially reduced, and the dairies that had routes could maintain the routes instead of giving up all their business to the big supermarkets which paid basically nothing for milk.

The company already had a contract with the Omaha, Nebraska dairy company for buying a bunch of these refrigerators, because the Omaha company looked upon these refrigerators as its salvation. The company had a small plant on an old prison building on the Wisconsin-Minnesota border where they were producing a limited amount of refrigerators, but they were looking for sixty to a hundred million dollars to step up production and go national. I contacted the Omaha dairy and discovered they were very high on the project.

A background check on the promoters also indicated no problems. I also found that someone was making a small refrigerator using the device to cool beer kegs. And some of the breweries were making five- or ten-gallon aluminum pressurized beer kegs. The refrigerator was ideal for cooling those beer kegs. I bought one and of course, some of the beer, and it worked fine. It turned out that the aluminum beer kegs were very costly. There was a six dollar deposit on the beer kegs, which was nowhere near what the cost to the brewery was, and people found they could use the beer kegs once they were empty for other purposes, so the breweries were losing their shirts on that and the whole idea died.

Nevertheless, the promoters out of Minneapolis appeared to have a reasonable game plan. I flew to Minneapolis twice to see the plant and talk to them. One trip was in January. After I rented a car at the airport, I drove into town. I was amazed to see little flecks of ice crystals floating through the air. It was that cold! I wasn't surprised, then, to see a sign heralding the temperature at a chilly thirteen degrees.

Through some Harvard Business School contacts in Minneapolis, I found a fellow alumnus who was interested in taking control of the money in the company. Of course, he had to put a little of his own money in.

I was amused to find that the company was headquartered in the Foshay Tower, which had been the tallest building between Chicago and Seattle for many years. The tower was modeled after the Washington monument and was built by Wilbur Foshay around 1928. Foshay's business was to create gas and electric utilities. He promoted a little public utility company that went belly-up, the first such company to go bust in the summer of 1929. Some said that triggered off the Great Depression.

The Harvard fellow was going to run the company. I had some qualms as to how fast small dairies could adopt this refrigerator, particularly whether they had the money to buy the refrigerators. I did not think the customers would buy the refrigerators themselves. In fact, the dairy company did have to buy the refrigerators.

We put together a capitalization that our investors agreed to back, then we returned to the Minneapolis group, showed them our plan, and they hit the ceiling. They said, "That's absolutely ridiculous!: They felt that with all the risks they'd taken, they should get "X-percent" of the company and the money coming in should only get a small percentage.

I said, "No, it's not going to be like that." I gave them until ten o'clock the next morning to say yes or no, but frankly, I was having more and more qualms about the whole thing.

Early the next day, they called to say they could not accept our plan; that we had to accept theirs or the deal was off. I quietly said, "Thank you, gentlemen. Goodbye." I hung up the telephone and breathed a sigh of relief. In retrospect, the small dairy operator was unable to finance the refrigerator even though the price was only going to be about forty dollars per unit.

~

One day I got a telephone call from Joe King asking me to go out to Riverside to meet a man who had an aluminum rolling mill manufacturing company. He needed capital for expansion. Joe assured me it was a real company, although I'd never heard of it. So I went out to Riverside and the owner toured me through the plant, and—my gosh! It was a real company!

From my manufacturing days in Pittsburgh I thought of steel rolling mill manufacturer Blaw-Knox and Masa Manufacturing Company, which made huge mills, all steel. This company made some pretty big stuff, too, not quite the magnitude of the steel mill rolling equipment, because the presses required to roll them are significantly less than those required to roll steel. His company had a complete line of rolling mill equipment for the aluminum industry including a sheet-foil mill. Their customers were people like Alcoa and Reynolds.

They would start with aluminum and get these slabs, then bring it down all the way to aluminum foil, which was being more and more widely used. And they also put into operation a continuous casting mill. They would continually cast it into thin sections, which could move directly into a rolling mill with the final product being aluminum foil. The company's stock was closely held by three or four families. However, they were expanding rapidly and they desperately needed money to handle the capital costs of expansion. And to Joe King, this looked like a real winner.

He turned the company over to a corporate financier to handle the set up and registration. The corporate finance market was lousy at the time, so they set up capitalization, which was very attractive to the investors. They were offering shares of the company and Joe was approached by American Metals Climax who indicated their interest in purchasing the company.

The die was cast—we had to go ahead with the public offering, although we kept quiet about the interest on the part of American Metals Climax. The company was a public company for about six months, when American Metals Climax decided they just had to have the company. Naturally, we kept company management informed, and when about six months were up, they indicated they were prepared to sell.

Two of the families were going to get some real bucks in their hands. We didn't know that one of the four families didn't want to sell any part of it at all. But Joe King negotiated a buy out and all the stockholders came out smelling like roses. In short order, a meeting was set to approve the sell out to American Metals Climax.

We sent a memo out several weeks in advance that the shareholders meeting would be held at the company headquarters in Riverside, California at a certain date. As the day approached, the dissident stockholders made more and more waves. They let everyone know that they had just enough clout to possibly upset the meeting, and they were determined to make waves.

On the day in question, the lawyers and I showed up well before ten a.m. We had our watches set, and exactly at ten, the president pounded the gavel, called the meeting to order, found the quorum to be present and asked for a vote. The vote came in favor of the buyout, he pounded the gavel again, saying the vote was cast, that the majority of the stockholders had voted for the sellout, and at this time, he was calling the meeting closed. He pounded the gavel again and that was it.

Two minutes later the door opened and a couple of guys in expensive suits came in. They announced that they were attorneys representing the minority stockholders, and asked, "When is the meeting going to start?"

The president of the company said, "Gentleman, the meeting is over. It was scheduled for ten a.m. If you wanted to oppose anything, you should have been here at ten."

The angry response was, "Well, we got delayed in traffic."

And of course, the deal went through. I think it had taken all of forty-seven seconds to call the meeting to order, take the vote and close the meeting. And no legal action was taken because everything was done above board. It was a good deal all around.

Another interesting project we had underwritten was developed as an offshoot of a company that John Ellis had brought to Eastman Dillon. The basic premise of his vision had something to do with trash disposal. The details are sketchy, but it was a typical *skyrocket—it* went way up, problems developed and it tanked! The company went under.

Along the way, however, the company had developed a trash-to-energy proposal and Ellis got behind it big time. Through some friends, he arranged for some trash to be brought from the Boston area to east Braintree, Massachusetts, where it would be sorted out, run through various processes, then finally burned to make energy. The energy would then be sold to a power company somewhere. There were some take-or-pay contracts written and the project was attractive enough so that a revenue bond was issued to pay a great deal of the cost of the project.

E.D. bought into the project with some equity. It was called the East Braintree Massachusetts project. The project went into operation, but problems arose—all kinds of problems—people who were supposed to pay for trash to be taken to the companies developed less trash, so instead of the money coming in for taking the trash, we actually had to *buy* trash at times.

Maintenance costs for the mechanical equipment were vastly higher than anticipated. But since the project was a limited partnership, its significant appreciation and tax benefits to the partners of Eastman Dillon were considerable. In fact, it was so profitable that as such, we couldn't afford to kill the project off. As of a year ago, in 2001, the East Braintree Massachusetts project was still going in order to protect the Eastman Dillon partners from tax reversals.

Not all venture capital deals were disasters. Eastman Dillon was approached to put up the initial equity capital for a new concept. Historically, cargo had always been off-loaded from ships, piece-by-piece. Someone came up with the idea that instead of doing that, what if cargo were loaded into containers that would then be lifted out of the ship and put onto the dock, then loaded onto a truck to be taken to the destination. Specialized ships would be built to handle the cargo containers that were to be built in American shipyards.

The first shipping service would be between the continental U.S and Puerto Rico. The Maritime Commission would put up the mortgage money on the ships, on a sweetheart basis, and the Eastman Dillon group would buy the equity on the ships.

Once the mortgage was paid off, the ships would be free and clear, and theoretically the value of the ships would be significantly in excess of the amount of the equity. The deal was done. The ships were built and put into service.

Of course, problems quickly arose. The dockworkers didn't like the containerization—it reduced the number of man-hours. Worse than that, it was more difficult to steal from containers in big bulk. There were all kinds of port problems, particularly in Puerto Rico where the unions were particularly strong. The deal and the concept were eventually successful, of course and containerization has monumentally affected shipping life as it stands today. The equity in the ships was bought out when the mortgages on the ships were paid off, and it all worked out quite well for the investors. But Eastman Dillon did successfully finance the start-up of what became the rapid revolution in containerization in maritime shipping.

It is unbelievable what's happened since then. There was not the fantastic payoff for us that one might expect, relative to what has happened to the entire containerization process since that time, especially since our investment was actually the equity in the three ships that started it all. But it worked out to a profit of probably three or four times the money we invested in, over a ten-year period, which is not that bad.

Las Vegas was still a relatively low-key gambling operation with a great Mafia presence in a couple of the hotels and casinos. Two families privately owned the electric company as well as the telephone company. Due to its proximity to Hoover Dam, the power company had part ownership of a Hoover dam generator, which offered the company extremely cheap electric power. However, the rapid growth of Las Vegas demanded more power still, and the Southern Nevada Power Company started expensing off the capital costs of an additional generator. The company had been small. Since rates were so low, the company had never been audited by the Nevada Public Utilities Commission or the IRS.

When I first visited the firm, I met the president in the office, a two-room shack on the south side of what was then downtown Las Vegas. He literally kept the books himself. He saved incoming letters to use again for internal correspondence. He would use the backs of incoming letters for memos and other internal communications and documents. When I met him, the IRS had just audited the man for the first time. He was advised that his books and records were unacceptable and that he could not expense off projected future capital requirements.

As a fellow utilities buff, I immediately began to develop a great rapport with this man, although I was amazed with the nonchalant way he ran the company. When the IRS confronted him with a significant tax liability, he finally realized he had to have some additional capital. After the meeting, I agreed that Eastman Dillon would arrange a private placement for him, a private offering with no need for a prospectus. It wouldn't be a public offering, but rather a private, direct sale.

I drew up a simple contract in the form of a letter of agreement covering Eastman Dillon's fee for handling the negotiations. Incorporated into the letter of agreement, I mentioned that the owner would have to undergo a formal audit by a national securities firm before securities could be sold. Also, that there would of course have to be ongoing annual audits. When I took the letter of agreement to him, he read it over and threw it back to me, saying, "What are you trying to pull? I never agreed to have annual audits in the future!"

I had not discussed this fact with him, because to me it was so obvious that anyone lending money on a long-term basis would require an annual audit. But for now, the deal was dead. Four months later, however, with the IRS knocking at his door, the utilities owner agreed to conventional terms. E.D. placed his bond issue with an insurance company for four and three-eighths percent interest, probably a quarter percentage more than the quality of his issue would warrant. But after all, it was Las Vegas.

Las Vegas had a very small propane-air gas company. It had gone bankrupt at least once and was now owned by a Los Angeles fuel trucker who made his money on hauling the propane to Vegas. There was also a small gas company named Southwest Gas, with gas systems in Barstow and Victorville. It also operated on propane and was owned by three people, one of whom worked for Southern California Gas Company. He ran these properties on weekends. Natural gas was just coming into California from Texas and a line was being built across the desert and into both northern and southern California. This brought natural gas to Barstow and Victorville.

The operator of those properties, Harold Laub, checked out Las Vegas and got in touch with Bob Evans and me at Eastman Dillon. Laub believed that the Las Vegas Gas Company could be bought cheaply and that a branch pipeline could be built from the southern tip of Nevada up to Las Vegas, picking up the gas intrastate to avoid Federal Power Commission regulations. I checked out his figures and it made sense when we looked at the potential of the Henderson Nevada industrial development.

This was where the magnesium for my incendiary bombs had been made and I knew the potential of the area. And we all knew of the clear necessity of the power company to build a power plant because there no longer was any available excess Hoover Dam power.

We found that the Las Vegas gas company owner could be talked to only while he was sober, but that had to take place before eleven a.m. Bob, Harold and I negotiated the purchase of the Las Vegas Gas Company for only three- to four hundred thousand dollars, which was more than it was currently worth.

We quickly organized two companies: The Nevada Natural Gas Pipeline Company, which would build a ten-inch pipeline to Las Vegas, and the Nevada Southern Gas Company, to take over the old

Las Vegas system. The latter company would also build a modern gas distribution company in Las Vegas. I went on the board of the pipeline company and Bob went on the board of the gas company.

Eastman Dillon arranged both debt financing and common stock offerings of both companies. Simultaneously, the power company reluctantly agreed to buy gas from us. To fuel a new thermal power plant near Las Vegas inside of eighteen months, plus to handle the growth of Las Vegas, the power plant load, and the Henderson, Nevada demand made the brand new pipeline capacity inadequate so that we had to immediately begin the first of many increases in its capacity.

Simultaneously, the power company expansion needed to meet the needs of the city required massive equity capital, which we were happy to raise. The ownership between the families that controlled both the power company and the telephone company was not identical and the phone company-holder family with the largest interest was suspected of trying to squeeze out at least a portion of the other two interests.

The telephone expansion, like that of the city, rendered it impossible to continue as they had in the past. In my last meeting with the controlling family who was looking for money to install a large new manual switchboard, I commented that nobody should be buying manual equipment, but I was immediately corrected. I was told there would always be plenty of *telephone girls* available. This was in the early '60s. The Las Vegas Stromberg Carlson manual switchboard, which the telephone company installed with money raised through new investment banking connections, was the last manual switchboard installed in the United States and was thrown out and replaced by new automatic equipment within eighteen months.

One of my fellow directors in the Nevada Natural Gas Pipeline Company, Nevada's only gas company group in the early days, was a man who owned a local lime company. They made mostly chemical quality lime, and became a modest company of the gas pipeline company. The limestone deposit was large, but only a small quantity of it was the high quality required for chemical quality lime.

The city of Las Vegas was of course expanding wildly at that time, as it has ever since. Large quantities of cement were required, and there were no local cement mills. The nearest one was in Mohave and very difficult to get to. It was a huge drive, about two hundred fifty miles to bring that cement into Las Vegas.

There were also a couple of cement mills in the Los Angeles basin, about two hundred twenty-five miles away. Cement is a very sensitive commodity, and distant mills had to eat a portion of the transportation costs to remain competitive against mills that were closer and had lower transportation costs. We agreed that a cement mill in the Las Vegas area would have certain advantages economically over the mills further away, and in addition, would be an excellent customer for the pipeline company.

After tossing the idea around for some time, a few of us got together and raised about thirty-five thousand dollars. The lime company put some money in and agreed to sell limestone to the cement mill, and some of the directors of the gas company put some money in. We hired an engineering company to make a study of the market and to find out what it would cost to build a modest-sized mill.

We formed a Nevada corporation, the Tri-State Cement Company and put the money into that. The engineering study indicated that the market would be Las Vegas alone, that we could not afford to ship the cement into the Los Angeles market because the shipping costs would eat us alive. The area in Nevada north of Las Vegas was barren. There was no market there. The Glen Canyon Dam was about to be constructed, but there was a new cement mill about to be constructed in Arizona, which would probably satisfy that. Transportation from Las Vegas to the dam site would be difficult and expensive.

The study recommended that a mill on the low-end of the economic size range should be built. Just then a couple of new Las Vegas casinos had come on line. They were built and pretty well financed and the city had a temporary slow down so the Tri- State Cement Company was put on hold. Nationwide the stock market had gone into decline, so the Tri-State Cement Company still remained in a drawer in the Paine Webber desk in Los Angeles. It was forgotten, the engineering report became dated, and Las Vegas took off, but it was too late. The stock holders died off one by one and finally, I was the sole director of the company and remained so for a number of years.

Occasionally I received letters asking if there was any market for the stock, which of course, there was not. It never became a public company, and the whole thing was forgotten. Up until recently, the Tri-State Cement Company's bank account was charged every month by the Bank of America, until finally, the account was eaten away to nothing.

We didn't pay the Nevada state fee for the corporation, so the charter was suspended. Today, the Tri-State Cement Company still exists, but only in a folder about two inches thick in the hutch behind my desk. I have the corporate seal. I have the stockholders' book. Anytime I want to issue a hundred thousand shares of stock, all I have to do is get the seal out, get the stock certificate out, write myself a stock certificate, put the seal on it and "Bingo!" But the company is inactive—it's disappeared.

Of course, if the company had been built, it would have been a great success, because the expansion of Las Vegas was vastly beyond what anybody could have anticipated. The cement mill could have run at one hundred percent capacity all the time, and a couple more kilns would have had to be put in to meet the demand, but that also is hindsight.

~

I was one of the few businessmen who consistently went to Las Vegas and made money. Why? I never gambled. I would get paid my expenses and directors' fees and never gambled. I realized early on that the odds only favored the house. Bob, on the other hand, was firmly convinced that one could have sudden streams of good fortune. Usually, he would set a reasonable limit for his losses. He liked to play Craps and Twenty-one.

Occasionally he would get carried away and I would receive a mysterious telephone call from him saying something like, "I've spotted a Hammond organ in a store in Vegas and thought it would be something that Hope should have." Then he would add, "The dealer made me an offer I couldn't refuse." So I would cover his losses but he always paid me back. He'd send me a post-dated check and by the time I received it, I could safely deposit it into my account.

Jack Mackie frequently went with us to Las Vegas. Jack had been born in Carson City, Nevada, and had done about everything he could do early on, including running some gambling games before he had made his way into the investment business.

Jack had an unlimited storehouse of Nevada-related stories. One of his favorites was about the time he called on an elderly woman in a nearly defunct mining town. He would sell her shares in Bank of America, in those days, with a five percent mark-up. The old woman used to say, "Young man, these here stocks had better be good! I earned this money the hard way, lyin' on my back!"

Following the success of our introduction of natural gas into southern Nevada, when the pipeline was built from Utah northwest into the state of Washington, we took the opportunity to organize a new pipeline company to tap this line and bring gas down into Reno and central Nevada.

This was the Nevada Northern Gas Company. We built distribution systems in the northern Nevada towns, with the exception of Reno which already had a system and which became a wholesale customer. I was a director of this company. After a number of years, because management in all four companies was the same, they merged both pipelines and the Las Vegas Gas Company into Southwest Gas.

Subsequently, they acquired a small gas company in Arizona and Southwest Gas ultimately acquired the gas operations in virtually all of Arizona to become what is now one of the largest gas companies in the country. Somewhere along the line, Southwest Gas became subject to the Federal Power Commission and I had to leave the board. The FPC claimed it would be a conflict of interest for me to stay on the board of directors.

Later on, I was doing some research and writing some reports on various companies. I had so much fun during the break up of the public utility holding companies identifying individual companies being spun off and trying to find those that seemed to be particularly appealing. There were yields available of nine and ten percent, and prices of book value.

It wasn't long before I was invited to join the Los Angeles Society of Financial Analysts. At the time, the society probably only had sixteen members or so. I believe it was the second or third oldest society in the country, after Chicago and San Francisco. The society would have occasional luncheons and invite people from various companies to speak, those who wanted to push their shares.

Also, we would have one or two bashes a year, where all the members would get together and tell tall tales about their successes and have a drink or two. A couple of the guys always got into a big craps game. We met at the old athletic club, and things were *very* informal in those days.

As the securities industry grew, the society grew, their events becoming more formal. We had a monthly meeting, then two meetings a month, usually at the Biltmore Hotel, always accompanied by what we referred to as *Biltmore gull* – (chicken). Occasionally we would get a speaker who would step up and want to pay for a decent lunch, and we would have a lunch at the California Club.

In those days, investment research and corporate finance were so intertwined, but still, we didn't misuse information. Our reports were not at all written for the purpose of turning a company into an investment-banking client, unlike the scandals in recent years. I would write up a company like Florida Power and Light and I might own some of the stock myself, but irrespective of that, I could not be faulted in any way regarding the amount of stock I owned and the impact on my report. I owned the stock for a long time because I thought it was a good investment, and my write up recommended the stock for the very same reasons. I think I wrote up one good company with the comment that "a power company investment will help pay your utility bill."

One time we were introduced to a small local company called US Chemical Milling Company. It was exactly what the name indicated—they knew of a way to reduce the weight for aircraft and missile use with the use of chemical milling which was, in some instances, cheaper and more effective than machine milling. I wrote a recommending their shares, beginning the report with the phrase, "weight is the enemy of everything that flies."

U.S. Chemical Milling grew substantially. They made more and more money and stock went up and up. I kept seeing references to my phrase, "weight is the enemy of everything that flies" with the increase in the price of shares. The aggressive young man who ran the company used shares to make numerous other acquisitions, none of which were handled by us, so we received no criticisms for recommending the shares to make the acquisitions. The share price became fairly volatile, and we stopped recommending the shares. Their fiscal year ended at an odd time, like the end of July or August. They used a local accounting firm, not one of the big seven national firms which existed at that time. We had checked out the local accounting firm, and they seemed to have a good reputation.

One afternoon, I received a telephone call from the partner of the accounting firm. He requested a meeting. We set up an appointment for the next day. After closing the door to my office, he said that they had a serious problem. They had found that the U.S. Chemical Milling had been *fussing around* a bit.

They had reported a sale and some *funny checks* in accounts payable on their books. He had sorted the matter out and found that in the fiscal year just ending, they would fall significantly short of their expected earnings. U.S. Chemical Milling was refusing to pay its invoices for accounting work until the accounting firm came up with an annual report that met *their* requirements. All of this happened around the mid-1960s.

An eastern securities firm with a branch in Los Angeles was aggressively pushing U.S. Chemical Milling to do a public offering, making a market in the shares and pushing them up. Bob Owens and I decided that this was time for Eastman Dillon to get the customers out of the shares and quietly began recommending the sale of the shares, saying that we thought they had arrived at a price that we thought was not supportable with the outlook for earnings for the company. U.S. Chemical Milling acquired new auditors. In those days, apparently, the SEC did not look into the reason for a change in auditors. The price of U.S. Chemical Milling continued to rise, and the firm in question did, in fact, do a public offering.There were additional shares of U.S. Chemical Milling offered without any mention about the accounting irregularities that had somehow been papered over.

The principals of U.S. Chemical Milling developed a vending machine they promoted. First of all, they issued themselves and their underwriter a bundle of shares at a dollar a share, then did a public offering at about six dollars a share. For a short time, the vending machine company shares moved a *big* premium. But just before the six months was up, when those who got the dollar shares could sell them, suddenly the whole balloon collapsed.

U.S. Chemical Milling got into so much trouble. It turned out they had some orders that were not, in fact, bona fide orders, as they had been cancelled. The manufacturer discovered they couldn't sell their vending machines and the bubble collapsed just as the six-month period arose and the stock dropped from well into the teens down to a dollar a share.

If that weren't bad enough, one of the writers for a local financial publication had bought some of the vending machine shares at the inflated price, and when the price collapsed, he became very unhappy with U.S. Chemical Milling, the vending machine company and the underwriter. He wrote a number of nasty articles about the underwriter without, of course, disclosing the reason for his wrath.

The Computerization of America

In the late 1950s and early '60s, computerization captured our focus. From the original colossal IBM computers that occupied whole floors of identical tube units, with massive amounts of refrigeration required, the machines quickly began to reduce in size. Other companies began to get into the business. Honeywell, Bendix, RCA and General Electric all began to develop large computer divisions. Xerox, flush with cash from the success of its photocopying machine became involved in computers in a big way. These machines were more modest than IBM Unisys; nevertheless, they were very large and quite costly.

Eastman Dillon was an investment banker for both Bendix and Honeywell. In fact, E.D. had a large Honeywell machine that processed its work in the early 1950s. Since ownership, programming and maintenance of a computer would not be practical for a modest-sized company in those days, somebody came up with the idea that individual companies should tie in to a large computer via a sort of Teletype network. It was assumed this could readily be done.

Honeywell came to Eastman Dillon with the idea that they would provide computers and set up organizations that would tie into those computers. Eastman Dillon would finance the projects, and this would open up a brand new area for computer usage. Somewhere along the line, the name Remote Computing Corporation was secured. I thought it was a wonderful name. Capital was secured from the partners of Eastman Dillon with some of our clients, on a risk basis, and the company was started in Los Angeles at One Wilshire Boulevard.

It was going to be a service bureau with no real computing on site, but since I was local, I was nominated to be Eastman Dillon's director on the board of the new company. We were to build the company up until it was available to the public. We were all positioned to make a lot of money. The concept was so good that several other companies simultaneously started doing the same thing.

Several of those companies either went public or at the very least *tried* to go public. Remote Computing did not, but in fact it turned out to be a terrible business. One of our largest investors was a private investment company whose principal owned a large department store on Market Street. We found out that all the customers required a significant amount of additional highly specialized software; thus our income was always short.

Fortunately, Honeywell and Bendix wanted so badly to move some of their computers that they bent over backwards on rent adjustments and things of that sort. Around 1967-1968, Remote Computing was just about breaking even, and one of our friends in San Francisco put the arm on the remainder of the old First California Company to do an underwriting.

Remote Computing actually got together the background of a red herring and made a filing with the FCC. Once, they had an early red herring, but then the whole securities market went to hell in a handcart in the late 1960s. Remote Computing struggled along until finally, the San Francisco investors decided they liked the business for one reason or another and made enough to buy out all the initial investors for cash.

The purchase didn't make us whole, but it was much better percentage-wise than one could expect, so we all accepted the offer. The San Francisco group became sole owners of the Remote Computing Corporation and I left the board of directors.

Remote Computing struggled along as the new owners continued to put venture capital into the company. I think out of all the companies that tried to do that sort of thing, only one survived, and they survived only because they got out of that business and went on to some engineering project. This was in the 1980s.

They paid off all the bills; gave some retirement pay to those who had worked so long and struggled so hard to make the company go; and took over an abandoned night club in Palo Alto where they hosted a going-out-of-business party for all of their former employees. They hired a noisy band, offered cocktails and the works, and we went out with style.

Around 1987, I got a call from corporate finance in New York, asking me to check out a company they had run across, a company called Extra Soft. The firm was into point-of-sale software and was run by a married couple. The woman had been crippled by polio and her husband was a terrifically talented computer programmer. They had planned a large exhibit at a computer show in Las Vegas in a few weeks' time. The couple had worked for Sears Roebuck trying to computerize a bunch of the store's cashiers and had already done a good deal of software work for them.

For years I had been thinking that point-of-sale software was something that should be developed, but for some mysterious reason, very little work had been done on it. I went to Las Vegas and was quite impressed by the principles of it. It was still very primitive—this was before the availability of barcodes. The couple had a business plan of sorts, certainly not very elaborate, but the amount of money they required was less than a million dollars.

I recommended to New York that we finance them, and New York put together a small group of potential investors, which was basically a collection of some of the partners with a few outside clients. I was asked to go on the board of directors to represent the shareholders.

With the usual clarity of hindsight, I can now see all the mistakes that we made. First of all, the company was grossly undercapitalized; secondly, it should have had a top management team rather than the two principals. We should have had at least five million dollars to work with, rather than pillar-to-post minimal assets, in order to run the company properly.

Of course, predicting the near future and the 1999 dot-com boom, you could have capitalized that company for two hundred million at the drop of a hat, and pissed it all away. We only made one sale of the software license and that was to a Japanese company. They wanted to express that as income, and I told them they couldn't, as that was a non-recurring event.

So we didn't play it up. When the company ran out of money, even though everything was being *poor-boyed*, we had a rescue party to get more money from Eastman Dillon and other partners. We raised about two hundred and fifty thousand dollars in additional funds through subordinated notions, but we ran through that money quickly. I'd go up to the company's headquarters in San Jose every quarter or so, but it was a hard battle. We never set ourselves high enough; we never had the capital to do that. So we decided to wind it up.

The biggest sale we ever made was to a chain of photographic stores. We retained a fellow to sell the company for us. He struggled and struggled and finally found somebody in the area, a company that had gone public and was doing very well in point of sale, connecting vending machines to the Internet. We sold the company to them. Basically, the company had no assets. We paid off all the creditors and gave a modest bonus to the two principals. I believe I was the largest investor in the company and I got paid sixty cents to the dollar for my senior notes and forty cents to the dollar for my junior notes. They gave the shareholders something like ten or fifteen cents a share and told them that if they had the sales receipts, they could capital the loss.

The company consistently lost money and the state of California refused to recognize our losses against the sales price, so we had to pay capital gains tax to the state because we sold the company at a profit above the book value. We were unable to use the accumulated deficit. It really annoyed us. This was really a case of being in the wrong place at the wrong time. Seven or eight years later, we could have hit the boom and the bubble of the late 1990s, and with that boom we could have raised enough capital, but who knows what we would have done with the money?

ICN Pharmaceuticals

Not long after we opened the Eastman Dillon office in San Marino office in 1958, I was approached by one of the salesmen who insisted I meet with a contact of his by the name of Milan Panic, a recent immigrant from Serbia and quite a promoter.

His company, International Chemical and Nuclear Corporation (ICN) sold radioactive chemicals for diagnostic purposes for nuclear medicine. He had also initially sold company stock to local individuals at a dollar a share. Unfortunately, the half-life of the product was shorter than his sales ability and the company had nearly gone bankrupt.

He had moved on into attempts to develop nucleac acid biological pharmaceuticals. I was put off right away by the junky equipment in Panic's primitive facility near El Monte. But the salesman pushed hard on one of my New York partners, insisting that this fellow was a *comer*. I was encouraged once more to meet with Panic. I was led to believe that the man had cleaned up his act. Panic claimed to have developed a memory enhancement pharmaceutical. The drug had been tested without formal clinical trials and according to Panic, had shown surprisingly amazing results. This was years before the Federal Drug Administration developed and enforced extreme controls on pharmaceuticals.

Panic was now able to provide audited figures. On the strength of these, which showed at least nominal profitability, E.D. made a private placement of less than a million dollars of his shares. His stock had reached a price of four dollars or so, based solely on the strength of Panic's talking to selected local stock salesmen.

My partners urged me to go on the board of ICN, which had recently acquired a facility in Glendale. In one meeting, Panic began behaving like a suddenly loosened spring, hopping all over the place. He became extremely vocal about the presumed benefits of the rapid developments he had underway in nuclear biology. He had largely abandoned radioactive chemicals and was pitching the possibilities of revolutionary developments based upon nucleac acids. One of his last efforts in Glendale was to make some radioactive chemicals through the use of some plutonium as a source. How he obtained plutonium no one will ever know. But there came the day of the brief "panic" party when colleagues learned Panic had had a *small* plutonium spill. Apparently, he covered it up successfully before word got out.

As Panic aggressively pushed the growth of his company, there naturally followed a desperate need for more capital. I wrote up a very low-key discussion of ICN for presentation to a group of speculative institutional investors. It was to be presented at a meeting in New York. The meeting was designed to sell five million dollars of ICN stock, which was now trading for around fourteen dollars a share.

To my absolute horror, the meeting in Eastman Dillon's New York office turned into a professional embarrassment. Panic literally threw away my remarks and launched into his own tirade. By the time he had finished, I was mortified and watched helplessly as some of the potential investors dashed out of the room to place orders ahead of the crowd.

Panic renamed the company ICN Pharmaceuticals and went on an aggressive expansion spree using ICN shares as paper to make acquisitions. He bought a Cleveland based manufacturer of expired patent and generic drugs then went on to acquire a Swiss company whose Italian subsidiary was a large penicillin maker. Then he acquired a German pharmaceutical company, a Brazilian company and a Mexican company. There was a board meeting in Switzerland, then the board met with the Italian company, and finally held another meeting in Amsterdam with a Dutch bank who controlled a manufacturer of glass pharmaceutical and perfume vials. Those company figures looked very good until I figured out that under Dutch law, they were allowed to mark up the inventory on the basis of valuing unsold over-runs to anticipated sales prices.

When I pointed out that this was wholly unacceptable in the United States, accounting-wise, and that the SEC would never approve the use of such figures, the senior officer of the Dutch bank became very upset. He said I was accusing him of dishonesty.

Panic was looking to expand into Japan. Because of the worldwide scope of ICN, he had convinced himself that the company needed its own *adequate* air transport and he proposed to buy an airplane, a British Aircraft Corporation 111. The plane was almost equal in size to a DC-9. The seller convinced Panic that he should take a trial flight in the BAC 111 and Panic arranged for the board to fly it to Tokyo. Our wives were invited to accompany us. We flew from Los Angeles to San Francisco, then to Honolulu and on to Wake Island and finally Tokyo.

My son Jim, now around eighteen, expressed his concern in learning that Hilda and I were making these long, over-water flights in a two-engine aircraft. On the last leg into Japan, the Tokyo air controllers tried to divert our plane to Osaka. It was obviously a non-scheduled airline and the Japanese were suspicious about our intentions. The pilot claimed he was concerned about fuel and we were allowed to land at the old Tokyo airport.

It had been a whirlwind year and we had decided we needed some time alone. After a week in Japan, Hilda and I left the ICN group and went on our own to Okinawa, which at the time was still under U.S. rule. Then we flew on to Guam and down through the Marianas Islands. The Islands were fascinating to us now, especially since it was the mid-1960s and two full decades after the end of the war.

The airport perimeter was still lined with the wreckage of Japanese airplanes, bombed out during attacks on the island during World War II. The DC-6 was refueled by a native in a G-string and we took off for Micronesia. The weather was oppressive with the temperature at ninety-five degrees and humidity the same.

After stops in Pelau and Truk Island in Micronesia, we made a brief stopover in Bikini Atoll, where atomic testing was done after World War II. Still considered a top secret-type island, I was unable to take photographs there to add to the thousands of slides taken during my various trips around the world. Bikini Atoll had other explosives on the island during the war and had been heavily contaminated. The island was still used as a base station for rocket course planning. We spent a week and a half in Hawaii before heading home.

I had become bitterly opposed to some of the actions Panic was now taking. I considered Panic's board to be made up of mostly patsies and I remained the single voice of reason and too often, the sole voice of disagreement. I was firmly convinced that to acquire a corporate airplane would represent an extravagant expense. The ongoing cost was around four million dollars a year.

Panic had made several acquisitions and had guaranteed a floor price for his shares. This was a practice I had always opposed since the risks were that the company almost always had to buy in shares at the floor price at a time when their market value was vastly lower. Plus, the company would be assuming an obligation without anyone knowing the timing or the amount, irrespective of the company's financial position at the time.

Panic also wished to buy in his own stock, since the shares had dropped from the upper thirties to the upper twenties, and he still had some cash in the till. He would argue in the most irritating manner, "Beee-el, my stock has never been so cheeeap! And it's the best investment we can make right now!"

I would try to explain. "Your own stock is not a valid current asset." I said that time and again. Panic wanted to take out a major loan in Switzerland, which would be in Swiss franc denomination. I pointed out that the Swiss franc at the time was the strongest currency around and that in exchange for cheaper interest charges, Panic would be running the vast risk of dollar depreciation against the franc.

As a result of my reasonable, valid objections, I was eventually advised that Panic no longer desired my presence on the board and that I would not be included on the upcoming slate for ongoing directors. I had no recourse but to express my objections to Panic's approach to these problems. We simply had too many differences. Another one of my partners accepted a nomination to the board in my place. It was the late '80s and I had been involved with ICN for many years.

As the ICN stock price collapsed, reaching a low of a dollar seventy-five, the chickens came home to roost with a vengeance and the board and company were subject to shareholder, lawyer-inspired litigation. As usual, the lawsuits were largely settled by directors and officers insurance since no criminality was involved. Subsequently, ICN has historically experienced wildly varying ups and downs. Many of the acquired subsidiaries were sold off at bargain prices to meet urgent financial needs.

One result was that a promising, large developmental laboratory in Orange County was closed down and written off without regard to the potential of work underway because the company could no longer afford continuing research and development.

Panic had various personal problems that were quite serious. His wife was a fine woman who ended her life in a messy suicide. One of his sons committed suicide due to reputed drug use. Panic was sued multiple times for sexual harassment, which was probably justified, according to all the accounts of evidence presented.

In addition, during the course of Panic's company activities, ICN acquired a Serbian pharmaceutical company. That company briefly made huge profits selling to Serbia and Russia, only to lose them through inflation of those currencies and through the seizure of the plant in Serbia when Panic fell out of favor with Milosovich, the Serbian dictator.

To this day, Panic continues to be the subject of controversy over his financial dealings.

The Real World of Mutual Funds
(The Day the NYSE Forced Me to Give Away a
Million Dollars)

Back in the early 1950s, the mutual fund business was a modest business, to say the least. There were a fair number of funds around. The Massachusetts Investors Trust may have been the first American mutual fund. The Investment Fund of America was a reorganization dating from 1932. It had been growing and growing and had some options outstanding, so I managed to buy some for pennies. There was a fund group out of Philadelphia, but it was really low-key. Eaton and Howard was out of Boston and had a San Francisco office. That is where Kay worked (the young lady I met on the boat in 1937). Other than that, the mutual fund business was a fairly low-profile business.

The salesman liked to sell mutual funds because there was a nine and a half percent load on virtually all of the funds, and the payout to salesman was typically fifty percent of that load. Plus, there were many customers for which the diversification of a fund for small amounts of money was ideal. There were a few specialized funds around as well as a few industry funds, but it was not typical to have specialized funds in those days.

A former fund wholesaler I knew thought he saw an opportunity to start a regional fund, so he organized a fund called the California Fund Management Company. He was going to run a mutual fund which would invest primarily in California based company stocks. He had done some statistical work, which demonstrated that California based companies were doing better than companies nationwide. On that basis, he expected to build a fund and reap lots of sales.

Around 1959, the mutual fund business was beginning to take off, so I decided to put in ten thousand dollars. He wanted to raise seventy-five to a hundred thousand for the management company, and said his projections showed that if the firm could get up to twenty-five million, it would be self-supporting. He had some reasonably good sources of recommendations in California stocks. He wasn't the best stock picker himself, so I put ten thousand in. He ended up raising about sixty-five thousand dollars.

Well, he never got the fund up to over twenty-five thousand; it wasn't that good. It was rather an obscure fund, and while I never sold any of the stock myself, still it was the First California Company. Ethically I couldn't recommend the shares myself. As a matter of fact, he couldn't have any of the salesmen recommend the shares. But as it went along, he lost a little money and the management company got down to zero capital. He managed to keep the SEC at bay and the company continued to exist. And then the First California Company came back to Eastman Dillon, and I had been at Eastman Dillon by that time for three or four years.

Some questionnaire came along and in answering it, I mentioned that I had ten thousand dollars in the California Fund Management Company. Well, by gosh, that put a *cat among the pigeons*. Somehow the New York Stock Exchange saw that and became extremely upset. They gave Eastman Dillon all kinds of hell for allowing me to have that stock. I pointed out that I had never misused my position, but it made no difference. They demanded that I immediately sell the stock.

Of course, there was no market for the stock; it had virtually zero book value and I had already lost my ten thousand, but they insisted I sell it somewhere. So I handed Con Gertmenian a hundred dollars to buy the stock from me at a dollar a share – a hundred dollars for a hundred shares. It had cost me ten thousand dollars. The New York Stock Exchange didn't believe I sold the stock, but I gave them a letter from Con saying that he had indeed bought the stock, it had been transferred into his name, and that was the end of that. I had already written it off.

Three years later, all of a sudden, Doug Fletcher left Blyth and Company and decided he wanted to get into the fund business. He looked around for a vehicle and discovered California Fund Management Company. He negotiated to buy the stock from the fellow who originally owned the company, and then turned around and offered all the shareholders their original cost, should they want to sell.

Con called me and said, "Bill, someone wants to buy my California Fund Management Stock and they're offering me ten thousand dollars. What should I do?"

Without hesitation, I said, "Con, take it!"

So Con sold his stock for ten thousand dollars - stock which he had paid a hundred dollars for - a hundred dollars I had given him. He tried to return it to me, but of course, I refused to take it – a deal is a deal. Of course, he was happy as a clam. The next thing I knew, Doug Fletcher took over the California Fund Management Company and changed its name. Meanwhile, the mutual fund business suddenly became wildly successful and Doug started a closed-end fund which totally took off.

This is an example of the way it's done: If someone buys really obscure stocks, you can get your basic position on the stock for, let's say, twenty-five dollars a share. If you're an aggressive buyer, you can move that stock up to seventy dollars a share, which makes your performance look terrific.

Doug Fletcher's company started doing wonderfully well with this mutual fund. He had a manager who was able to play that game very well. They also would buy closed offerings; for instance, if the company had a stock selling at twenty-five dollars a share but they needed more capital for expansion, they would negotiate with this mutual fund to sell the it with "xyz" shares of stock, lower the stock at twenty dollars a share under the market, then the mutual fund would mark the stock up on its books, even when the stock was lettered, or not saleable - to the going market price. Then if they got aggressive, and built some more stock they could boost the price of the stock, so this fund took off like a scared pigeon. It was an open-end fund.

They got probably a hundred million dollars in a really short period of time, then the management company decided they would go public, so they started a closed-end fund, took that public, and their stock went way up. If I had held my original California Fund Management Company stock and not taken the offer they made to

Con, but stayed with it at the time when the shareholders' management company was called, my ten thousand dollars would have been worth a million. So basically, *the New York Stock Exchange forced me to give away a million dollars!*

The bubble did burst, however. The mutual fund shares eventually went way down because of all the junk that was in the portfolio. There were all kinds of SEC investigations but no money had been stolen, and the closed-end company survived and is now listed on the NYSE. It has done very well. Doug Fletcher bought a fancy house down on Virginia Road not far below me. He finally sold that house. I think he's living in Santa Barbara, probably basking in the glory of earning a lot of money from that deal.

Meanwhile, Con felt guilty about all the money he made, so after the four of us decided we wanted to go to the Far East, Con said he wanted to pick up some of the expense. So Con, Doris, Hilda and I took off to the Orient and Con ended up picking up about two-thirds of the entire trip!

It was our first flight to Bangkok. It was a wonderful trip, but not without its challenges. The plane had mechanical problems in Honolulu so we were put up in a hotel and after sleeping for a couple of hours, were called at five a.m. We flew from there to Guam then on to Hong Kong, but of course were already delayed, so we missed our connections there. After checking into the Mandarin Hotel, we spent a wonderful day in Hong Kong. We did a pretty thorough job of visiting the city in a limited amount of time.

We finally got on the plane about eleven thirty at night and slept all the way to Bangkok, arriving at some ghastly hour. We were driven to The Oriental, a brand new hotel on the river and slept until two in the afternoon. A few years ago, when I returned to Bangkok, they were in the process of tearing the whole thing down. In Singapore, we stayed at the Shangri-La and had a wonderful time.

Measurex

In late 1977, one of my New York partners asked me to go to San Francisco to meet with a man named David Bossen. It seems Bossen was interested in developing a revolutionary direct-digital control system for paper manufacturing machines. Bossen had been manager of Industrial Nucleonics which controlled such machines through analog technology. This technology was clearly becoming obsolete.

I met Bossen and his technical associate in San Francisco. Bossen explained that while working for Industrial Nucleonics, he had urged them to convert from analog to digital. However, the controlling owners felt that theirs was the only game in town with virtually a hundred percent of the business, and that the cost of conversion to digital control was not warranted.

As general manager, Bossen was promised the ability to acquire a meaningful stock interest, but the controlling interest of what was still a private corporation had never brought him more than a token participation. He had left the company a year earlier without taking any proprietary information since the company had ignored his attempts to bring them into the digital world. After a year of looking around, he decided he wanted to proceed with the development of direct-digital control of paper manufacturing machines.

A friend with IBM had suggested that his company look into the process, but the idea was rejected because the market was too small and too specialized according to IBM standards. The two linked up and prepared a business plan for a new company to develop the concept.

It took me only twenty minutes to recognize this as the best business plan I had ever reviewed. The concept was well thought out and the initial financial requirements were very modest.

The plan proposed an initial three hundred fifty thousand dollars to be spent on circuit design and construction of a breadboard prototype for the actual accounting concept. Following proof of the theory, a second comparable sum of money would be used to design a prototype controller and a third similar amount would be used to build and install the first digital computer-activated paper machine control. Bossen and his friends were to put up a modest amount of the start-up money. E.D. would raise one million one hundred thousand dollars to be scaled in one-third at a time, as needed.

For this, Bossen and his friends received thirty-seven percent of the equity with the balance going to the venture capital start-up investors. I had enough technical background on computers and digitizing to recognize the validity of the concept and its potential improvement over analog technology. I was enormously impressed by Dave Bossen, who had attended both the Naval Academy *and* MIT *and* had successfully run Industrial Nucleonics! I strongly recommended to my partners at E.D. that we finance this deal - a deal I believed to have all pluses and virtually no negatives.

Even the equity participations were highly favorable to the investors, unlike those of today, which tend to treat investors as bothersome interlopers who should welcome the opportunity to get ten percent of the equity in exchange for their *largesse.* The E.D. Commitment Committee immediately accepted the deal with a good portion of the investment being taken up by individual partners of the firm and the balance placed with a few legitimate venture capitalists.

The operation went better than originally forecast. The prototype breadboard worked right off the bat with results, which were better than expected. The company, named Measurex, rented a modest facility in Santa Clara where they would develop the design of the prototype machine.

Things progressed so smoothly that several paper manufacturers immediately expressed interest. The initial prototype controller was placed on a container- board paper machine in the Bay area. It was online and exceeding expectations within three days of turn-on as compared to weeks of adjusting and necessary coddling required for the old analog machines.

The new enterprise faced only one minor disadvantage. It was customary in the industry to offer a six-month trial period for new developments, with payment to take place once the company successfully met specifications. Orders starting coming with a rush, presenting Measurex with significant potential cash flow problems. They knew they had a success on their hands, but the six- month delay between producing the machine and receiving payment was daunting.

The commercial banks refused to see through the reason for this delay, even though the day-to-day results showed that there should be no problem with the equipment being purchased. To get around this snafu, several Bay Area venture capital participants set up limited partnerships to provide the short-term capital to pay Measurex for the machines. They would not only receive a reasonable return on investment, but an option to buy unquoted Measurex shares at an attractive price.

With their financial problems eliminated, Measurex took off spectacularly. Within a year's time, the banks were quite willing to buy short-term paper secured by sales receivables. The venture capitalists did well, too, and the dilution resulting from this method of financing was acceptable to everyone involved.

Initially, the Measurex equipment controlled only the basis weight of the paper web. This was particularly critical because controlling and minimizing the variations in basis weight represented immediate and substantial savings to the paper maker. When a large paper machine consumes several million dollars of pulp a month, any reduction in the amount of pulp necessary to make a given amount of paper while improving quality represents large immediate savings.

Added to other savings such as fewer breaks in the paper web going through the machine and more uniform quality to the user, the potential benefits all around became a mandate for the paper maker.

Initially, the Industrial Nucleonics Company called their analog product Accuray. This name was based upon their use of radioactive sources. With the sudden immediate success of Measurex, Industrial Nucleonics kept its head in the sand until they lost a major portion of their market share. Then they were forced to develop "me, too!"

digital controls of their own. They began to adopt the slogan, "Wait for the new, improved digital technology."

They also changed the name of the company from Industrial Nucleonics to their trade name, Accuray, and managed to go public on the strength of the earnings remaining from their ongoing sales of old-style equipment and their very profitable replacement parts business. After rising materially in price from the public offering, the share price collapsed when the full impact of Measurex hit.

Ultimately Accuray got their house in order but by that time, Measurex's ongoing development program had left the company in the dust.

Developments such as opacity control, brightness control and absorption characteristic control continued at a fast pace with Measurex controlling approximately fifty-five to sixty percent of the total worldwide market, even though the Germans and the Finns also were in the mix, competing with an edge on Measurex in their own home markets.

Even at that time, Japan had a very large paper industry. The Japanese took a look at this highly specialized, lucrative market and still decided it was not for their electronic specialists. They figured that paper machine controllers represented more and more software and less and less hardware in terms of dollar value. The Japanese are great at duplicating or improving large volume products but dislike trying to compete where limited volume and specific tailoring are required.

Ultimately, Harnischvegar, whose subsidiary is the world's largest paper machine maker, approached Measurex with the suggestion that they acquire a twenty-five percent interest and promote the Measurex equipment as their preferred recommendation for installation on their machines. After looking at the pluses and minuses and reaching a standstill agreement, Harnischvegar acquired that interest. However, it turned out that some of the qualms of the board of Measurex were well justified. Competitors continued to go out of their way to downplay Measurex.

Earlier, while on our board, Bill Gossel had saved Harnishveger from impending bankruptcy. As president, he was a very knowledgeable and valued member of the Measurex board. When he retired from Harnishveger, a fellow whom I will refer to only as "Mr.

217

X," took his position. The successor was an aggressive hot shot who had graduated from Harvard Business School and worked for the Illinois Central Railroad.

Mr. X looked upon the Measurex investment as not having the *sex appeal* that he wished potential acquisitions would bring to Harnishveger. So Measurex bought back the shares held by Harnishveger, Mr. X retired from the board where he was odd man out - and Measurex retained Bill Gossel as advisory director.

The great Asian industrial boom was in full course in the late 1990s. And several paper companies were aggressively expanding. This was very good for Measurex. But we did recognize that the pace could not be continued since the paper business is not only capital intensive but also cyclical. When the economy is down, everything paper related slows down. When demand decreases, pressure prices increase.

Around this time it became apparent that a major upgrade of the software programs would shortly be needed. The cost of this would reduce our earnings to zero for a year's time. Honeywell was a major factor in many control areas. But the company had a nominal impact on the paper business. They had, however, recently developed some extremely sophisticated software advances. These could readily be adapted to Measurex' perception of future needs.

The board acquired an investment banker to search for a potential merger. The banker appropriately selected Honeywell as the most logical buyer, one who could offer true value rather than over-valued stock.

While a stock-for-stock deal could be tax free, and a cash deal would be subject to capital gains tax, the pluses for the latter exceeded the risks of a share exchange for those companies willing to reach out and meet the price. Honeywell acquired Measurex for thirty-five dollars a share. The timing was perfect. The East Asia boom collapsed. Among other things, Harnishveger basically lost its shirt due to Mr. X's pushing the sale of paper machines to bad credits. This was around 1997.

Between Mr. X's drive to continue to expand plus making several other mistakes such as paying too much for cyclical business, Harnishveger was eventually reduced to bankruptcy.

The Measurex experience was fantastic. I served on the original board of directors and continued to serve throughout the life of the company. The Measurex board was enormously cohesive and constructive. It was truly independent and the directors had created a safe environment for the thought process. No member was afraid to speak his mind, not that I ever had a problem in that area.

Being a global company, Measurex attempted to have one board meeting a year in a foreign country where we had significant business dealings. In later years we combined the board meeting with the sales award meetings for those who made or exceeded target. This provided an incredible incentive to the sales staff. First-class deluxe meetings were held in Portugal, Spain, Switzerland and Vienna.

Once we had to quickly move a meeting to Monterey when our security people learned that there might be an attack on a cruise ship in the Aegean Sea. In fact, there was such an attack with horrifying results. On October 7, 1985, four terrorists representing the Palestine Liberation Front hijacked the Achille Lauro, an Italian cruise ship. The ocean liner carried more than a hundred passengers, most of whom were elderly. They were in Egyptian waters. The terrorists demanded that Israel free fifty Palestinian prisoners and to prove they were serious about their demands, they shot an elderly Jewish man, then threw him overboard in his wheelchair. At the time, we had planned a cruise around the Greek Islands. We were only too happy to change our venue.

Our last such meeting took place in Paris simultaneously with our acquisition by Honeywell. For a week we stayed at the Grand Hotel in Paris. We booked the entire Paris Opera House for a reception and dinner dance.

I enjoyed the traveling aspects of my work immensely. One of our board meetings abroad was in Leningrad, now St. Petersburg, where the board declared what was probably the first dividend declared there since early 1917. The Russians bought all the equipment we had on display at the trade convention, some of which still lay unused in boxes a year and a half later.

One of our most outstanding meetings was in Beijing at the invitation of the Chinese paper industry. China had more paper machines than any other country in the world. This was an impressive statistic until analysis showed that over ninety-five percent of them were obsolete or completely uneconomical to run.

However, the Chinese government was aggressive in building a modern paper industry and was very receptive to Measurex, which became a substantial supplier. Board members were invited to stay at the state guesthouse compound, an enormous complex in the heart of Beijing. The compound had lakes, gardens, even such grand amenities as a bowling alley and a swimming pool.

We came to realize that the compound housed some very prominent guests during our visit. Queen Elizabeth and Prince Phillip happened to be staying there as well, though obviously residing in more regal facilities. We saw them numerous times in Beijing and in Souchou, where the ceramic army is buried. Our hosts closed down the monument for the Queen to visit privately, then reopened it just for us.

Our visit to the Great Wall was cut short by the arrival of the Queen and the royal party. Shanghai was spruced up for the royal visit and we missed her by a day, but in Hong Kong, we were present when the Queen arrived on the royal yacht. We watched, fascinated, as Her Majesty disembarked right in front of our hotel rooms and saw her lay a wreath on the war memorial directly underneath our balcony. That evening the city presented the most spectacular fireworks display I had ever seen - and rightly so, since fireworks were invented by the Chinese.

Witnessing a Birth
The Savings and Loan Industry

For many years, savings banks were essentially non-shareholder owned mutual companies. The role of the savings bank was merely to loan money. Marketing strategists realized early on that monies could be more aggressively used. Thus was born the savings and loan industry. These institutions were either mutual or shareholder owned. In the latter case, shareholders were typically local entrepreneurs who were mostly interested in promoting savings and home ownership.

However, some realized that the savings money could be more aggressively invested in riskier ventures than pure home ownership, ventures such as commercial buildings. Also, as a quid pro quo for making monies available, ownership participation in financed real estate could be acquired for making certain loans.

In some states, savings and loans had to be mutuals. However, in other states, California, for example, with California Savings and Loan, the institutions were allowed to be shareholder owned.

Until the 1940s, both savings banks and savings and loans were exempt from federal income taxes. Obviously, this presented an extra opportunity to entrepreneurs, although without exception, there never developed an actual market for ownership shares in shareholder-owned stock savings and loans.

With the great expansion of home ownership and commercial development starting in the 1950s, the special advantages of savings and loans permitted them to offer slightly higher interest rates than the typical savings bank. With inflation and sudden prosperity at hand,

221

deposits in savings and loans began to increase rapidly, with an even larger rise in their profitability.

Commercial banks were alarmed at the rapid growth of savings banks as well as savings and loans, and moved quickly to secure the elimination of their tax-exempt privilege. However, by this time, these organizations had achieved a momentum by carving out a niche, which ensured their rapid growth. The commercial banks then chose not to aggressively pursue savings accounts.

In California, one of the most aggressive savings and loan companies was Great Western. Lehman Brothers recognized what was happening and very quietly made a minor public offering of Great Western shares to a relatively limited number of sophisticated investors. Though the offering had been public, it was handled in a low-key manner and only a nominal market developed on the shares.

A man by the name of Mark Taper had immigrated to England from Poland in the late 1930s to escape the Nazis, then made his way from England to the United States. He had achieved success in England as a builder and arrived in the States just as the enormous housing demand was taking place in California. With the expansion of the war industry in the early 1940s, Taper, who had been dabbling in real estate, instantly recognized the potential of low-cost, subdivision development. He built thousands of homes in the Los Angeles area for workers who toiled in the burgeoning war plants. These houses, of course, needed mortgages and Taper soon realized that ownership of a savings and loan could provide a ready source of funds to assist in the sale of the homes he built.

Over the next two decades, he bought control of a number of savings and loans, which he consolidated in early 1961. Under government insurance rules and because of the rapid growth of his deposits, he needed to match deposit liabilities with an adequate level of capital. Through a Bank of America contact, Mark was introduced to Bob Evans.

I suddenly found myself in the picture on the ground floor of the savings and loan business. I met with Mark Taper and his associates to learn the fundamentals. Lehman had never publicized their offering of Great Western and I was literally flying blind. Intrigued, I tackled the challenge with great gusto and wrote the basic underwriting memorandum for my partners, describing the savings and loan business and the growth opportunities I thought it represented.

Mark Taper renamed his company First Charter Financial since one of his acquisitions held the first savings and loan charter issued in California. With my memorandum as a base, Eastman Dillon negotiated a public offering with Taper and organized an underwriting syndicate of basic security firms to handle *the first truly public initial offering for savings and loan shares.*

The offering came at a price Mark Taper wasn't happy with but which, at the moment of the actual offering, appeared to be excessive. However, at the end of the first day of offering, the general market tone turned around, the sticky offering became a success, and the *short position* Eastman Dillon had taken suddenly became an expensive burden. *(A short position is the offering, by the managing underwriter, of more shares than actually are being issued by the seller. The reason for a short position is that in those slow days of stock markets, some shares would be sold to reluctant buyers who would turn around and seek to dump their shares. A short position gave the managing underwriter a home for these shares with a stabilizing bid, so that the weakly sold shares could not otherwise be sold and depress the market.)*

With First Charter, the sudden turnaround in the hours approaching the anticipated end of the offering resulted in an unexpected demand for additional shares and instead of the short position having to buy in shares to protect the market, Eastman Dillon, the managing underwriter, was suddenly faced with the need to cover the short by going into the open market to buy shares. The short was covered at a sufficient premium to wipe out a significant portion of the underwriting profit. Thus - a sticky deal became an expensive success for the underwriters. And it turned out to be a good buy for the purchasers. Subsequently, the so-called *green shoe* provisions were typically incorporated in underwriting agreements to cover short-position risks.

That cost was more than offset by the publicity and good taste that the successful deal left. When a deal works out in such a manner, it hopefully lays the groundwork for further offerings of the issuer.

Mark Taper was an interesting person. He was quietly very charitable but he was a hard man with whom to negotiate. He fought for every penny, but having made a deal, there was never any argument or double talk. He never went back on his word. He ran First Charter exceptionally well and his loan-loss ratios were negligible.

Based on the success of the First Charter offering, numerous other savings and loans were taken public in California. Eastman Dillon was then offered numerous opportunities to underwrite other such companies. The business was so vast, there was no competitive concern about one underwriter handling such issues.

Frequently a group of promoters would quietly buy all—or a controlling block of shares—of a closely held unquoted savings and loan, raising the capital through the creation of a holding company. They would then offer publicly sufficient shares of the holding company to raise capital to pay off whatever money had been borrowed, frequently to advance additional capital to the operating savings and loan to meet its growth requirements. Naturally, Bob Evans was invited to serve on the board of directors of First Charter.

Another deal brought to Eastman Dillon came to us from John Griffith, a real estate developer who lived in San Marino. It began as a savings and loan named Far West and was incorporated into Far West Financial Corporation. Again I did the write up, the deal was successful, and Lloyd Gilmour went on that board as a director.

Not long thereafter, the historic climb in interest rates began. Mortgage rates went up. Housing demand was enormous and the savings and loans competitively offered higher and higher interest rates to the public who showered them with money. Consumers were largely withdrawing funds from commercial banks savings accounts which paid significantly lower rates.

At one time, Far West one-upped the competition, offering five percent on deposits. Money flooded in so fast that our office literally had boxes full of mail – stacks and stacks of envelopes containing checks waiting to be processed to open accounts.

Within a year, Bob Evans was approached by a man who had access to controlling blocks of stock in the Southern California Savings and Loan. Southern California Financial was organized and they secured interim financing to take up the savings and loan shares with Eastman Dillon, with friends joining the highly regarded real estate developer as the purchaser. The original office of Southern

California Savings and Loan was in downtown Los Angeles where, at the time, there was little or no walk-in business.

Company headquarters were moved to Beverly Hills and I was invited onto the board of directors of the holding company as well as the board of Southern California Savings and Loan. Although my underwriting memorandum had been successful for securing the additional private capital to make the purchase, the savings and loan market turned it down before the new owners could fully implement their legitimate operational change intentions. Therefore, it was not feasible to take the company public. However, the profitability was such, there was no problem with rolling over the short-term loans.

Nevertheless, Eastman Dillon management was uneasy, as was the new owner. In casting around for a purchaser, one of E.D.'s contacts found a major Texas insurance company. The chairman of the board held brief negotiations with the savings and loan holding company, then proceeded to buy it without referring the matter to his board of directors.

When the facts came out, there was a violent reaction. At that time, there was an ongoing battle between insurance companies and savings banks and savings and loans because of the relative liquidity of savings and loans deposits versus tying up money in annuities or life insurance policies. By this time, I had left the board of the savings and loan upon its acquisition, and did not follow closely the subsequent history of Southern California Financial Corporation.

For years, I had been sort of an odd man out in the western region, backing up Bob Evans Sr., doing corporate finance work and occasionally making investment recommendations, largely to the western region. Handling my own investments, I had been reasonably successful and had obtained a reputation, which, in my opinion, was unwarranted when a major vacancy occurred in the Research Division in New York.

Lloyd Gilmour approached me in the mid-1960s to head up E.D.U.S. Research. Frankly, I did not consider myself qualified because among other things, the job would involve managing a number of corporate research specialists. That breed was becoming increasingly specialized and financially demanding. Personnel management is not one of my fortes and I really did not want the job, although I was told I could keep my home here in San Marino.

Hilda was not enthusiastic about the thought of moving to New York. We agreed that I should discuss it with the boys and in a long conversation with Jim and John, they indicated that in their opinions, I would be giving up several years of my life for a little more money. In other words, "Don't go!" When I told Lloyd Gilmour our decision, he stated he was very disappointed but did not throw me out of the firm.

~

In the late 1970s, Lloyd Gilmour became ill and resigned from the Far West financial board. I was elected in his place. There was still one remaining outside shareholder of the actual savings and loan-operating subsidiary of the holding company - Morton Seidel. Control of Far West was still held by the John Griffith family, old-line California WASPS. John Griffith was getting along in years and wanted to make his estate more liquid. His son was an up-and-coming officer of Far West. The board had made several attempts to sell Far West. One bid was from a New York promoter who had earlier made and lost a fortune in the computer-leasing business. In the meantime, he had secured control of a major Philadelphia based insurance company. Insurance companies were honey pots for promoters in that they controlled vast sums of money, affording aggressive owners quite interesting opportunities. A bid was made for Far West, which on its face appeared attractive to the board. However, the arrangement would have placed the holders of Far West bonds at risk should the new owner misuse the company by looting the assets.

The board of directors and I were sufficiently uneasy at this prospect and decided to reject the offer. Our intuition proved to be correct. Many years of subsequent actions by that promoter resulted in the ultimate receivership of the large insurance company he controlled.

A subsequent sale of Far West to another savings institution was negotiated at a satisfactory price. However, the sale could not be closed without securing numerous regulatory approvals. While these were being sought, out of the blue came an offering from a group of Canadians who offered to buy 24.9 percent of the shares of Far West at a price only slightly below the other announced sale price.

The deal had no strings and a tender of shares in excess of the 24.9 percent limit would be pro-rated. Since the price was a premium to the going market price of Far West, the tender was heavily oversubscribed. And three Canadian brothers by the name of Belzberg ended up with a controlling block of stock. The Belzbergs had started in the furniture business in Alberta and had developed the Canadian equivalent of a savings and loan empire in their own country.

When Griffith told the board that he intended to fight the Canadian offer, I pointed out that any such battle would be futile since there was no legal impropriety with regard to the Canadian offer and that the offer required no United States approval at the time. The Belzbergs requested positions on the board of directors. John Griffiths was determined to engage in a proxy fight against them. I stated that under California law, with cumulative voting, they could not be denied seats without a messy contest or a legally indefensible reduction in the size of the board of directors. That meeting was conducted in the Eastman Dillon conference room and the Griffiths and other board members finally acquiesced to me, but certainly not with any show of grace. The Belzbergs proceeded to get permission to buy additional shares and ultimately ended up with slightly over sixty percent, which they used to revamp the board of directors, of course, adding some of their friends.

I was not removed, simply because I pointed out to them that I represented the remaining forty percent of public shareholders, since the stock was still listed on the NYSE. Far West moved its operating headquarters to a new building near Irvine. Bill Belzberg became president and quickly established his own office in Beverly Hills. Meanwhile, interest rates exploded through the inflation of the Nixon, Kennedy and Johnson Vietnam War years. U.S. government, long-term bond rates reached fourteen-and-a-half percent and short-term rates offered by savings and loans, at times, exceeded eighteen percent.

These rates far exceeded the returns on the current investments of savings and loans who frantically sought income sources to attempt to match their income needs. Simultaneously, someone developed a theory that high-yield bonds could be issued by conglomerates. Aggressive use of this concept provided funds through the sale of junk high-yield bonds to permit promoters to push buy outs of going businesses at excessive prices. The new concept of "earning" before interest depreciation taxes and amortization was pushed as a holy grail.

The Morgan Investment Banking Group threw their historic conservatism to the winds and produced a treatise that high-yield bonds could be a safe investment. An old-line securities firm named Drexel Burnum had retained an aggressive bond promoter named Michael Milken who established a Drexel office in Beverly Hills. Within a few years' time, he had developed a huge and enormously profitable business offering junk bonds. As the business grew, standards were dropped and interest rates offered rose from peak to peak. Offerings were frequently based on projected or assumed cash flow without regard to economic fundamentals.

Drexel became greedier and greedier under Milken, who developed various means of offering and encouraging bond issues that were frequently unsupportable. In order to meet the demands for increasing interest payments by savings and loans, Milken found managers of several savings and loans and lower rate insurance companies who would readily buy his bonds because of the presumed income they afforded. At the same time, in a roaring real estate market, promoters discovered that they could heavily leverage land, apartment and commercial buildings; and offered to pay huge interest rates along with ownership participation to institutions willing to lend money through deals that should not have been considered justifiable risks.

Early on, Milken approached Bill Belzberg as a potential buyer of his offerings. Belzberg was wide open to such appeals because these appeared to be a solution to the interest differential problem. From day one, I publicly opposed buying any such bonds, particularly from Drexel Burnum. I believed these deals to be economically unsupportable and that while I had no specifics, I was extremely dubious about the ethics and financial practices of Milken. He was reputed to be making hundreds of millions of dollars in bonuses from his participation of the profits from his division. My cautionary advice in opposition to such purchases was constantly overridden.

I wasn't surprised when the Drexel bond issues collapsed in price, as did the overheated real estate market. Savings and loans nationwide promptly suffered severe losses and capital deficiencies. I believe that many of these were from honest mistakes, but I felt strongly that a large portion of other losses were the result of fraud.

This is a classic example. Friends of a savings and loan would swap a property back and forth at increasing prices. They would obtain loans from promotional savings and loans institutions that could not be supported, but which would afford all kinds of creative opportunities for kickbacks. In one such case, a Texas savings and loan company ended up with ninety-three percent of its loans in default.

The Federal Savings and Loan Insurance Corporation insured savings and loans deposits up to one hundred thousand dollars. The FSLIC became alarmed way too late when the capital of insured savings and loans was depleted and runs on deposits occurred. This was in the late 1970s. Losses were enormous as innumerable savings and loans were taken over. Far West Financial, with its portfolio of low quality bonds and aggressively financed apartment developments, was no exception, although in the Far West case, in all fairness, I maintained, unequivocally, that the Belzbergs never took anything on the side. Nor were they responsible for any morally improper business dealings.

On one gray, gloomy day, I attended a board meeting of Far West Savings and Loan where my board met with representatives of FSLIC who stated that they found Far West with a grave capital deficiency. It was FSLIC's intention to seize the savings and loan. They made a substantial investigation but of course, never found any improprieties. They began by criticizing two or three real estate transactions as being imprudent, but which later turned out upon investigation by their liquidators to be not only completely above board but profitable as well.

The Far West Financial separate holding company had sold additional stock to the public and was itself solvent. The price dropped to a few dollars after the seizure. All of the officers and directors, including me, were the subjects of a lawyer-inspired, class action suit brought by attorney Bill Lerach of San Diego.

We battled this action as best we could, and in the end, no improprieties were ever found. The suit was finally settled when we allowed Lerach's firm to represent us in a suit against Drexel Burnum.

The ultimate result was that we agreed in future to have the audit committee meet quarterly rather than semi-annually and that all future bond purchases should be approved in advance. And for this, the Lerach firm, on their contingency, received more than twenty million dollars. The upside was that Far West received substantial sums, which through a quirk of their legal setup, remained in the holding company's possession rather than reverting to the FSLIC.

Bill Belzberg ran the holding company, in my estimation, as a typical Canadian promoter. His belief was that outside shareholders were merely nuisances. I continued on Belzberg's board because Far West remained a company with public ownership, and I thought the public was entitled to a watchdog.

I agreed to most of Belzberg's direct corporate proposals, as I believed the risks on these to be reasonable. However, I strongly opposed Belzberg's insistence on a long-term employment contract, which I thought ridiculous for a family-controlled business. Although I realized there did appear to be some apparent antipathy between Bill Belzberg and his brothers, who each owned approximately twenty-one percent. Even worse, Belzberg insisted upon receiving a significant stock option grant. More irritating to me, as an example of what I considered pure greed, Belzberg insisted on receiving director's fees. He was not pleased when I pointed out that I knew of no other public company where corporate officers received such fees. As a result of this difference of opinion, in 1998, I was advised that the board of directors was being reduced in size and that my name would not be included for election in the forthcoming annual meeting. I was forced out, dignity intact. I never backed off from my principles, believing them to be correct.

Union Securities

In the 1930s, Joseph King was given two million dollars to form a subsidiary of Tri-Continental Investment Company, a closed-end mutual fund on the New York Stock Exchange. The subsidiary was named Union Securities Company and it became very successful in the area of corporate finance.

Union Securities, although being quite profitable, was costing Tri-Continental too much, because with a business subsidy, the parent company had to pay dividend tax on its investments. Until that time, the tax had been less than what Union Securities was making. However, Tri-Continental had become highly profitable as an investment company and the tax on their dividend income became greater than the Union Securities profits. Joe King and Lloyd Gilmour of Eastman Dillon were long-term friends and the two companies were similar except that Union Securities specialized in areas not covered by Eastman Dillon.

Tri-Continental could have sold Union Securities to the highest bidder, but the amount would have been nominal because the buyer would assume that the producers of Union Securities would not be able to work well with a new master.

A deal was negotiated for Eastman Dillon to take over Union Securities on a friendly basis for nominal consideration and a percentage of the profits on business from ongoing historic relationships. In the summer of 1956, Eastman Dillon bought only the ongoing business. The assets of Union Securities, which were more than thirty-two million dollars plus substantial values in ongoing profit participation in oil deals, were retained by Tri-Continental.

Eastman Dillon partners decided to change the company name to Eastman Dillon Union Securities. The Union Securities personnel smoothly integrated with E.D. with only a nominal loss of valuable people. This was probably one of the most successful merger-acquisitions in the securities business. This was motivated by Lloyd Gilmour's insistence that the Union Securities people would become partners and would be able to participate in to a degree that would have been impossible with the old Union Securities Tri-Continental organization.

On the west coast, Bob Evans and Jack Mackie proceeded to open offices, welcoming quite a few staff members from the First California Company. The new adoptees had become increasingly unhappy with that firm. Jack Mackie, who had started with us in Los Angeles, was essentially a San Franciscan at heart. As such, he was always yearning to return. In 1962, he finally moved back to the City by the Bay to run a very successful office. We continued to work together.

One of the problems of the adoptees was that the historic Bank of America practice of referring business to First California Company had worn thin. In addition, the basic profitability of the over-the-counter securities market was gutted. Public pressure and the National Association of Securities Dealers resulted in the publishing of inside market prices. Historically, published prices had included a five percent markup. This practice was discontinued with a major impact on over-the-counter trading profitability.

Intent on starting an office in Seattle, Jack Mackie and I visited the city several times. Boeing was in one of its periodic cut downs and the lumber industry was being hurt by the end of the depression. Nevertheless, there were a lot of people in Seattle and we figured there was a lot of opportunity there.

In 1974, a Seattle colleague told me about a manager in his office who was looking to make a move. (I've forgotten the young man's name, so we'll call him John Smith.) He had been with a moderately large firm and had done some underwriting. His office was very profitable but the firm, which had its headquarters in New York, was losing money. Smith's efforts had earned him a substantial bonus which upper management denied. This was a very bad mistake.

Several of us went to Seattle a number of times to work out details. We met with Smith at his home located at the bottom of a hill that led down to the shores of Lake Washington. There had been a sudden snowfall in Seattle, and with our rented car, we didn't dare go down that hill for fear we wouldn't be able to drive back up. So we parked the car at the top of the hill and trudged down through the snow to the house where we were to meet. Our negotiations were successful, and New York approved the acquisition of John Smith who would be responsible for opening our new office in Seattle.

Smith was well regarded in the community, and as soon as it got around that Eastman Dillon was opening an office there, several producers from the Seattle office of Blyth and Company approached Jack and me, asking to come aboard with us at Eastman Dillon Union Securities. Suddenly everyone wanted to board the new ship. There had always been a mutual understanding that Eastman Dillon, Blyth and Dean Witter would not raid each other's offices for salesmen. But several salesmen approached us to indicate their dissatisfaction with their managers. Their office had not been terribly successful, not only because of the manager but because of some problems with the INA merger. We didn't feel we were acting inappropriately when we offered a couple of them positions in the new office.

Our next challenge was to cast around for suitable quarters. Seattle was in a downturn so there was plenty of office space available. We found good office space and entered into negotiations for a lease. Almost simultaneously, the INA people decided they had to do something with Blyth and negotiated the sale of Blyth to Eastman Dillon. It was suggested that the Eastman Dillon office that was already being created for their personnel move into the Blyth space.

However, Blyth, historically, had had a limited number of sales people in the Seattle office, each of whom had a *real* office, affording them each the privacy they desired. During the morning, when business was slow, if he didn't feel much like working, the salesman could close the door, put his feet up, and remain undisturbed. Our new digs would not afford them that level of privacy. The offices would have to be open and shared with several salesmen. That was their complaint. And their complaints were unacceptable to us.

In addition, the Seattle manager of Blyth was not particularly effective, and had not endeared himself to our new manager. A couple of the remaining Blyth salesmen expressed the opinions that they considered Eastman Dillon to be a *wire house*, similar to Merrill Lynch, and they wanted no part of working for a wire house.

Blyth also had a Portland office with a weak manager, and we solved some of these reoccurring problems by transferring the Seattle manager to the Portland office. We intended to take over the latter office once things were settled in Seattle. The Seattle manager reluctantly agreed to the transfer, vocally expressing the feeling that Blyth was much more senior than Eastman Dillon, that they were much more recognized in the international banking community, and that he should be chosen to run the new Seattle office after the merger, once the company name was changed to Blyth Eastman Dillon. The name change was a challenge as well because Eastman Dillon was significantly larger than Blyth at that time and theoretically, that name should have come first.

Our new Seattle office was quite successful from the beginning. We did eventually move into the Blyth facilities, but we quickly tore out the walls and opened the space. We lost a few salesmen, but with a good manager, we also gained a bunch of effective salesmen, so all in all, it was a very successful operation.

The transition, however, was not without obstacles. I was in charge of the whole west coast operation, which spanned from Houston and Dallas to Oklahoma City, to Denver, up to Seattle and even included Hawaii. Blyth's principal west coast operations were in Los Angeles, San Francisco, Portland and Seattle. Their west coast operation was managed by Dick Klieg in the Los Angeles office on Spring Street. Those quarters had been there since the beginning of time and Dick and I had known each other for years. We had never been close friends, but we had exchanged ideas and had some good discussions, so there had never been any antipathy between us.

I could see that the Blyth operation was old fashioned. They actually had a lady who came in every day and served tea and coffee to the salesmen. Every office was nearly autonomous with safes installed in every office where their securities were individually held for safekeeping. They had a terrible time each month when they had to reconcile accounts. It was a very expensive operation, very inefficient.

Right away, Eastman Dillon started moderating those things and began to move Blyth into our own systems. The Blyth computer operation was primitive, and we moved Blyth onto our operations, with some problems, although not excessive ones. Of course, the Blyth back-office staff in all the west coast offices had to be let go.

With Eastman Dillon's superior computerization and different operating systems, there was no way in the world we could continue Blyth's costly method of operation. In Los Angeles and San Francisco, the Blyth retail, institutional and corporate finance people were moved in with the Eastman Dillon people. We had been doing very little corporate finance, so I was quite happy to welcome Blyth's corporate finance people on board.

Over the years, Dick Link had picked up Blyth's stock whenever it became available. He had acquired a relatively large percent of stock, more than most of the other seniors. In the acquisition of Blyth by INA, he became a substantial holder, in terms of dollars, of INA stock. He made no particular effort to push me out as manager of the western region and decided to retire.

Dick lived on the west side of the Pasadena Arroyo and for his farewell party, invited a group of the Eastman Dillon people from the Los Angeles office to his home for dinner and drinks. Several of us showed up, along with a few of the Blyth people. We had a pleasant dinner and a few drinks. Gradually, everybody left except me. Dick had been drinking fairly heavily. He kept asking me how I expected to keep all the Blyth people on the payroll and I kept pointing out to him that there was no way I could do that, that there were people whose jobs no longer existed because of the necessary systems changes. Quite inebriated, he continued to ramble.

Then he got onto the subject of his secretary, Doris Babinski, whom I had known for many years. I knew that Doris was *coveted* indeed, but she was not back-office staff. Dick launched into a tirade about how I had to take care of Doris. I had no problem there, because I had long before recognized that Doris was a wonderful executive secretary, so I kept assuring Dick that I would be sure to take care of Doris.

I was good to my word. A year and a half after our talk, my own personal secretary chose to retire, and I immediately recruited Doris to be my secretary. It worked out wonderfully well.

When I had first been approached in the late 1970s to take over the management of the western region of E.D., I agreed to accept that responsibility contingent upon my being given a strong sales manager. The New York office promised they had the perfect candidate: Tom Thomas, an up-and-comer who had made a spectacular mark in the Bridgeport, Connecticut office. Having been recruited to the New York office, he was quickly recognized for his abilities to promote sales.

I also wanted someone to handle detailed administrative duties and for that, we all agreed that Robert Bothner, who ran the successful Long Beach office, would be ideal. The team of Baum, Thomas and Bothner took over management of the western region of the firm and successfully ran it for many years.

One of Dick Link's problems was that he never traveled to the other Blyth offices in the western division. He had kept himself holed up in Los Angeles, so the various branch office managers never saw him.

When our team took over, I made sure that Tom Thomas, Bob Bothner and I regularly visited the offices. I personally made sure to visit all the offices at least once a year to meet with all the personnel. I soon grew tired of this, so I encouraged Tom Thomas to become regional manager so I could take life easier. However, in a relatively short time, New York decided they needed Tom back east to do sales work there, and he was promoted from Los Angeles to New York for a more important job. Once again I had to reassume leadership of the western region, which I did for another year or so.

The Begats of the Investment Banking Business from Blyth to UBS PaineWebber

Around 1970, Charlie Blyth died. Since Blyth was a corporation, the firm was not permitted to be a member of the NYSE. The company had many valuable investment banking accounts including Pacific Gas and Electric and Pacific Lighting, and was, of course, a major national underwriter. Most of Charlie Blyth's shares in the company were purchased by seniors who held major participations. Most of them were approaching retirement and quite frankly, were greedy. The upcoming junior officers, on the other hand, were not given the opportunity to significantly increase their ownership.

The Insurance Company of North America (INA), located in Philadelphia, decided they wanted to become involved in investment banking. They made an offer for Blyth through an exchange of shares. The seniors accepted the terms and Blyth became a wholly owned subsidiary of INA.

The result was a fiasco. By the early 1970s, the investment banking industry went into a tailspin with a sharp depression and market decline. The juniors who had been looking forward to being able to acquire a major participation in Blyth were locked out because all the shares were owned by INA.

As a result, the competent, aggressive up-and-comers, who were positioned to become the future of Blyth, left in droves. INA was upset because none of its own people were qualified to move in and take charge of Blyth.

Historically, NYSE rules permitted only partnerships and sole proprietorships to be members. Corporations could not become members. The theory was that the unlimited personal liability of partnerships reinforced the integrity of NYSE membership. A disadvantage was that this rule restricted access to the outside capital a corporation could acquire.

Among the other disadvantages was the fact that partners were unable to enjoy various tax advantage retirement programs. Nor could they share in the appreciation that would be available to the shareholders of a successful corporation.

Around 1971, the NYSE, under pressure, permitted member firms to incorporate.

E.D.U.S. did so. For my partnership interest, I received shares of the new corporation. For some time, William Boothby had held one of the larger partnership interests and upon incorporating, became president of Eastman Dillon U.S.

Boothby, a Philadelphia resident, commuted to the office in New York. Many of his Philadelphia acquaintances were senior officers of INA. As a result, in 1974, Blyth and Company merged into E.D.U.S., changing the name again - this time, to Blyth Eastman Dillon and Company.

This was a strategic move. Historically, the Blyth name was better known. Equally important, a name beginning with "B" would be placed before the names of competitors in *tombstone* ads. These are ads for the stock offerings after the offering is made and positioning is very important.

INA ended up with an approximate thirty-five percent ownership interest in the ongoing firm of Blyth Eastman Dillon. Several INA executives went onto our board. INA pressured us to enter certain areas of the investment business, which we had thought unattractive. Those areas turned out to be expensive loss leaders in the unsettled security markets that continued through most of the 1970s.

INA became increasingly unhappy with their investment and some capital cash injections they had made. They thought that a further merger with a larger firm that had a bigger retail securities business could solve their problem.

They secretly negotiated a deal with PaineWebber in which Blyth Eastman Dillon would be acquired for PaineWebber shares, which were listed on the New York Stock Exchange. The deal was pushed through and we became Blyth Eastman PaineWebber.

We had offices ranging from Houston and Oklahoma City to Seattle and Honolulu with Tom Thomas doing most of the sales promotion. After several years, I gradually relinquished my duties as manager and Tom Thomas took over, only shortly thereafter, to be promoted to the New York office. Reluctantly, I had to take over management duties once again. Not long thereafter, the PaineWebber merger became effective, so PW management took over and I gladly gave up any and all administrative responsibilities, although I maintained an office in downtown Los Angeles in what became the principal local PaineWebber office. After a few years, PaineWebber collapsed the Blyth Eastman subsidiary into their firm and Blyth Eastman disappeared as a separate entity.

In the depths of the early 1970s poor market, PaineWebber shares had declined to a dollar seventy-five. Fortuitously, I had bought some stock around that price and then acquired additional PaineWebber shares as well as a cash payment during the merger.

Even though I had given up my management duties several years before, I continued to maintain a presence in the downtown Los Angeles office. I dabbled a bit in corporate finance and stock picking and by agreement, took a nominal salary. In 1984, I found it difficult to justify my corner office and a secretary, so by agreement, I negotiated office space in the PaineWebber Pasadena office. Without any reluctance, I gave up the daily drive to downtown Los Angeles.

I also decided that with the move to Pasadena, I should rent a separate office for my personal affairs and to provide space for my secretary. Offering to purchase my office furniture from PaineWebber in Los Angeles, I was told it would cost more to calculate its depreciative value in order to sell it, so the company kindly made a gift of the furniture. Doris moved with me out to the Pasadena office, but eventually she was forced to retire due to illness. Actually, I no longer had any executive responsibilities at all. I would help out a manager if he needed me to assist him in selling a deal, but for the most part I was completely on my own.

Dr. No - My Well-earned Alias

At one time, there were separate stock exchanges in Los Angeles and San Francisco. In the 1950s, they merged into the Pacific Coast Stock Exchange with trading floors in both cities. Eastman Dillon had a membership in the Pacific Coast Stock Exchange. That membership was assigned to me when I first joined the firm. Although that permitted us to have a trader on the floor, I never acted as a trader for the firm.

The Los Angeles Exchange was located in an art-deco building on Spring Street. It was built specifically for the stock exchange with facilities for the Exchange Club on the top floors. By the 1970s, the building had become obsolete, and with the transfer of the Los Angeles financial community from Spring Street, the L.A. branch finally moved to new quarters just north of the freeway. I helped negotiate the lease. This move actually completed the final demise of Spring Street.

In San Francisco, the Exchange occupied what had been the Sub-Treasury building, a classical two-story structure with huge vaults in the basement. At one time, gold had been stored in the vaults. The building had been the principal asset of its predecessor, the San Francisco Stock Exchange. During the merger, the San Francisco building had been spun off. One share of stock was awarded to each of the eighty members.

The Exchange entered into a net lease of the building and the building corporation sold off the air rights for a substantial sum and distributed the proceeds. The building shares were transferable, but with the provision that Exchange members were offered the Right of

First Refusal on any sale. To my surprise, one day I received a notice that one share was being sold at a price of four thousand five hundred dollars. When I inquired of the president of the Exchange, he told me the history and said that undoubtedly, the inherent value was substantially higher. In addition, the shares paid a dividend of more than two hundred dollars a share. After clearing it with my partners, I bid for and bought the shares.

Subsequently, as additional shares occasionally appeared, I would buy them on the same terms. I eventually ended up with eight shares. One day I was advised that an offer had been made to buy the corporation for a much higher amount. The largest stockholder was a lawyer who represented Bechtel Corporation.

The buyer paid cash plus a mortgage-bearing interest at ten percent, even though the theoretical value of the building and its location, etc., was significantly higher. The long-term lease, the historic nature of the building and the prior sale of the air rights made the offer very attractive. I accepted.

Immediately thereafter, in 1980, I began serving on the board of governors of the Exchange and was elected Vice Chair of the Pacific Coast Stock Exchange. I served for one and a half terms, until 1985, as a paid professional. Both before and after my position as vice chair, I was elected to serve on the Listing Committee and did so until the year 2000, when the Stock Exchange disbanded. That committee controlled the listings of stocks on the Exchange.

Although the Exchange itself was a minor one compared to the NYSE, the listing of a stock gave automatic *blue-sky clearance* of new issues in all states. This privilege was valuable in that it reduced new issue costs for public offerings. Of course, this attracted questionable companies. Since I had been involved for years in both security analysis and corporate new issues, I had what I believed to be substantial insight into the likelihood of a proposed offering being viable, thus affording the investors a fair shake.

Most of the other committee members were from the trading floor and their approach to a listing was, "Would it trade actively?"

I enjoyed analyzing proposed new issues and other potential listings through seeing the detailed information that was required to be filed. From the start, I took the position that the public interest should be paramount. Exercising my rights, I took strong positions whenever I saw a proposed listing that did not meet my standards.

Almost invariably, I was able to convince the others whenever someone was trying to misuse the Exchange. I know I made many lawyers, issuers, and *schlock underwriters* unhappy, but I maintained my standards and invariably, I was always able to carry a majority of the committee. Hence, because of my frequently firm negative positions, I became known as "Dr. No." I am certain I saved the public millions of dollars through killing poor underwritings sponsored by promoters whom we turned down.

The Bob Evans Family

E. J. "Bob" Evans always had a penchant for trading houses and did so as easily as he traded cars. The first house he bought was in Encino in 1946 around the time we moved to Pasadena. Although relatively small, his little estate had some unique amenities including several horse corrals. It wasn't long before he sold that home and moved to another one.

The Bank of America had foreclosed on a beautiful house on the Bel Air Country Club Golf Course in West Los Angeles. The house's former owner had made a fortune tooling sugar during World War II, successfully creating a knock-off of Lifesavers. The candy was called Hollywood Stars. At the end of rationing, however, the real Lifesavers candy became readily available and his business died a sudden death. Sadly, he lost his home to foreclosure.

The bank put the house on the market and when Bob learned about it, he made an inquiry. The bank offered Bob a sweetheart deal and he bought the house immediately, paying around a hundred twenty-five thousand dollars. Today it must be worth at least five million. The house was beautifully situated on an appendix road coming off Wilshire Boulevard. It was far enough away from the boulevard so as not to be bothered by traffic noise. There was a guesthouse on the property where Hope's parents lived. Hope had good taste and the main house was beautifully furnished. Of course, Bob was already a member of the Bel Air Country Club, so he thought it was meant to be.

But before long a real estate agent approached Bob saying he had a buyer for a fine house and he asked Bob to show his home. Bob, being a salesman *and* a sucker, said, "By all means!"

So this Texas oilman who had sold some oil properties for a lot of money brought his wife to see the house. They were entranced by it, and rightfully so. The oilman asked Bob what he would take for the house. Bob mentioned some figure he thought to be grossly excessive and the man stepped right up and said "Sold! I'll buy it. Just one thing…you can take your personal possessions, pictures, silverware, linens and things like that, but all the rest goes with the house."

Bob Evans was hooked. Although he was offered a lot of money, the value of that house far exceeded what he was paid and he sold that beautiful house for a song. Still, he had earned far in excess of what he had originally paid and with the proceeds, he then bought a house high up in the canyons. Actually, it was in a terrible area because it was a great fire-hazard.

Later, as Bob approached retirement, he became quite interested in Rancho Santa Fe. He and Hope ended up renting a house there while building a lovely large home.

Throughout his adult life, Bob Evans, Sr. was a compulsive smoker. There were times he would have a cigarette in his mouth and there would be two lit cigarettes in the ashtrays on his desk. He would be smoking, the telephone would ring, and he would grab the phone while lighting another cigarette. Unfortunately, soon after he retired, he was diagnosed with lung cancer, and before long, he was gone.

When his will and trust were read, I found that in addition to being his executor, I also had been named trustee for an irrevocable trust to benefit his wife, Hope. From there, the trust went on to Bob, Jr. and his wife Bev upon Hope's death. When Bob Jr. predeceased his mother, those arrangements became more complex.

Robert M. Evans, Bob, Jr., although a go-getter, unfortunately did not have some of the better qualities his father possessed. He had originally started with Dean Witter and Company but eventually left to come with us and work for Eastman Dillon. He was aggressive, he was confident, he was a good salesman, and he rapidly made his way up from the E.D. office in San Diego to the Los Angeles office. By the time his dad retired, young Bob had legitimately worked his way up to justify the position of manager of the division and he was immediately nominated for that position. Bob, Jr. ran the western region for a number of years with a good measure of success.

Young Bob managed the offices and the salesmen, working everyone very hard. Every quarter we held a sales meeting, usually in Los Angeles, but almost always, there was an open bar. In my mind, this was a great mistake. Bob, Jr. was, unlike his dad, a bit of a boozer. He even held an open bar during the daily meetings. The salesmen never became drunk during office hours, but they certainly weren't as bright in the afternoons as they might otherwise have been.

It was a bit frustrating, as I would prepare presentations on various stocks and issues in which the firm was participating, or stocks which I thought were attractive for purchase, and the salesmen were so relaxed by the time I had finished my discussion that I was never really sure if I was getting through to them or if my efforts were wasted.

For some reason, Bob decided to go off on his own. He started a money management business that became only modestly successful. The firm primarily handled various kinds of specialized insurances, annuities and such. Setting up an office in Pasadena, he built the small organization very quickly. Then something happened to cause him to liquidate the business. I never knew the full story.

He and Beverly had been living in a huge house in South Pasadena and eventually sold it to move out to Encino. One day I received a telephone call from Bev, saying that they were at home when young Bob had suffered an embolism. He died within the hour. They had recently returned from a vacation in the Caribbean and hadn't been home very long at all.

Young Bob and I had always been good friends and Beverly proceeded to read me from his will in which I had been named trustee under various trusts. I was flabbergasted because earlier on, he had asked me to take care of Bev if anything ever happened to him. I had agreed, thinking he was just talking about investment recommendations, but I never agreed to become his trustee. So there I was, out at her house the day after his death, reading the will and confirming that I had been made his trustee. Bob Jr's will called for the creation of an additional irrevocable trust to benefit Bev until her death, with the assets then going to their children. The trust was funded with only about three hundred thousand dollars. The First

245

Interstate Bank, originally named as trustee, refused to assume the responsibility, so we went to court and I was officially appointed trustee.

Unfortunately, they were not good trusts, they were continuing trusts with the income to be held for Bev, but ultimately, on Bev's passing, the assets of the trust would go to their four children, which could have been years and years away. Bob had never really trusted any business affairs to Bev. He had managed all their money himself, and what a mistake. Bev could watch a nickel like you couldn't believe, and she was very competent, but she could never lay her hands on it to manage it because of the nature of this trust. I guess Bob thought that she would squander that money. The fact that the trust continued on until her death when the children would take it over was a great mistake, and he did her no great service at all in setting things up that way.

Having lost her husband and her son in a relatively short period of time, Hope tried to go on with her life. She left their large home to rent a beautiful apartment in the center of Rancho Santa Fe. But one day, several years later, probably in the mid-80s, I received a distressing telephone call from Bev. She was beside herself with grief.

Hope, who had seemed in apparent good health, had invited some friends in that afternoon to play bridge. The ladies had decided to go to the Inn at Rancho Santa Fe for drinks before dinner and Hope went into her bedroom to change. After a while, not hearing anything from her, a couple of the ladies went in to check on her and found her dead, lying on the bed.

They called Bev who immediately called me at the office. She was beside herself and didn't know what to do. I told her to give me enough time to pack a few things and to pick me up at the house.

I called Hilda, dashed home, grabbed a suitcase and Bev soon came by. We drove down to Rancho Santa Fe and arrived at the apartment to find that Hope had already been moved to the mortuary. I helped Bev make arrangements for the cremation and a modest funeral, adhering to what we knew were Hope's wishes.

To the absolute horror of Hope's friends, Bev and I stayed at Hope's apartment in Rancho Santa Fe, wrapping up loose ends, going through jewelry and things of that sort. We made a quick inventory of the furniture and figured out which clothes were to be given away to

Goodwill and which ones Hope would take. Once everything was done, I returned to Los Angeles.

Once again, I ended up as executor and trustee for two separate irrevocable trusts for the benefit of Bev Evans, with total assets of only approximately six hundred thousand dollars. But there was no way to break the trusts and give the money to Bev to manage, although again, I knew she would do a fine job with it.

The Impact of the Blyth Acquisition
and the SEC Hearing

The New York Stock Exchange had historically operated like an old-fashioned European guild in the sense of ethics and such. They wrote their own rules, but some things were written in concrete, one of which was that the unit of trade on the New York stock exchange was one hundred shares. Exchange members fixed the commissions at X-amount per hundred shares. If you had a trade for five hundred shares, the commission was five times the commission for a hundred shares. If you had a trade for ten thousand shares, the commission was a hundred times the amount for a hundred shares, with no reduction being allowed.

With the ongoing expansion of the U.S. economy, the development of institutional business and the development of mutual funds, the activity of the New York stock exchange grew and grew, and the amount of money being made by the one hundred share commission rule was unbelievably fantastic.

A number of the firm's institutional salesmen began making vast sums of money. Because commission splitting outside the exchange was not permitted, they created devious ways to permit outside organizations to turn up orders and participate in the honey pile. They had two-way tickets and four-way tickets for over-the-counter stocks, and things like that. Of course, they also created devious means by which to split up this vast amount of money.

An organization run by reasonable people would have recognized that there were serious problems being created here, and that

248

something would have to be done to stop these excess profits. Of course nothing was done because the owners of the exchange were so bloody single-minded to getting hold of that money.

Finally there were some scandals because of the excesses and the Securities and Exchange Commission got into the act. After the hearings, the SEC mandated that commissions be scaled down to match the increasing sizes of orders. Further, the SEC decided that for a short period of time, fixed commissions should be banished altogether, and all commissions should be negotiable. Securities firms were given a year or so to prepare for the transition to negotiable commissions. Naturally, there was a great uproar on Wall Street. Because of anti-trust laws, there was no way that the various securities firms could mutually agree on scales of commissions that they all would be required to adhere to.

Therefore, it was very apparent it was going to be catch-as-catch can, but how great or how deep the commission cuts would be, nobody really knew. Nor did anybody know what the long-term impact of all this would be. Various firms set up commissions and overseeing groups to monitor the situation, and Blyth Eastman Dillon - out of the blue - tapped me to undergo a study. They wanted to know what was going to happen and asked for my recommendations.

I spent several months drafting and redrafting reports and opinions, talking to members of the firm and some of the salespeople, trying to come up with what might happen. But it was a very amorphous process. You could not consult with other firms because of potential anti-trust considerations.

Early on, I arrived at this conclusion. Blyth PaineWebber's institutional business at the time was relatively modest. We were a well-balanced firm with a retail business that was adequate to balance off the investment-banking business and support that on the basis of retail alone. Our typical customer was not an active customer. Our typical order size was larger than that of the Dean Witters and Merrill Lynches of that time. I thought we had to come up with something that would be distinctive. I had the idea that if we paid our customers on their free credit balances on their accounts we could attract more customers that way and we could afford to pay them an amount of money equal to at least the appropriate loan rate for margin loan and margin securities.

I proposed that we would re-forest our accounts and that customers with free credit balances arising from the sale of securities after the five-day settlement period would receive in excess of some large amount in interest, on a daily basis, which was equivalent to the brokers' loan rate on bank loans.

My overall report begged the question as to where these commissions would end. I was optimistic on the upside, but I strongly recommended four-star interest payments to customers, and after a long meeting of the executive committee of the firm, this was agreed upon. Thus, Blyth Eastman Dillon formally announced the four-star account payment of interest on free credit balances to the customers. This was revolutionary at the time!

However, others promptly picked up the strategy and several firms immediately went into the checking account business. My report was bound and circulated to the senior members of the firm. One of the things I remarked upon was the fact that underwriting spreads were fixed by the SEC and could not be discounted so long as the offering was made until that offering was closed and freed up all sales from the management syndicate by the various participants, that it must be at the public offering price and that the spread could not be discounted to the customer.

When so-called D-day arrived, and fixed commissions were abolished, there was a fair amount of confusion, but commission rates have dropped down sharply and the boutique firms, in essence, went out of business.

Several other firms developed new institutional departments. On the floor of the NYSE, some of the floor traders happened to get together, and tried to keep prices up. Finally, there was a scandal of some sort, which brought the SEC into the act, then the federal government for a full-blown criminal investigation. A number of firms were named. They were primarily floor traders.

I don't think Blyth Eastman Dillon was named to begin with because our floor trading was very modest. We were not big block traders. But one day, out of the blue, I was served with a subpoena to go back to New York to testify before a grand jury with regard to a commission fixing issue on the New York Stock Exchange. I was required to supply old diaries and things of that nature, but I had virtually nothing of the sort in the office, never having been involved in anything with which they might be concerned.

At the time, I was a member of the National Association of Securities Dealers, NASD, Board of Governors, so I arranged to have my appearance in New York tie in with a meeting in Washington DC with the NASD board. I had a couple of teleconferences in New York with some of the partners of one of Eastman Dillon's law firms.

I already knew that council would not be permitted to represent me in a grand jury appearance, although he could stand outside the door if I needed to consult with him. This appearance did not bother me at all because frankly, I had always conducted my business affairs above board and with great integrity. I had never done anything I would later have to hide. I flew to New York and after a brief final meeting with our council, went into the grand jury hearing. The council did, in fact, sit in a room outside while I went into the jury room. What an interesting experience! I had never attended a hearing before, let alone been so personally involved in one.

There was indeed a jury and they sat in a box to one side. About half of them appeared to be African-American women and the others were sort of hard to define. After I was sworn, I was apprised of my rights, which I already knew, of course. The assistant prosecutor then started out and produced a bound volume on the report on commission changes, discounting what Blyth Eastman Dillon should do. He asked me if I recognized that document. Of course, I said, "Yes, I wrote it."

Then he asked me various questions, none of which had any real relevance to the world I was involved in. He asked whether I had asked for counsel from other brokerage firms as to what we should do with commissions. My response was that I very carefully avoided that because I was well aware that anything of that sort would be illegal.

After about two or three hours, he finally got to the section of the report where I mentioned the SEC's fixing of the new offering spreads, that one could not discount the spreads, that if one were making a public offering, one had to offer it at the same fixed price to all buyers.

He kept harping on the fixed prices until finally I said, "Sir, it is an SEC rule, and the SEC has ruled that all public offerings must be made at the same price. The underwriters are not allowed under SEC rules to discount that price at all. Only when the syndicate is broken can the stock be freed and sold for what the stock will bring."

Well, that killed that. After a few more questions, I was thanked and excused. By this time it was already past five in the afternoon, and I was bushed.

Our attorney met me outside and we retired to the offices of Eastman Dillon. I had a stiff drink, then dashed for the airport as I was late for a meeting in Washington. My NASD Governor associates during the subsequent few days had a wonderful time debriefing me as to what had happened before the grand jury. My conscience was clear. In fact, going down in the elevator with the lawyer, I made the comment that I had thoroughly enjoyed the experience, having had no problem at all. Somebody apparently from the government was in the elevator, too. He said, "Well, it always helps to have a clear conscience."—Boy, was that true!

Professional Associations
Paying My Dues

Early on, when Bob Evans and I were still with the First California Company, we represented the firm in the Investment Bankers Association - IBA. I gradually made my way up through the Society of Financial Analysts, which had grown in size through the years. The IBA had a California section. Of course, there were large numbers of modest-size investment banking firms in the state at that time. The California IBA met at the Santa Barbara Biltmore, an absolutely glorious, wonderful place. Bob and I always attended those functions, bringing Hilda and Hope with us.

Since Bob and I were leaving First California Company on May 1, 1956, we were not going to be allowed to attend the forthcoming convention of the IBA. I pushed Eastman Dillon higher-ups to realize that we should make ourselves known as quickly as possible, and they pulled out all the stops to get us in the IBA again, this time as representatives of Eastman Dillon. They had to bend the rules a bit, but we found ourselves, inside of six weeks, being able to attend the IBA meeting at the Biltmore.

As a member of the Financial Analysts Society of Los Angeles, I went on the board, working my way up to assistant something-or-other. I was given the job of recruiting the luncheon speakers and decided we should have more money in our treasury. So I arranged to have all the luncheon speakers pick up the tab for the luncheons and we actually made some money for the Biltmore Hotel for the luncheons, plus, we began to develop a decent balance sheet for the Society. I became vice president, then president a year later.

Similarly, over the years, I worked my way up in the Investment Bankers Association. From a board member, I moved up to vice chairman, then chairman. The chairmanship was a pretty big job. I had to organize a meeting at the Santa Barbara Biltmore, which went pretty well. During the year, I also coordinated several cocktail parties. And then I had to conduct the whole damn thing for one year, all the events, which was fun. I wasn't the best chair they ever had, but we got through it somehow. In good times, particularly, it was easier. The last of the great, good years was in 1967 or 1968. The industry was flush, and we had the annual meeting of the investment bankers' society at the Honolulu Hilton in Hawaii for the first and last time.

In the late 1930s, at the insistence of Congress and the Securities Exchange Commission, the securities industry overseer was known as the National Association of Security Dealers, generally known as the NASD. The NASD was headquartered in Washington, and various divisions were set up. The western division was headquartered in San Francisco. Their mandate was to regulate the over-the-counter securities market, the stock exchanges having their own supposed regulatory requirements. Initially there were no requirements in over-the-counter companies being mandated to file company reports, nor did they have to initially file a 10K.

All broker dealers and those dealing in over-the-counter securities had to be registered with the NASD. Various rules were established, particularly one restricting the markup of over the counter stocks to five percent above the offering price available between dealers.

I became very good friends with the head of the west coast NASD. I forget his name, but he was around for years and years and years. He had been in the business in Oregon. He was made out of sheer gold and was as ethical as he could be. While the stock exchange had arbitrated between members, then held arbitration between members and customers to settle disputes, initially, there was no such arrangement for the NASD. So the NASD set up arbitration arrangements in the various divisions.

I was invited to become a member of the western division NASD Arbitration Committee. The committee consisted of five members, two from the industry and three from outside the industry. They wanted to be sure there was complete fairness to those appealing any member argument.

I found membership arbitration fascinating. Most of the cases that came up would be between a stockbroker dealer and an honest customer, indicating of course that the customer was wrong and the dealer was right. We found small dealers marking up securities from ten to twenty percent, with a total spread of maybe as much as twenty to twenty-five percent.

We found one dealer in Pasadena who had two small companies that shared a market he controlled. One was Fletcher Aviation, which had been an airport that had been converted into industrial properties. It was located down at the edge of El Monte. His clientele was primarily elderly widows with plenty of money but not much in the way of intelligence, and he would switch them back and forth between stocks, marking the stocks up to the maximum plus an extra amount, each and every time. We finally nailed him after many long, long, long hearings. After the first two hearings, he simply did not show up, relying upon his attorney to be present. The attorney was not too happy representing his client, who was obviously, guilty as hell.

After several days of this nonsense, the attorney finally told us he had no more questions. We asked him if he had anything more to say and he said, "No."

So we adjourned the hearing, went into a meeting, found Mr. X guilty-guilty- guilty! - then fined him the maximum amount we had ever fined anyone at that time. I believe it was ten thousand dollars, and we were delighted to proceed by simply throwing him out of the business.

When he got word, we were told he screamed bloody murder and threatened to have his attorney disbarred. Thank God, the NASD and SEC both supported our decisions. We had shown the guy to be an unmitigated crook.

His attorney went on to be appointed to the Security Commission of the state of California. He made a good commissioner. In fact, we had the opportunity to meet at a later time.

Bill Burgess, a friend of mine in Los Angeles, had a company called Electronic Specialty Company (ES Co.) that made converters. At the time, they were focusing on converting AC into DC, which made electric razors run more efficiently. Although a company of modest size, ES Co was quite successful and eventually went public. ES Co had many financial difficulties, and went up and down, up and down. They became involved with a product that had some crossover runs and they were about to go belly up.

Somehow Burgess had gotten in touch with U.S. Time Corporation in Waterbury, Connecticut, an old clock company founded in 1857. This was the company that made the Timex watch, which had become extremely successful. U.S. Time was interested in diversifying into electronics and wanted to invest in ES Co to help them out of trouble, giving U.S. Time an opportunity to gain control of the underling.

U.S. Time was prepared to make a substantial capital investment in ES Co, but as a quid pro quo, they wanted an option on the balance of the company's authorized, but unissued shares at the approximate market price. That price was higher than was justifiable, in case ES Co didn't get the loan from U.S. Time Corporation. At the time, California regulation and security issue for California companies said the offering must be "fair, just and equitable"- whatever that meant.

The local office of the California State Security Commission suddenly took the position that the issuance of the options on shares at the existing market price to U.S. Time Corporation would be unfair. They refused to issue the permit. Time was of the essence, so I was asked by Bill Burgess to intervene because I knew the head of the Commission, who just happened to be the lawyer I had met earlier. I agreed that I would go to San Francisco with Burgess to see if I could be of assistance.

The head of U.S. Time Corporation, a Swedish gentleman by the name of Lemkuhl, came to Los Angeles to meet with us so we could all go together. Unfortunately, the weather was abominable and all the flights to San Francisco were cancelled, so Burgess, Lemkuhl and I got on the old Lark (the California coastal train) and took an overnight trip to San Francisco. In the club car over drinks, I got to know Lemkuhl a little. I was fascinated to learn about U.S. Time Corporation, although he was very closed-mouthed and had to be encouraged to talk about the company. Regardless, I was certainly impressed.

In San Francisco we sat down with the commissioner, and in half an hour's time, he threw his hands up and said, "Oh, they're bloody fools! This is a rescue party! The deal that Lemkuhl and U.S. Time want is a real deal. I'll order the issuance of the permit right away."

Mission accomplished, we headed home. The weather was still lousy, so we caught the Lark back to Los Angeles that night. I don't believe we billed Electronics Specialty for anything other than my expenses on the trip up and down. I was so enormously impressed by Lemkuhl, I'm sure that at the time, I considered my efforts to be paid in full with an expense check.

In going through the pink sheets, I happened to look up U.S. Time Corporation and was surprised to see that there was an offering of one hundred sixty-three shares of U.S. Time Corporation for about twenty dollars a share. Only one dealer was offering the stock. My experience in that sort of situation with peer companies is that usually the prices were very reasonable. However, there was nothing on U.S. Time that I could see in any of the security manuals.

I immediately bought the hundred sixty-three shares at the offering price and wondered what I had bought. Several weeks later, the certificate of my purchase came through, and to my amazement, it was not only the shares of U.S. Time Corporation, showing that it had indeed been incorporated in Connecticut in the 1850s, but along with the U.S. Time corporation shares were shares of International Time Corporation, Delaware Time corporation and Timex Limited, a Bermuda corporation. All the shares were tied together.

That meant that no share in one company could be sold without a similar number of shares in the others, being sold as a block. I wrote U.S. Time Corporation for their annual report and soon received a mimeographed page consisting of a balance sheet and a surplus reconciliation. There was no profit and loss statement included in the package. These were the days when over-the-counter companies with modest numbers of shareholders did not have to file anything with the SEC.

When I received a report of Timex Limited of Bermuda, it turned out that U.S. Time Corporation, aka Timex, had transferred all its foreign operations into the Bermuda corporation and they were making various amounts of money with plants around the world. Even then, sales of the Timex watches were highly successful. Being a

Bermuda based corporation that was not a subsidiary of U.S. Time Corporation, they could accumulate money without having to pay U.S. income tax.

The balance sheet of U.S. Time Corporation was pure gold, also. Obviously, they operated the company quite conservatively. There was a limited market in U.S. Time Corporation shares, and the market started going up slowly, slowly, slowly, from thirty to forty to fifty dollars - when all of a sudden, I received word that all three companies were splitting the shares ten for one.

International Time Corporation of Delaware was a nothing company. Since U.S. Time Corporation had such a limited number of shareholders (less than three hundred), they didn't have to file an SEC report. But they were zealous in keeping the number of shareholders below the reporting requirements. (I believe the maximum was five hundred.) Somewhere along the line, I learned from the company that if I ever wanted to sell the shares, the company preferred that I sell the shares back to them rather than offer the shares to the public in the open market.

They informed me that they would pay a small bonus over the public offering price, but they did not want a proliferation of shareholders that would put them under U.S. government and SEC regulatory requirements. Because the shares had appreciated so much, I started giving a few shares as donations to academic institutions such as Cornell and the Harvard Business School with instructions to call the company to sell the shares rather than offer them in the open market. From time to time, I sold a few shares myself - always in the same manner.

In the early 1980s, the personal computer business was beginning to develop. An English promoter had developed an inexpensive computer. The Timex affiliate of U.S. Time Corporation, with a major plant in Scotland, decided to get into the computer business with this product. Apparently, Lemkuhl was once more concerned that somehow the price of the stock and the number of times it had split would force the company to become subject to SEC regulations. So he called upon three major New York investment banking companies to value the shares of U.S. Time Group and made a private offering in order to get all the shares back in.

He had three prices set by the three firms and naturally, chose the highest of the three prices. Then he made a cash offering to all the shareholders, did a squeeze out, and I lost my U.S. Time Corporation shares. The computer business didn't work out, and Timex, which still exists, had some problems recovering from that fiasco. Lemkuhl had to absorb the loss and all the problems that went with it while we stockholders cashed out and smiled all the way to the bank.

With regard to Electronic Specialty Company, Lemkuhl had not bought the whole company, he had merely bought control of the company, and so Bill Burgess continued to run it. With Lemkuhl's consent, Burgess aggressively expanded the company and ES Co grew and grew.

Suddenly, and seemingly out of nowhere, the company was raided by a disreputable raider. Burgess fought as hard as he could. He put the money up and gained control of ES Co. Then Burgess resigned and sold all his stock in the company. The company remained a public company, but in due course, the fellow who had rated it ran it into the ground. There was a total reorganization, a huge scandal, and in the process, Bill Burgess finally got back in. He continued to run the company for a while and eventually retired in Palm Springs.

The Discount Retail Business

In the early 1950s, a group of government employees in Los Angeles got together and decided to form a small buying cooperative. Their idea was to pass on the savings to fellow government employees. They named the company Fedco and the store was successful almost from the start. It was a true cooperative with no shareholders. The members had ownership so that equities might be developed. They opened their co-op to more and more people, and began to opened branches, one of which was in Pasadena. Almost anyone who had any kind of recognizable relationship with the state or the federal government could become a member. Fedco began to receive a great deal of favorable publicity.

Enter Sol Price, a lawyer who was working in the firm of Tony Procopio in San Diego. Price was frustrated with the legal system and wanted desperately to become an entrepreneur. After hearing of Fedco's success, he decided he would try to replicate the co-op in San Diego. He gathered a little capital from eight of his friends and started a company called FedMart. When he opened his first small store in the dock district of San Diego, it was immediately successful - so much so that he decided he had made a mistake in setting it up as a cooperative.

Somehow, in those first few successful weeks, he turned it from a cooperative into a stock corporation. The company was managed spectacularly. Lucky for him, Price didn't know there are many things one should not do in the retail business. Not knowing the business, he did them anyway and wonder of wonders, his strategies were very successful. FedMart grew by leaps and bounds and eventually needed more capital.

At our San Diego office, Bob Evans was introduced to Price and they got along famously. In a very short time, I was writing up a resume on FedMart. A statement was filed with Eastman Dillon Union Securities as the lead underwriter; the deal came, was very successful, and went to a premium.

My associate George Jessic had worked on the prospectus. He was so taken by Sol Price that when Sol made George an offer he couldn't refuse, (nor one we could meet) - George left us to become Price's assistant for FedMart.

The company grew rapidly, opening a number of branches in California, Arizona and Texas. And Sol Price realized his dream. He had become an entrepreneur. He really wanted to own real estate, and rather than renting stores, Price put more money into real estate for his stores. He knew that real estate would be a solid asset although real estate ties up liquid assets, which can be a problem.

To join FedMart, as was the case with Fedco, consumers were required to pay a small two-dollar admission fee, but almost anybody could get a permanent membership without having to be a government employee. But Price wasn't through as a visionary.

Somewhere, Price got the idea that a life insurance company would be profitable, particularly if he had the types of customers who were middle-aged and long-lived. So FedMart created a life insurance company and we raised capital for the life insurance company. The stock in that company also took off.

Bob Evans had gone on the board of directors of FedMart when the company went public, whereas I got the monthly financials. We didn't have much contact with George Jessic anymore, as he was pretty close to Sol who was very aggressive. Finally, Price discovered that he had too much involved in real estate and the insurance business turned out to be tougher than he thought it would be. They began to miss projections and Bob Evans became unhappy. I tried to cover write-ups on the company, but I really couldn't do it because the company was so busy with projections. We began to lose confidence in Sol because his interests were too widespread and he couldn't focus.

Finally, he pushed us to do a favorable write-up on his company and do some further financing. Bob and I agreed we could not write something recommending the company, so Bob was *sort of* invited off the board of directors. FedMart transferred its business over to the Stotts firm. Of course, the Stotts manager very respectfully asked if we would object to their taking over Fed Mart's business and Bob, with a heartfelt sigh of relief said, "Please feel free to talk to Sol. It's quite all right and I understand completely."

Stotts proceeded to do a write-up on FedMart. I don't recall whether they did any financing or not, but the FedMart figures started getting worse and worse as Sol continued to miss his projections. He was over-extended in his real estate and his company got in a tremendous amount of financial trouble. It became evident that FedMart would need to be taken over.

A German entrepreneur had begun buying more and more stock in FedMart until he eventually gained control. He had a couple of rows with Sol Price, and finally forced him out. Sol had been smart enough to insist on an employment contract so he brought a suit against the German and was successful in winning a judgment.

Nevertheless, the German did take control of FedMart, and stories began circulating about how Herr so-and-so required his employees to stand at their desks at attention when he came into the office. FedMart went down, down, down, and was finally liquidated.

One would think that Sol's disaster in being forced out of his own company would have put him out of the retail business, but he was a survivor. In a relatively short time, he bounced back. He still thought that he could make a deal if he could sharpen up the discount operation so in 1976, he and his son Robert raised two and a half million dollars to start a new company in San Diego called Price Club. The warehouse was located on Morena Boulevard in a remodeled airplane hangar.

Once again, he was spectacularly successfully. Although he lost three-quarters of a million dollars the first year, he expanded into two locations with nine hundred employees and made a profit in 1979 of a million dollars.

Price had learned from his earlier mistakes and had surrounded himself with better merchandising people. He was very aggressive and the Price Club grew rapidly throughout the state of California. It became a public company in 1980 and the stock multiplied like a rabbit. Four years later, Price Club sales exceeded a billion dollars. The Price Club stores were much larger and the pricing was indeed aggressive. He had changed the business from the standard retail store selling at discounts to introducing new departments and services: pharmacies, gasoline stations, and the like.

Ultimately, Price Club gained the attraction of a similar company that opened up in the Pacific Northwest Seattle area. It was called Costco. Costco made a hefty offer and in 1993, acquired Price Club. Costco has become a very successful operation and continues to be a very strong company.

Earlier I talked about Bob Evans having done the underwriting for the Thrifty Drug Store Company. This company was operated by the Boruns brothers. The Thrifty drugstore chain became very successful in the western United States, and Bob was on the board of directors, but after a while, Thrifty began having some problems. The Boruns were aggressive, having started in the 1930s with one drugstore and eventually creating a chain of fifty. The Walgreen drugstore chain, located out of Chicago, wanted to move into California, and when Bob found out, he negotiated the acquisition of Thrifty by Walgreen's.

The Boruns thought that if the person with whom they were negotiating was not in tears by the end of the meeting, they had not made a tight enough deal. They were so tight that the private-placement bond issue Bob negotiated finally wound up with an interest rate expressed in a sixteenth as the fraction, rather than the usual eighth or quarter of one percent.

The Walgreen deal was negotiated tight-tight-tight, subject to due diligence by Walgreen. They started their due diligence and it wasn't long before we started looking at merchandise behind the front counter and on the shelves only to discover that most of the merchandise was dated or dusty. When Walgreen found out, they quietly pulled out of the deal. Bob recognized that the Walgreen pullout was justifiable and never raised serious objections. His trust in the Boruns was certainly reduced.

Bob used to tell the story about how, after the appeal of prohibition, he and some friends started a small distillery out here on the coast. He said they made some liquor and the Boruns wanted to sell it in their liquor department at Thrifty. But Bob said, "That whole place is so damn tight, we'd never make a dime off of those guys!"

He closed up the distillery and for years, every time we'd drive down to San Diego and go by where the distillery had been, he'd tell the story of how Thrifty squeezed him dry.

At a much later date, long before the Blyth-Eastman Dillon merger, the Boruns were aging and expressed interest in liquidating their estate, so Blyth and Company negotiated the sale of Thrifty to the Southern California Edison Company. Edison wanted to have a business in which seasonality was not tied into their profits. They believed that Thrifty would be the answer. Certainly, Blyth did not discourage them. This strategy, however, turned out to be a disaster. Public utility companies do not know how to run businesses. And the drugstore business and the electrical business were poles apart. Thrifty spiraled down to the ground until finally, Edison sold it to somebody at an enormous discount from the price at which they had purchased it a few years before.

~

One of my least happy experiences involved a fine young man who, with his wife, set out from New York to establish a municipal department in the Los Angeles office. They stayed at our house for a while when they first came out. They were fine people, but unfortunately, over the years, the department did not work out. Not long before the Blyth acquisition, New York decided that the municipal department in Los Angeles should be drastically reduced in size. This young man (whom I shall call Joe) had been made a partner of the firm. It was decided in New York that because of the failure to perform for the department he would be asked to resign his partnership.

In November in the early 1970s, I received a call from Jack Powers in New York, who is in charge of all the sales, saying that Joe was going to have to be relieved of his partnership. He said that the fellow would be asked to stay on, but probably would resign. Jack said, "Of course he works for you. So do you want me to come out and tell him this or would you do it?"

Obviously he did not want to do it. *I* certainly didn't want to do it, but as head of the region, I figured this was a duty I could not shirk as much as I hated the thought of delivering the news. Joe had already been advised that his department was not up to snuff, that he was losing money, but he was unable to correct matters. I put it off as long as I could, realizing that Christmas was coming up, so finally, a day or two after New Years, I called him into my office, sat him down and closed the door.

I said, "I'm sorry, but New York has decided that they must ask for your resignation as a partner because the municipal department has been losing money and does not appear to be turning around."

Although Joe had been warned that things had to be improved, he had never thought it would come to this. This news was obviously a shock to him. And it was terrible for me. What I didn't realize at the time was that his mother had been visiting he and his wife during the holidays and was going back east the next day. He knew he would have to tell her that he had been asked to resign his partnership. I never had any few days as bad as those leading up to when I had to sit down face to face, with this nice young man, and tell him the bad news. It was very difficult indeed. As we had anticipated, he decided to not stay on and resigned.

Two and a half months later, when we became Blyth Eastman Dillon, INA offered to buy a significant interest of the firm. Soon our stock was being bought out by INA at a very satisfactory price.

A number of months later, after the INA deal, a lawsuit was filed against Blyth Eastman Dillon, of course naming me, and claiming that Joe, our former partner, had been fired so the remaining partners would see a significant increase in the light of the forthcoming INA acquisition.

Under NYSE rules, the subject went to arbitration before the New York Stock Exchange. I was called back to New York to testify. The arbitration was held in the New York Exchange office building, adjacent to the Exchange. The arbitrators were all required to be members or allied members of the Exchange. This young man insisted we had cheated him by forcing to turn back his partnership.

I knew Joe's attorney well. He was well regarded in Los Angeles, and he did a pretty good job of representing the young man. On the other hand, we had the facts to present to the arbitrators, and they understood exactly what went on; the securities industry is a fickle business. It was a really difficult situation. Joe was there and he was not happy. I certainly was not happy and Jack Power was also not happy.

We had made a very valid claim that the INA set up of Blyth really had come up out of the blue, we had no discussion of it until early spring. However, Joe's attorney made a good point of our decision to let Joe go, having been decided in late November, and that we had not told him about the decision until January third or so.

He asked why we had waited and suggested that it was because we knew of the forthcoming Blyth merger. There's an adage in the legal business that an attorney should not ask a question of a witness unless he knows in advance what the answer is going to be. I told the arbitrators that we agreed to delay the actual notice until after Christmas and I waited until a day or two after New Years to tell him, because I did not want to destroy his Christmas. The attorney paled at hearing that answer, and the arbitrators obviously fully absorbed it. In a short time they handed their ruling down, denying Joe's request for compensation in the amount of what he would have received had he still been a partner when the merger took place.

Jim and John

After Jim graduated from eighth grade at Polytechnic School, we began researching boarding schools. The local high schools weren't all that good, and in looking around at private schools, we found two that might do.

One was Cate School, which was founded as Santa Barbara School in 1910. It was renamed for its founders in 1950. We also discovered Thacher School. From its very beginnings in 1889, Thacher had a solid reputation for its academics. Located in the Ojai Valley, the campus is eighty-five miles north of Los Angeles. Thacher was not posh by any means. Their buildings were quite rough. They had horses on the property, and a decrepit old barn called the rough house. Once Jim saw all of that, however, he was sold. So Jim entered boarding school for his freshman year at Thacher.

Hilda and I quickly became familiar with the two-hour drive from San Marino. The Ojai Valley is beautiful, running all the way up from the Pacific Ocean between Santa Barbara and Ventura. It was a hard route driving along the hillside. Of course, there was no freeway in those days. We would drive part way, up through Newhall, and turn off onto the highway then onto an overpass that ran by some stinking old oil fields. It was easy to tell that there were sulfur springs in the vicinity. This was the site of the first oil development in California. It began in the 1870s and started what eventually became the Union Oil Company. We would drive on, coming up over the hill and down into the old white valley where Thacher was located.

Jim settled into boarding school right away, displaying no apparent homesickness. It seemed that the Thacher administration

267

believed a boy could learn a great deal of discipline by having to care for a horse. I never thought I would end up buying a horse in my lifetime, especially a second-hand horse, but I did. He didn't cost much, a couple hundred dollars at the most. The horses had been in the Thacher School family generation after generation, so there was no adjustment period for them, either. Jim didn't seem to mind taking care of the horse, although I believe he was a bit relieved when the time came that as an upperclassman, he no longer had to spend part of his busy days mucking out the stall.

Jim did well at Thacher, especially in the sciences, even taking a summer science course one year. And early on in beginnings of the computer age, he learned how to operate the new equipment.

Since summer camp had offered me such a wealth of experiences as a boy, I wanted to be sure my sons had the same opportunities. We sent Jim to Camp Agawam in Maine for two summers, in 1952 and '53. The camp is located on Crescent Lake in Casco, Maine. Camp Agawam is one of the oldest summer camps in the country, having been developed in 1919.

Thacher School owned a camp in Northern California on the east side of the San Joaquin Valley. Camp Silver Pines was way up in the High Sierra. In 1954, we enrolled Jim and he had a great time. Naturally, the camp was very rustic. Other than muddy water, there was not much else, but he loved it. John got to join him at Silver Pines the next summer.

I had recently purchased a brand new Lincoln Continental, a huge, long car. In those days, cars did not come with air-conditioning, so I had air-conditioning installed and Hilda and John and I took off for the north by way of San Francisco. We were going to pick up Jim after camp.

All I remember is driving into Redding, California and the car being insufferably hot. I was cursing the air-conditioner for not being able to work, that is until we stopped at a gas station and while I was opening the hood to check everything, I happened to look up at the temperature on the window of the gas station store and realized it was a hundred ten degrees. No wonder that poor air-conditioner couldn't keep the temperature in the car down!

After cooling the car and ourselves a bit, we drove on up into the mountains along a lumbering road, and I was pleased that the car made it all the way to Camp Silver Pines. Just as we were parking, we saw Jim coming across the little pond in a rowboat. He rowed us over to the camp and we spent a night there in a poor excuse for a guest cabin. It was damn cold and damn uncomfortable. There was no hot water for a shower or anything of that sort, but the boys loved it, of course. John followed in Jim's footsteps and went to camp there later on.

The next time we went up there, however, we flew into Redding, rented a car in Redding and drove Mr. Hertz's car up that rough road. When we flew back from Redding to San Francisco, we checked into the Clift Hotel. I am sure we looked pretty scruffy, but they accepted us because I had been there many times after I had started going to San Francisco for First California Company. In earlier years, I had always stayed at the St. Francis Hotel, which my father preferred, but when Hilda's father was doing some work on the San Francisco school system, he suggested The Clift.

He was right. It was a much better hotel and of course, in those days, fifteen or twenty dollars a night was what you paid for a good hotel room.

When Jim graduated from Thacher, we took a tour of colleges in the east. We arrived at Cornell on a beautiful morning, and again, he made up his mind right away. The other colleges that we visited were nothing in comparison, partly because he had already decided that Cornell was the place for him.

Jim quickly learned to cope with winter, and before long, he was telling us that *everybody* at Cornell had a car. After a great deal of persuasion, Hilda and I relented, and Jim bought a British two-seater, four-cylinder Sunbeam Alpine. He dearly loved that little car and drove it a number of times cross-country. ROTC at Cornell was still required and Jim signed on for Air Force ROTC. By the time of his senior year, he had earned the rank of squadron commander.

Jim had learned to fly in southern California at El Monte airport, but he didn't fly much at Cornell. He was heavily involved in other things, mainly rowing. Jim was very active in the Cornell rowing crew, which was in those years quite successful.

Having chosen mechanical engineering, a rather difficult academic program, he was doing double duty by also participating in such a highly demanding physical sport. But Jim worked hard at both.

He didn't make the first rowing crew, but the second crew at Cornell was pretty damn good in those days. He started when there was ice on the lake and kept rowing until the lakes became so iced up, the lightweight rowing boats wouldn't make it anymore.

Phi Delta Theta wanted to pledge Jim. The engineering campus was close to the Phi Delt house when I was there, but the new engineering campus was at the far end of the main campus and a long way from the Phi Delts. Kappa Alpha, on the other hand, had a brand new house right down the ravine from engineering, and whatever the final reason, Jim chose Kappa.

Jim certainly proved to have his grandfather's architectural genes. As a young kid, he was fascinated by the construction of the log house next to our home on California, and then when the pool house on Oak Grove was being built, he was there all the time, helping the construction workers as much as they would let him. At school, there were a couple areas of the Kappa Alpha house which he thought needed improvement, so he and his roommate took down some country-brick walls, moved things around and renovated a few rooms all by themselves.

In June 1965, John graduated from Thacher and Jim graduated from Cornell. Jim had already been accepted in the graduate program at Stanford University in aero/astronautics. He signed up for a large course load in order to graduate in only nine months because he wanted to start pilot training in June of 1966. However, this summer, he was scheduled to work for the Douglas Aircraft Company. He was to work on the extension for the DC-8.

Periodically Jim would stop off at Long Beach Airport where he learned to fly a helicopter. One day he took me to the airport where we rented a helicopter for an hour and a half. He piloted me all over eastern Los Angeles and even over San Marino. We flew up to Mt. Wilson and landed right on top! Even though Mt. Wilson is surrounded by desert, as much as ten feet of snow has been recorded on Mt. Wilson. It is the site of some of the most important discoveries in astronomical history. The 100-inch telescope was completed in 1917 and held the record as the world's largest telescope until 1947. What a view from there!

Taking off again, we flew all around. It was funny going around in a little bubble helicopter. Of course, Jim was the pilot and he didn't trust me to fly the craft. Rightly so because helicopters are infinitely trickier to fly than airplanes, but I would probably have managed.

After graduating with a master's from Stanford in the summer of 1966, Jim joined the Air Force to begin his pilot training. He was sent to Laredo, Texas where he went through basic compliance school, even though he was qualified to fly, already. He kept quiet about his helicopter ability, but he worked very hard and did very well. He was number one in his class so he had first choice of what he wanted to do and where he wanted to go after graduation. He wanted to fly bigger airplanes and chose the C-141, which was then by far the largest transport plane the Air Force had.

Jim flew C-141s for three or four years as co-pilot, working his way up to aircraft commander. He flew all over the world making some of the most unique deliveries, not only for the military but also for the State Department.

Once, he delivered a snowmobile to the Shah of Iran just before the Shah got kicked out. It was more like a small snow weasel, according to Jim, and was a New Years gift from Nixon. Most people are not aware that at the time there was lots of skiing in Iran. There are several tall mountains in the country. He also delivered some sort of brewing device to South Africa, took a load of barbed wire from Korea to Vietnam, all kinds of weird things.

Occasionally his plane flew as backup for Air Force One, with a lot of Secret Service officers on board. Jim's unit was based on Norton Air Force Base, in the foothills right next to San Bernardino. He was only a hundred miles east of San Marino, so he came home occasionally. He had worn the legs off that little Sunbeam Alpine, so he got rid of it and bought a Mustang. Once while driving down from a lake, he was forced off the road and the Mustang was totaled. He replaced it with a Cougar, which was destined to become Hilda's car when he went off to Vietnam.

All Air Force officers were required to do a stint in Vietnam, so Jim was eventually shipped out to Vietnam with great trepidation on the part of his mother. He was assigned to a super-secret reconnaissance detail. He flew an EC-47, the military version of the DC-3. They used that plane from 1966 – 1974 throughout Southeast Asia during the Vietnam Conflict. The EC-47 was packed full of *super-super-secret* equipment. Jim was not allowed to enter the back of the airplane in case he was forced down. He had no knowledge of what they kept back there.

Some of the bases from which he flew were safe. On other ones he had to live in bunkers and was prohibited from spending any time with others on the base. Jim flew the EC-47 for a full year and flew a mission, which had taken him into a restricted area. For his service, he received the Flying Cross. Because of the way he earned it, his citation is still classified!

After a year, he came back to the States to McQuire AFB in New Jersey where he instructed on C-141s but he continued to fly to Vietnam, which certainly didn't make Hilda happy. I believe Jim would have liked to stay on as a test pilot for the Air Force, but he left the military and went to work for the Federal Aviation Administration in at JFK Airport in New York. He became a civil air carrier inspector assigned to Eastern Airlines.

During that time, we had an emergency at home. My mother was visiting. Hilda was standing across the street from our home trying to direct my mother's driver so he wouldn't hit another parked car. Unfortunately, the driver backed into Hilda and the accident crushed her leg terribly, just above the knee. She was fairly crippled after that and rarely traveled anymore.

Jim did not care for the government bureaucracy and happily, in June 1972, he had an offer from Eastern Airlines to work on training programs for the DC-9 and the Electra. He was actually hired by former astronaut Frank Borman who had retired from the U.S. Air Force. In December 1970, Borman was named Senior Vice President of the Operations Group. He wanted to build up a staff of administrators with qualifying experience.

Jim was ideal for that job, so he started with Eastern in Miami. However, Eastern was operating under union rules, and of course, Jim had no seniority. After a while, Eastern experienced budgetary cutbacks and was forced to relieve personnel with less seniority, regardless of their capabilities.

Jim had trained some pilots for Air Jamaica, which was being operated by Air Canada, and they liked his work so much that they offered Jim a job starting as captain. Naturally, the union made a complaint that the job should go to someone with seniority, but Air Jamaica was beyond their touch, so Jim began as a captain and flew

DC-9s from New York, Philadelphia, Washington, Toronto, Buffalo, and occasionally Detroit and Syracuse, ending up in various ports in Jamaica.

In 1980, Jim was offered another deal with Eastern. He could have gone back earlier, but he was doing so well with Air Jamaica, he stayed with them for six years. But Eastern was buying bigger airplanes and Jim was interested. Eastern had acquired some DC-10s for a route they had purchased from another airline that had gone belly up and they had bought some routes in South America and also started service from Miami to London. It was a terrible mistake. Jim was trained on the DC-10, but later, Eastern realized they couldn't afford to keep those planes operational after all, so they cut down the route and Jim got transferred to the Lockheed 1011.

Eastern was raided by Frank Lorenzo who had run Trans Texas and Continental into the ground, then took control and started looting Eastern for benefit of the revitalized Continental Airlines. Jim flew the London flights a number of times until Eastern sold that route to Braniff, another one of Lorenzo's deals. Jim ended up flying DC-10s from Miami to Buenas Aires to Santiago, Chile, primarily, until Eastern lost the right to land in Peru for some reason.

Meanwhile, he was living in an apartment in Miami and one day at the pool, fate changed his life. He met Judy. They began dating and in short order became engaged. Hilda and I went to Miami for the wedding. Jim bought a townhouse on a lake on the southwest side of Miami. After living there for a year or two, Judy became pregnant and they bought a lot further down in the SW corner of Miami. Jim and Judy started building a house—and I mean *really building a house!* They did a vast amount of work themselves, building their house to California standards designed to withstand hurricanes and such, which it successfully did over the years.

There were a few empty lots in his area, one in particular across the street. Jim was concerned someone might build a house that was not to his liking, so he started building a house on spec. Before he had finished it, he had it sold! Once people saw that house, they asked him to build others, so he ended up building six or seven other houses in that general area—all custom-built houses. Each one was brought in way under cost. They weren't built on concrete blocks, which was typical for Florida real estate at that time, but truly built to California

273

standards and quality. All of them stood up to the various hurricanes that have hit since that time.

In the meantime, the drug situation in Miami was getting worse and worse. There were some escapades near Jim's house that he wasn't very happy about, so he decided he wanted to bring Judy back to California, particularly since he could commute from California to Miami with his flights. He bought a house on two lots right on a golf course here in Pasadena. He lived in the house and had the lots legally separated, then started building another new home on the vacant lot next to the one he lived in. He built that house beautifully; it's enormously efficient. He lives there today. When he moved into the new house, he sold the first one.

He commuted to Miami regularly. In fact, the airline liked it because he was always in L.A. as a standby. He continued to fly Miami to Buenos Aires and sometimes had to make tight connections to make it up on the flight up from Buenos Aires to catch the flight from Miami to Los Angeles, but he almost always made it.

Finally, Frank Lorenzo got into a hassle with the airline mechanics who threatened to strike and close the airline down. Lorenzo stonewalled the mechanics who were true to their word. For all practical purposes, that put Eastern out of business. There were a few non-union pilots that hung around. Jim was not union but he did obey the union rules. The mechanics were right. Jim continued to work with Eastern until their demise in 1989 and as fortune would have it, at least for me, agreed to come to work with me in my office in the investment banking business.

Dwight James Baum II – "Jim" - showing off his homebuilt replica
of the 1901 Oldsmobile

Jim with his pilot training class in Laredo, TX in 1966.

Jim receiving his aircraft commander award in 1969: USAF C-141

Jim's wonderful family: (l to r) Dwight J. Baum III, Jim's wife Judy, daughter Lauren and Jim (Dwight J. Baum II) in 1997.

Backtracking to the fall of 1965, we'll catch up on John's life. He had been accepted at the University of California of Los Angeles and the Berkeley campus as well. He made a very wise decision and chose the University of California at Davis. That was a good decision because for one thing, the Davis campus was very calm. This was a time of the campus riots and those sorts of incidents were particularly engendered by the *gentle folk* up there at UC Berkeley. U C Davis had been originally an agricultural school but had fully developed into a university, so the social environment was different. John took engineering there and learned to fly. He even headed up the aviation club at UC Davis and got his commercial license there.

When he graduated, with a Bachelor of Science in Aeronautical Engineering, he got a job with the Lockheed Aircraft Company, working on the brand new Lockheed 1011 jet transport. The plane wasn't yet in production, but he continued to haunt the employment offices of the various airlines, particularly United Airlines. They used to say it was hard to get him out of their heads, he was calling them so often. He started working for United as a flight engineer.

Very early on, at John's first flight after his graduation from United Flight Training School, I was bound for New York on the noon flight out of LAX . I drove to the airport, walked up the steps to get into this brand new DC-8, and there at the door of the airplane was this fine young man who said, "Welcome aboard The Friendly Skies, Mr. Baum."

It was none other than *John E. Baum* and it was his first flight as flight engineer for United Airlines. I was in first class, of course! The captain saw me talking to John in the doorway and asked who I was. John said, "That's my dad." The captain invited me up to the cockpit. I stayed in the cockpit all during the taxi run and out to the takeoff point, where I returned to my seat. It was a wonderful experience, indeed. Prior to the flight, John had called home and Hilda had said she thought I was going to be on that flight. That's why he knew to be at the door to welcome me on board.

By that time, Jim had left the Air Force and was working for the FAA as an Air Carrier Inspector based out of JFK. And with the depression in early 1971, John got furloughed from United and so he also worked out of JFK for a few months as a sky marshal for the U.S. Treasury Department, enforcing the Air Piracy Act. Those were the days hijackers were trying so desperately to get into Cuba. They weren't terrorists and weren't really interested in killing people: They were just determined to get to Cuba one way or another. Jim and John roomed together with another pilot for about six months in a townhouse in Greenwich, Connecticut. Then Jim was hired to fly for Eastern and moved to Miami while John was hired back by United as an Inflight Services Supervisor based in Los Angeles. Among his duties was the supervision of the flight attendant crew on the jumbo jets. He did that for around six years.

Once I flew to New York with John as the Inflight Supervisor and he introduced me to a number of young ladies. When we got to New York, I invited John and several of the young women to the Algonquin Hotel for drinks at the bar. It was a *cold, cold, cold* winter day! We walked all the way up Seventh Avenue near the park then down to the Algonquin. One of these ladies happened to be named Mindy. After that, John started seeing her more and more and more and guess what? She is now Mindy Baum - Mrs. John E. Baum! She had come to visit with him from time to time to our home in San Marino. We loved having her. Hilda and Mindy got along just dandy. And I came home one night from a trip and on the dining room table was a note in Hilda's handwriting. It said simply, "John and Mindy just got married!"

John got back into the cockpit as a flight engineer, then was promoted to first officer and finally graduated to be a full-time captain, flying the 737s and the shuttle, which he loved.

Captain John E. Baum

Hilda and Mindy. They got along fine.

Mindy and I during our travels.

The Baum Family Travels

Having collected a lifetime of fascinating memories from traveling with my family as a child, I wanted to be sure that my family had that same experience. And travel was a wonderful balance to my work.

Early in January 1954, Hilda and I took a two-week vacation to Guatemala and Costa Rica. It was a rich cultural experience. We stayed at the Hotel San Carlos in Guatemala and on the first full day of our trip, we hired a car and drove to the romantic colonial city of Antigua ending up at the Chichoy Pass. There we enjoyed the magnificent view of Lake Atitlan that rests five thousand feet below the pass. It was so incredibly beautiful that we returned to Lake Atitlan a couple days later to visit the fascinating Indian village.

We flew via Pan American to San Salvador where we toured El Boqueron, a volcanic crater, again, a magnificent view. We visited the Archeological Museum and went on to the Tropical Experimental Station, which I especially enjoyed. We spent the last few days of our trip in San Jose, Costa Rica.

In October 1960, while the boys were safely at school, Hilda and I went on a month-long trip to the Orient, traveling to Bangkok, Hong Kong and Japan. We took four half-day tours and visited the Temples of Bangkok, the Royal Palace and especially enjoyed the early morning tour of the klongs (canals).

We left Hong Kong on a midnight steamer to Macao and had a private stateroom on the boat. In Tokyo, we stayed in the new wing of the Imperial Hotel and the next morning visited the Imperial Palace

Plaza. We liked the Orient so very much that we returned twice over the next six years.

In 1966, on our last visit, we stayed at the brand new Mandarin Hotel. We were in a hotel in Osaka, Japan when we saw a painting entitled, "A Brief Moment" by Okada, a Japanese artist. We had been looking for a large painting to hang over our living room mantle above the fireplace but it had to be exactly the right size. We looked at the painting, then at each other. Without speaking a word, we both knew it was the right one. We had it shipped back to the States and it has been in the living room for more than thirty-five years.

We toured Singapore then went on to Perth, in western Australia. We spent a couple days time, rented a car and drove into the outback. We had a marvelous time. I'll never forget how strange it was to drive in Melbourne. I became hopelessly lost trying to get out of the city. I couldn't figure out what was wrong. I suddenly realized I was disoriented because of the shift in compass. The sun was in the north, not in the south. We got ourselves properly oriented, drove to Canborough and visited a wonderful museum there. We attended an hour-long session at the historian parliament, which is not at all sedate like our congressional meetings; not even as *tempered* as the raucous House of Parliament in London. What an experience!

Although the years have dimmed the chronology, there were so many moments I would never forget. I recall during one visit, in June of 1961, Hilda and I took the boys to Europe. We drove from Copenhagen to Hamburg then to Berlin. Jim was seventeen and John was fourteen. During the trip we took an auto-ferry. Once we drove off the ferry, we hadn't gotten very far before it became dark. There was a terrible rainstorm.

We finally found an inn where we chose to have dinner at the bar. After we had settled the boys into their room for the night, Hilda and I started paying canasta and to the amazement of a large number of Germans, we sat and played for about two and a half hours…Familiar things in a foreign land. In Berlin we stayed at the Kempinski Hotel.

Even before the wall went up, access to East Berlin wasn't easy at the time we visited. One of the things I remember was the famous Aus Vaterland nightclub where I had gone with my parents in 1931 and later with Jim Wyld and Bill Harry in 1936. It had been destroyed in the fighting in Berlin in 1945.

There was a large military presence throughout Berlin. But the nightclub had been rebuilt and was now called the Vassergarden (Water Garden) and featured *dancing waters*. Of course, Vassergarden was frequented by Germans as well as lots of tourists. In addition to the spectacle of the dancing fountain waters, which were choreographed to lights and music, there were other attractions at the Dancing Waters.

There were telephones between the tables and there were even tubes so you could send message between the tables. To use the telephone, you dialed it right from the tables, but if you wished to use the tubes, you had to go to a central place where the messages were dispatched to the recipients.

Jim spotted an attractive young lady there, and went up to ask her to dance. Actually, he was a pretty good dancer. They started talking and before we knew it, he was sitting at her table. He decided that when Hilda, John and I were ready to go back to the hotel, he would remain with his newfound lady friend. Hilda, of course, being a protective mother, had qualms about leaving him, but we agreed that he could stay.

We went back to the hotel and Jim finally strolled in around three in the morning. He'd had a wonderful time. I believe his new friend was from East Germany. Once we returned to the states, she and Jim carried on a correspondence for a while, but it eventually died off as most long-distance relationships do.

We traveled to Frankfurt where I picked up a Mercedes 220 at the airport. We drove on to Nuremburg, to Munich and Lichtenstein, and visited a few other towns before we flew to France. When we arrived in Paris, neither Jim nor John were too thrilled because the menu was completely in French and they didn't know what they were ordering. I remember when we got to London, Jim said, "Finally! We'll be able to read the menu!"

Unfortunately, at the first fancy restaurant we went to in London, there was more French on the menu than there had been in Paris. We had a good laugh over that. In London we stayed at the Stafford. We moved on to Copenhagen, where we had a terrific time at the Tivoli. The birds rode on the handlebars of people's bicycles all around Copenhagen. It's really a beautiful city and we had a wonderful time there.

In the summer of 1962, when John was fifteen and still a student at Thacher, I took him to Athens, Greece. We hired a driver to take us all over the peninsula. Our guide told us endless stories about Greek mythology, all in broken English, of course. He would be relating some great myth, then we would come upon some great architecture. He would interrupt himself by saying, "A parenthesis!--" Then he would proceed to tell us about the historical significance of that particular building or scene before continuing on with his tale. John enjoyed him as much as I did.

After spending some time in Athens, we went down the Peloponissos River, crossed the mountains over to Sparta then to Olympus. We took a boat across the water to a landing where we could see the Delphi Ruins, one of the most beautiful, fantastic places in Greece. Then we made our way on up to Delphi, which I always considered to be the most glorious place in Greece. After visiting Delphi, we returned to Athens and flew on to Izmir, Turkey. That was quite an experience. Everybody in Greece kept telling us that if we really planned on going to Turkey, we would be killed by the Turks. When we got to Izmir, everyone there kept saying, "You mean you've been to Greece and they didn't *kill* you? How lucky you are!"

Izmir is a beautiful port city. We stayed at a hotel called Killum, which I thought was quite appropriate for what we had been hearing. We had a great time.

John and I were taking in the sights, strolling past a club and a fellow tried to pull me in saying, "Come on in, this is the *best clip joint*!" I told him I wasn't interested and we continued on to a hotel to have a good dinner. On the way back, the same thing happened. John and I returned to our own hotel and after I was sure he was carefully tucked in, I went back to see the *best clip joint* in Izmar. I had a tape recorder with me because I wanted to record some of their live music.

I sat down at the bar and to my surprise, one of the proprietors came up to me. He spoke very good English. I had three beers and taped some music, and when I reached into my pocket to pay my tab, the owner said, "No, no, it's on the house." I don't know why he did that to this day, but what fun!

John and I went on to Zurich the next day, then on to Rome. We were sitting at a table on the Via Venuto and I was quietly having a drink. We were relaxing, soaking up the scenery, when a couple came by and the young man started patting his girlfriend's backside. John's eyes got as big as saucers and I had a good laugh over that.

Our next stop was Istanbul. There we boarded a Russian ship on the Black Sea Line. It took us four days to go to Varna, then Bulgaria. The ship was filled with a multi-cultural staff. They spoke a conglomeration of languages. It was an exceptional experience for John. We had to share a bathroom with the people from the cabin next to us. That was a strange experience for John as well, to share a very private room with strangers who didn't even speak our language. John and I decided that we were probably the only Americans on board.

While at sea, a man died on board. We were told he was a very prominent figure with the Communist party. Evidently, he was en route to Russia for heart surgery. The Bulgarians organized an honor guard and coordinated quite an elaborate event to remove the deceased. We had to disembark and wait two hours while they dealt with their emergency.

It was a hot day so we found at a café by the harbor where we could have a cold drink. An interesting looking elderly gentleman came by. We were told he could only speak four words in English. He came up to us and wrote on a piece of paper—*108!*

After much gesturing, we finally discovered that he was trying to tell us the old man in the corner of the café' was a hundred and eight years old. We had heard that people in Bulgaria enjoyed longevity but this was really something. The man was pretty well preserved, just sitting there nonchalantly, enjoying his drink. We were soon allowed to return to the ship and resume our travels.

After a brief stop in Romania, we went on to Yalta where we met a writer who did a fine job of showing us the video palace where the summits were held. The royal palace is also there. Our guide explained the backgrounds and what noble families had occupied the palaces and how they had been occupied by the Nazis: Also, amazingly, how in a few weeks' time, the palaces had been restored to good condition for the Yalta conference.

The Sierra Yalta was fine and it was easy to see how in the old days it was a wonderful resort area, but aside from that, not much could be recommended other than the general scenery. The beach was not sand, but rather rubble - like flat slate or stones. The beach was occupied by a large number of Russians. And if I may offer the observation --- Russian ladies are not made for bathing suits!

There were large crowds of patriotic prize-winning Russian workers and their families at the beach and none of them looked very happy. The accommodations were about tenth rate, although compared with the accommodations in Moscow that I had seen before, they didn't seem that bad.

John and I took a trip on a Russian hydro-flier. The operator was really very good, dashing up and down the coast at high speed. We drove us to a place where there was a cave at water level. He dashed into the cave and at the very last minute, put the boat in reverse and brought the boat to a complete stop inside the cave. It scared the B*ejeesus* out of John and me!

After our hair-raising experience, we wanted something a bit calmer. We saw what appeared to be a large, well-illuminated restaurant on a hilltop far above Yalta. We took a taxi up there to have dinner and it was a typical Russian place with the guests all speaking various languages, most of which we heard was the expression, "Nyet." The view was fantastic and the beer was okay.

I went looking for the bathroom which turned out to be an outhouse. It was a short distance from the restaurant. I went inside and discovered the most horrific public bathroom I had ever seen—at least as bad as the one I saw outside the Great Wall of China. It was ghastly—no running water or anything. I couldn't believe the Russians operated like that. I warned John that if he needed to go to the bathroom, he should go find a bush—it would be infinitely more sanitary.

There was no airport at Yalta, so we took a long car ride across the mountains and down to the flatland on the peninsula which joining the main part of the Ukraine. Then there was the Crimea. Then we boarded a plane. I'm thinking it was a TU-104. The plane had the typical mesh nets up ahead and up on top, and I believe only some of the seats had seatbelts. I think we may have had the last seats in the airplane; even perhaps that they may have kicked somebody off to put us on board, for some reason, but off we went to Moscow. The flight was uneventful. We stayed in Moscow four days. John and I flew to Moscow two summers in a row. It was fascinating.

When we arrived, we were taken to the Ukrainia Hotel. Since I had been there before, I knew my way around. We had no real problems at all when we arrived, except the usual vast amount of paperwork while checking in. But we were given a decent room and we settled in quite comfortably.

I took John around the usual sites—especially Red Square and the Basque Cathedral. We stood in line to see the bodies of Lenin and Stalin. They had not yet been removed. That was prior to the great cultural exhibit the Americans had arranged there. It was still under construction, but John and I went out to the site and breezed our way through. We saw a lot of the stuff under construction, including the kitchen where Nixon would later have his famous discourse with Leonid Brezhnev.

While in Moscow, I mentioned to our guide that I had been a physics major in college for a while, and that I was very interested in seeing the famous Moscow University Physics Department. The department is a huge collection of Stalinist gingerbread-type buildings located on the south bend of the Moscow River. She arranged a visit for me.

It was very interesting. The protocol was unlike most American universities in that I had to check in. But someone on the staff took me straight to the department, which was fairly modern. Most of the equipment was a conglomeration of Italian, French and American. I saw several American items. The Russians had copied them, so of course they hadn't been made in America. Rather, they were knock-offs of American models. The Russians were very good at that—if the equipment they're copying has a crackle finish on the panel, they put a crackle finish on the panel, irrespective of the utility of that finish. But they had some pretty good equipment there. Then they showed me the dormitories, which were pretty crowded.

They explained that one group from some foreign country was living quite parsimoniously because the Russian allowance was really more than they needed to survive, and with the money they were saving, they were able to send some back to their homeland. I was still very impressed with the first-class facilities of the physics department. I assumed that the rest of the university with regard to engineering and size was comparable.

However, on a subsequent visit with a guide, I visited the foreign languages and literature departments in downtown Moscow. This was another story altogether. I could only assume the facilities dated back before World War I.

Two of the halls were grandiose, built with a great deal of elegant marble, but the actual rooms for living were dim, dark, dingy and dirty. I surmised that literature would never receive the same kudos as the sciences, which were respected more for the ability to make rockets and those sorts of advances.

On one of the trips to Moscow with John, I wanted him to see the wreckage of the American U2 airplane piloted by Gary Powers in 1960. It had been shot down over Siberia as a spy plane. The incident had quite a negative impact on American-Soviet relations. I knew that the Russians had the display of the wreckage. It was located at a temporary Russian army museum. We had to encourage our guide to let us see it, but she eventually took us out there.

It was a very long drive to the site and we went through a part of Moscow that has log cabins. I wanted to stop and get some pictures, but the guide was very adamant about not doing that. I finally convinced her. I said, as diplomatically as I could, "Lena, I'd like to get a picture of this now, because I know when I come back at a later date, this will all be replaced by beautiful new apartment houses."

She reluctantly agreed and I took my pictures. We arrived at the army museum and there it was—the wreckage of the U2. Of course, there was a sign with some propaganda and unfortunately, it was all in Russian so I couldn't read it. She asked, "That was the American spy plane?"

I said, "Yes, it was flown by an American called Gary Powers."

She asked, "Oh, you know about that?"

I replied, "Oh, yes, we traded him off for a Russian spy." And I went on to explain. "We had captured a Russian spy in America who denied his involvement in espionage, but the evidence was conclusive. So he was put in jail in the United States, and when Gary Powers was shot down, we made a trade. We got our spy back for your spy." I told her that I'd forgotten his name but that he was the top Russian operative in America.

And she shook her head and said, "No, we do not do things like that!"

Then we went to the museum where we saw Russian scientific achievements. They had a color television display there that demonstrated the *great achievements* by Russians in color TV. Of course we noticed the tube was the RCA Color tube, which was already out of date in the United States.

We went into the computer exhibition and immediately noticed that every computer on display was obsolete. Actually, the only one I recognized was a knock-off of an analog computer from a company in which I had invested years before. The company had continued making it for a while, but now it was obsolete. I remembered that I had seen a photograph of the equipment in an annual report about five years before. I was taking a picture of it when a guard approached me and said, "Nyet, Nyet, Nyet - not permitted to take pictures—Secret!"

Then my guide shook her head and said in nearly perfect English, "Well, we have damn fools also in this country. You just met one of them."

We went on to a science museum, which I had toured once before. It wasn't the Smithsonian or the British Science Museum or even the Deutsche Museum, but nevertheless it was interesting and I thought John would enjoy it. On a previous trip, I had met an elderly gentleman who happened to be the director.

When I walked in this time, I was delighted to see that he recognized me. He escorted us around much of the museum. It really was an interesting museum because it showed lots of Russian development at various times, and I wished at the time that I could have read Russian. John was fascinated, too.

One thing that particularly amused us, though, was their Xerox exhibit. There stood a standard Xerox machine just like ours in the Los Angeles office. It was operating and visitors were permitted to put things down on the plate and make copies of them. There was a guard there and when people tried to make copies of money he scolded, "Nyet! Nyet!" Some of them began to make copies of their identification documents. When the guard suddenly spotted them, there was a big fuss about that.

Another tourist took pictures of something rather unique. We were at the Moscow subway. At the end of the platform, where the station is, there was a beautiful mural, all made of mosaic tile. It depicted a large group of young pioneers (the Russian equivalent of boy scouts and girl scouts) who were offering gifts and smiling up at Stalin.

In later years, during another visit, the mural was still there, except Stalin had been chiseled out, and the young pioneers were now making their offerings to a vast empty space.

In later years, back home, I had subscribed to a Russian magazine. which had an English translation. In one particular issue, there was an article that talked about the local Russian citizens going in to see this wonderful Xerox exhibit at the museum and being so careless as to put their secret identification documents down and make copies of them. After all, it warned, who knew if the people from the West—*the capitalists*—didn't have some secret device inside the machine so they could keep a copy to be used by spies. Oh, God, the paranoia!

~

John and I flew on to spend a couple of days in Prague. We arrived in Prague on a Russian airplane. It was 1962 and I shudder to think how old the airplane was. It was raining hard and we had to circle the airport twice before they finally set the plane down – hard - on the wet pavement. Neither of us was too happy about that.

On the way from Moscow, someone had given John a beautiful large orange. I don't recall why, but he decided to save it and placed it carefully in his backpack.

Later, at the hotel in Prague, he took it out and, without a word, handed it to the elevator operator. The stranger literally broke into tears. He said, "I have not seen such a beautiful orange as that in years and years. We don't have them in Czechoslovakia. I will take it home to my wife and we will thoroughly enjoy it. It will be the first orange we have had in a long, long time." I'm sure that was a memorable experience for John. I know I never forgot it.

We were on a mission. Two young men in my Los Angeles office were from Czechoslovakia. They had escaped a few years before during the insurrection when the Russians had forced out the temporary but somewhat democratic government that was trying to take power back from the Communists. One of the fellows in my office said his father spoke really good English and told me to look him up in Prague. He asked me to please give him a message and see what I could bring back to L.A.

I called the man from our hotel. The next day, he came to the hotel room with his wife. Although his English was impeccable, his wife spoke very broken English. The man talked with us for about half an hour. I got my tape recorder out and he recorded a detailed message to his son, saying that things weren't all that bad, that things were improving. It was a positive message.

Later on, we walked out together across the famous bridge over the river. In the middle of the bridge, we stopped. He said, "Tell my son not to believe a word of what's on that tape. I figured since you were American they probably bugged the room and I knew that they were probably listening to everything I said. Tell my son to ignore what I said on that tape. Things here are really terrible. The dedicated Communist party members get all the good food and products. The rest of us, particularly those of us with backgrounds in education and business, are barely able to make ends meet. Tell him I do very much appreciate the little money he was able to send us, although the exchange rate to the local currency is very unfavorable."

Next, we flew from Prague to Zurich on Swiss Air. Upon landing, they were passing out the current day's Paris Herald at the airport and we saw that Reese Taylor of Union Oil had died unexpectedly. Reese and his second wife Maggie were our neighbors in San Marino, and John was very close to one of their boys.

In the summer of 1963, John and I decided to tour Europe again, and of course, with the wealth of experiences we had shared the summer before, we had to include Moscow. John was sixteen, a great age for soaking up other cultures. John took some pens and some Beatles records with him, thinking that those would be of interest to young Russians. Were they ever!

Back in those days, the Russian ruble had a fictitious value of about a dollar thirty U.S. That wasn't its real value, but rather its mandated exchange rate. Of course, there was the black market, but they were cracking down on tourists using the black market, and they could be very hard-nosed if they caught you.

We stayed at the Ukrainia Hotel where I had stayed a number of times. It was a twenty-story building, actually separated by a boulevard that stretched over the Moscow River.

By the wall on the boulevard, overlooking the river, there were always money speculators there. As tourists were looking for a bus, they would accost them and offer to exchange money. The hotel was run by Intourist, a travel agency that handled travel to and from Russia, as well as within the country. At their desk, we could purchase airline and train tickets, even theater tickets. There were two or three restaurants in the hotel, most of which had the usual *Nget* spoken and about six other languages.

The elevators were self-service and always over-crowded. The system was that because they knew the elevators would always be overcrowded, they had a weight limit on them. So if too many people got on, the elevator simply wouldn't start until a number of people got off. Oddly enough, the system worked—one of the few things in Russia that did.

On the grounds of the Kremlin was a concert and meeting hall. It really was beautiful. I was certain the design was by a Swedish or Finnish architect because the quality of construction was perfect. It was quite large. We went to a concert, but in the middle of it, people suddenly started clapping. John and I looked up and there in the dignitary's box was Brezhnev. Everybody was applauding and the roar of the crowd was incredible. He stood up and bowed, then sat down and the audience calmed down.

The concert hall was perfect in every aspect—the lighting was excellent, the escalators had been made in Sweden, even the urinals in the men's room were stamped "Standard," which of course relates to the manufacturer American Standard. In Russian theater or opera, they always have long intermissions. There are large areas with restaurants and cocktail lounges. The facilities were so nice, and the Russians always wanted to take advantage of them because most of them lived with their entire families in one-room apartments.

It was July when we were there, and the night was very warm, so I suggested to John that rather than hailing a taxi, we walk back to the Ukrainia. It was almost a straight shot from the Kremlin down the hill to the hotel. It was still light outside because of the time of year.

We hadn't gone more than half a block when we were joined by several young men. They asked, "You are Americans or English?" They were delighted at our warm response, because they wanted to practice their English. Of course, we agreed.

So all the way back to the hotel, we talked. John would ask them a question and they would take their time to answer in their very best English. Then they asked John about American music and when John mentioned he had some Beatles records with him, they became so excited. They asked if they could meet with him the next day. One of them said, "We would like you to go to an apartment with us and we will trade some records with you. And you can listen to some Russian music."

John asked, "Dad, do you think that'll be okay?" and I said, "As long as I can go with you, that'll be just fine." So we arranged to meet them the next evening across from the hotel on the bank of the river.

I asked them, "Are you sure it's safe?"

They laughed and replied, "The secret police are dummies and they won't bother anybody if you use your head and don't do anything silly. So we'll meet you at the bridge there."

The bridge was only half a block from the hotel.

One of the boys said, "We'll go to my aunt's apartment and we can tell stories and exchange records and you can listen to some Russian music and stuff like that."

So we agreed to meet. I went down to the Intourist store, bought some boxes of candies and a couple of bottles of wine. The store was really inexpensive. The next evening, John and I met these young fellows on the bridge over the Moscow River by the hotel. They flagged down two taxis. John and I and two or three of them were in one taxi, and the rest of them were in the other, and off we went. And we drove and drove and drove—and ended up somewhere on the east side of Moscow. There were a bunch of new apartment buildings all around.

Just before we got there, the last half-mile or so, one of them warned, "When we get out and approach the apartment, don't talk English to us anymore," so we were careful to be silent when we got out of the taxi. They stopped at this apartment house and got out and put their finger to their lips to remind us to be quiet. The apartment building looked new. There was a lot of construction nearby.

They pushed the buttons that unlocked the door and we got into the elevator and went up a number of floors. The hallway smelled of urine, even though the apartment complex was new. When we got to the door, there were two young fellows there too, and we all went into this apartment. It was the largest apartment I had seen in Russia. It had a good-sized living room with a cot on one side, then a kitchen with a sink, a separate bathroom and a separate bedroom. Of course, they welcomed the candy I brought, and particularly appreciated the wine.

They turned the radio up very loud so they couldn't be heard, and the boys and John talked back and forth about all kinds of things from Beatles music to the secret police. They gave John a Beatles record that had been duplicated onto a piece of X-ray film. John gave them a couple of Beatles records, and they were so happy with that. We talked for about three hours.

I had my tape recorder with me, but there was too much background noise from the radio. I turned the tapes over to a radio station here in Los Angeles when we got back, hoping we could salvage some of the conversation but unfortunately, the background noise was so loud, the tape was useless.

Around eleven o'clock, we left. They escorted us to the square outside the apartment building, flagged down a couple of taxis for us, and we went back to the hotel.

For years I had been subscribing to three Russian publications: the Moscow News with weekly propaganda issues printed in English, another one which is an anti-western satirical magazine and Ogonyk, a so-called literary critical magazine, all in Russian of course. I couldn't read it, but I always enjoyed looking at the pictures. Since they were published solely for Russian consumers, the prices were pretty low.

John and I had spotted a building in Moscow that said Moscow News, in English, along with the name of the publication in German, French, Italian, etc. Since it was a propaganda publication, it was printed in many languages. John and I thought it would be fun to go into the magazine office and identify ourselves as American readers. We wanted to see what might happen.

We were taken by surprise when they welcomed us with open arms. We were escorted upstairs, introduced to the English language editor, and we talked for about forty-five minutes. At the end of our informal meeting, they said they would very much appreciate our writing a letter commenting on our being in Moscow and what we thought of it.

When John and I got back to the hotel, we sat down and very carefully composed a letter to the editor of the Moscow News. I commented that it was one of several visits for me and it was John's second. I said that we had very much enjoyed our visit, that the subway was everything it was supposed to be, that we found lots of things of interest, the concert hall was probably one of the finest in the world. And then we very carefully sneaked in some criticism.

We wrote about the problem of service in the restaurants. We talked about the fine ice cream and the unsanitary conditions of the drink machine that used common glasses without washing them between customers. I commented on how you could buy the two biggest Russian newspapers in New York or London, but you couldn't find a single foreign newspaper in Moscow other than Communist propaganda sheets.

I ended up by saying I looked forward to further visits to Moscow to see the progress that will be made in the future. We posted the letter and wondered about it for weeks.

About two months later, back at home, John dashed into my room all excited. "Dad, look!"

He was waving the current issue of Moscow News in the air. We looked up the editorials and discovered that the editor had published my letter verbatim. However, underneath the letter, he had taken the liberty of adding a few rebuttals. He discussed issues with supply, the reasons why Imperialist newspapers were not circulated in the *people's* victorious Soviet Union.

Our own State Department later published a newsletter commenting on the Russian press, and they referred to my letter and stated blandly that sometimes the Russians do print something different from what you would expect. I then wrote a letter to the editor of the American Magazine explaining the circumstances of our letter in the Moscow News. I got a very nice letter back from the editor saying, "Every now and then you win one, and you guys won one, getting them to publish your letter verbatim the way they did."

This time when John and I left Moscow, we went to Warsaw. We were about two hours late leaving Moscow. The reason was that Brezhnev was scheduled to visit Poland the same time we were. He was just leaving Moscow, so they delayed the departure of our airplane until Brezhnev was on the ground in Poland.

We got to Warsaw and were taken to a marginally acceptable hotel. Right in the middle of Warsaw was this huge, ghastly Stalin-type Russian building that looked like a giant gingerbread wedding cake. I learned it had been given from the Russians to their glorious compatriots in communist Poland. There was a great view of Warsaw from the top of the building. I had been there before, but I wanted John to see it. However, because Brezhnev was there, the building was closed to the public.

John and I had a reasonably good time in Warsaw. We saw the area destroyed by the Nazis—the Jewish neighborhoods were fairly demolished. When we were ready to leave Warsaw, we went to the guide and he said, "You're leaving now? Do you have a permit?"

I said, "What do you mean? Here are our tickets."

And he said, "Oh, you must have a permit to leave."

So we dashed off to some police office somewhere nearby. They sent us back and forth, finally stamped our papers, and we dashed to the airport. From that point on, we had no further problem and both breathed a sigh of relief when the airplane took off.

When we landed in East Berlin, we had to pay a special ten-dollar fee plus transportation to get through the wall into West Berlin to our hotel. We were staying at the Kempinski Hotel. We rented a Volkswagen and drove around West Berlin and even over through Checkpoint Charlie into East Berlin. John was sixteen, and barely able to drive at that time, but of course was dying to do so. And so, on a side street in East Berlin, he got his wish. I let him drive a little, but we were very careful to stay off the main drag.

West Berlin, even though it was isolated from the rest of Germany by Communist East Germany, was bustling. There were buildings going up all over the place, people were smiling and seemed well fed and there were lots of cars on the roads.

East Berlin was drab and dreary, totally reflective of the lack of spirit and wealth the Communist regime had brought to its people. A couple of the buildings on the main streets had been rebuilt, but there were still buildings off the main streets that were heavily damaged by the war. Those buildings had disappeared from West Berlin and that section had totally been rebuilt. There were some bars in East Berlin, but they were drab as well.

They had rebuilt the museums, but curiously the Berlin City Hall, which had been a ghastly red brick building built in 1880 had been rebuilt, brick by brick, to look as ugly as it had the day they completed the first construction. We went through Checkpoint Charlie a number of times. The Communist guards photographed our passports, and checked out every part of that Volkswagen, trying to see if there was anyplace in that car that we could have hidden somebody trying to escape into West Germany. We got a kick out of defying them.

We went over to Hamburg for a couple of days via London. We were going to fly home from Hamburg. While waiting for our plane in the airport bar, I discovered a bottle of Englehardt beer. John and I drank the beer, carefully packing it into a carry-on to take it home to Hilda. But on our way through the airport, I must have bumped up against the wall, for there was a shattering sound and I realized the bottle had broken.

Amazingly, a minute or so later, a guy from the bar came up to me. He had heard me talking about the family name, and he held out an empty bottle of the Englehardt beer and said, "So sorry about your losing that one." Now that's what I call politeness.

In August 1965, leaving Jim to fulfill his summer work obligations at Douglas, Hilda and I took John to Tahiti for a few days to celebrate his graduation from Thacher. We visited Bora Bora and an adjacent island at Captain Cook's Bay. We stayed in a very primitive, small hotel, the Montequilla. It was very rustic and only had ten rooms. Guests had to go to their rooms at eight o'clock because it cost too much in diesel oil to keep the lights on, so the hotel staff turned everything off in the bar at eight. Lights went out elsewhere at ten. If we weren't tired, we would confiscate candles or flashlights so we could stay up a little later. The influence oddly was French and the cuisine delicious.

Among the guests at the little inn was a wonderful Australian lawyer who was lots of fun. But there was the most irritating woman…an absolutely impossible old-maid-type schoolteacher. She was a terrible person. The Australian called her a bloody nuisance.

The resort had not been developed at all. Amenities aside, Captain Cook's Bay was beautifully pristine. One day, John and I took an outrigger canoe out on the bay only to discover that they were a lot harder to paddle than they seemed to be. The natives did very well of course, but John and I could only make the damn thing go in circles. John would forever remember the summer, not so much for all the fantastic places we visited, but as the summer the Beatles released "You've Got to Hide Your Love Away."

Although Hilda chose to forego the outrigger experience, she and I made an achievement all our own. Together, we drank up all the Tuborg beer on the island of Bora Bora.

From Tahiti, we flew to the big island of Hawaii to stay in the brand new Rockefeller hotel called the Mauna Kea. It was Friday the thirteenth. For some reason John hadn't wanted to dine with us, so Hilda and I celebrated our new comfortable lodging with a great meal.

We returned to the room after a lovely dinner to find that Jim had called from Los Angeles. He and John had been on the telephone for nearly an hour. The news from home wasn't good. The Watts riots had started. The entire Los Angeles South Central neighborhood was in flames following the arrest of a suspected drunk driver by California Highway Patrol officers. What ensued was six days of looting and destruction, with the National Guard finally being called out to control the situation. Thirty-four people were killed, mostly blacks from the neighborhood. We were glad to have missed it. John had gotten a blow-by-blow description from Jim as he watched it on television from the safety of our home.

On one trip, I rented a car in Cairo, Egypt. The road to the coast where I would pick up my ship was rough. I drove past the famous Mud Inn, perched on the mountaintop. I stopped at some temples and the pseudo-Egyptian guide beckoned me to come with him behind a couple of the walls at the temples, saying, "You must see, you must see this picture." He demanded ten dollars for his efforts. It turned out to be a carving, which I could easily have seen without forking over a tip. Then there were the guides in the tombs who insisted, "No photographs, no photographs," -then they would shrug their shoulders, put their hands down, and said, "Five dollars, okay."

Regardless of the scams by the local populace, the experience of witnessing the brilliance of the colors of the paintings on the walls of the tombs was incredible…not only in the Valley of the Kings, but also in the Valley of the Queens.

Somewhere in time, as things changed, some of my trips became trips with extended family and friends. After Hilda's severe injury to her leg, she was in too much pain to travel.

Following the acquisition by Honeywell, the Measurex Board of Directors, who got together occasionally, planned a jaunt to Istanbul. They were going to take a ship to the Greek Islands and to Athens. This was in the late '90s. But Hilda came down with lung cancer and I cancelled to stay home with her.

She had always been a heavy smoker, smoking up to two packs a day. I had told her all the time to cut down. She did everything the doctors said. She underwent chemotherapy, radiation, all of it. But it was too late. We had been married more than fifty years when she died in April 1999, a year or so after she was diagnosed.

Shortly after her death, the boys suggested I take a trip, so I checked with the Measurex people and found there was still a space available on the trip. The down side was that we had to book passage for two, so I invited Bev Evans to join me.

We flew to Istanbul. There was a fine hotel there that had been a jail at one time, up by the Blue Mosque. We thoroughly enjoyed visiting the Mosquee de Ste. Sophie (Sophia Mosque) and walked to several of the palaces. We spent two days there before boarding the ship again. It was a relatively small ship that only carried one hundred twenty passengers. We only had eighty on board, so we had lots of fun. People were not shocked with us at all. Our room had twin beds, of course! We got to Athens and booked ourselves into a large hotel there. Unfortunately, it was not conveniently located to the center of anything, so after two days there, I rebooked us into the Gran Vitania Hotel. In the meantime, Bev was having tremendous difficulty with her back.

I was determined to go up to Delphi once again. Bev stayed at the hotel resting while I rented a taxi and went to Delphi. I spent the night there and by that time, I was having problems myself, being very short of breath. We had walked around the monuments, which were set pretty far up the hill but regardless of our ailments, we thoroughly enjoyed the entire trip. I finally hired a driver to take me around.

When I returned to the hotel, I discovered that Bev was really laid up. The next day, I managed to get her onto an airplane. She couldn't even walk and was in quite a lot of pain. They had to use a forklift to hoist her onto the plane. But I managed to get her home all right.

Oddly enough, my next trip was a Measurex trip as well. I went from Los Angeles to Stockholm on a Norwegian-American cruise ship. It wasn't an exceptionally large one, probably eight hundred people on board.

How I had hoped to meet Bret Hahn in Holland. He was the outstanding African-American ambassador to Sweden during the days of all the fussing about Vietnam. When I arrived, I found out that he had left town for Washington. I had just missed him. So I spent some time at the Vasa Museum in Stockholm. What an incredible story that was!

The sixty-four-gun warship, The Royal Vasa, had sunk on her maiden voyage only fourteen hundred yards from launch. It was August 10, 1628 and a beautiful summer's day. A sudden squall had risen from the south-southwest, caught the sails that had just been hoisted, and simply tipped her over. Water gushed in through the gun ports and she sank, drowning more than fifty crewmembers and their families of the one hundred twenty-five aboard.

The occasion was meant to be a celebration and people watched from the dock in absolute horror as the majestic ship went down. After spending three hundred thirty-three years on the bottom of the sea, she was raised on April 24, 1961 and today is shown at the Museum.

For the next Measurex trip, I invited my friend Virginia to go along. We sailed from Los Angeles down to Puerto Vallarta, then to Cabo San Lucas and back to Los Angeles. Just a seven-day voyage. But Virginia got on very well indeed with the Measurex crowd.

I had always wanted to go on one of the French Canal barges. Pete Bancroft gave me the name of one. Again, the rate was for two people, so I invited Virginia to go with me again. After a reunion at Cornell, I picked up Virginia in New York and we flew off to London. We stayed a couple of days at the Stafford Hotel, saw a couple of shows, took the train (Chunnel) over to Paris where we spent four days at a very nice hotel. We strolled through several museums and took it easy before flying back home from Paris to the Newark airport. We spent the night at Virginia's house in New York and I flew home the next day.

My most recent trip was in September 2001. I had received in the mail a flyer from the American Clipper line offering an unbelievable rate for a trip to China and Vietnam. I would fly to Hong Kong, change planes, go to Beijing for a couple days, fly to Shang Hai, take a ship to a Chinese Island, then to a Japanese Island, then to Tai Wan, Hong Kong, and finally to the port city of Hanoi, Vietnam.

I leaped at the chance. I was scheduled to leave LAX bound for Hong Kong very late on Thursday night the fifteenth of September, but of course, on September 11, 2001, the world changed when terrorists hit the Twin Towers in New York City, then drove commercial airliners into the Pentagon and finally into a field in Pennsylvania.

Regardless, and unexpectedly, I discovered the flight to Hong Kong was still on. We were about the first people out of the airport since LAX reopened.

Once we arrived safely in Hong Kong, things were all mixed up because of delays, closures, and the like. I found myself scheduled for business class travel and decided to wait. I waited a few hours in Hong Kong for a first class flight to Beijing.

Upon my arrival, I met a couple in the hotel who were part of a group, and I expressed an interest in wanting to visit the Great Wall but told them I didn't want to go alone. There was just too much walking involved for my pacemaker, I thought. So three of us rented a car and driver to take us up to the Great Wall and we looked around a bit. We drove back down to the Summer Palace, walked through the Imperial City, and got back to the hotel around the time the group came back from their sight-seeing trip. Rather than stay with the larger group, we had gone on our own and seen everything with our own car and driver. We were quite proud of ourselves.

When we boarded the ship in Shanghai, there were about thirty-five people already on the ship who had come down from Japan, and by the time we were loaded up, we made a nice collection of about seventy-two tourists. It was a great, small fine ship—The Clipper Odyssey! The crew was great, the passengers nice. And we stopped at this Chinese Island where there was a big Buddha and we got to walk around a bit. Then we sailed over to a Japanese Island south of Okinawa. It was very tropical.

We spent a day there in a little port. It was really a long fjord, exquisitely beautiful. From there, we sailed down to Taiwan and over to the port of Hong Kong where our big ship was waiting for us. We proceeded on to Hanoi.

My travels weren't always without problems. Periodically, I had car trouble of the worst kind. These incidents reminded me of my father's letting his car roll into a ditch at the Hearst ranch when I was a young man. Once while visiting Germany, I stayed at a hotel at the tip of Lake Constance. The lake is also known as Bodensee and is bordered by three countries, Austria, Switzerland and Germany. It is Europe's second largest freshwater lake, covering two hundred twenty-square miles and it is absolutely breathtaking. There was an old monastery there. I drove all around the lake, going through Lichtenstein.

Driving on up Monte Sissone, above Liechtenstein, I drove into a snowstorm. I decided to take a back road through the mountains and ran right into a snowstorm. I turned around to go back down. It was snowing heavily. Halfway down the hill, I had the car in second gear. I was going very slowly, driving very carefully, trying hard to keep on the crown of the road on the hill when the car slid off the side of road and went WHAM!—into a tree! The impact smashed the front fender and damaged the headlight somewhat, but I managed to back the car away from the tree.

I got back into Germany and at the east end of lake, drove over the border into a little 'tag' of Austria. The German customs people were very upset that I was driving a Swiss car with a smashed front end, but they let me through anyway. I turned the car into Hertz in Zurich. Fortunately, I had full coverage insurance and hadn't done anything wrong. There was an unbelievable amount of snow on the mountainside and the road was so slippery!

Once, in a north Yemen village, our tour bus got stuck on a road so narrow, it was jammed between two walls. It took the whole village to squeeze the thing out so we could get out and go on. It was the only road that went through the town. The town's men folk were carrying daggers, but they grinned from ear to ear as they helped us get out of our sticky situation.

Another time, I picked up a car in Paris. They tried to give me a beautiful BMW. In France, we could get unleaded gasoline, but I knew that elsewhere, gas stations that carried unleaded gasoline were few and far between. The tank was almost empty when they turned it over to me so I traded it back in for a French Peugeot. I drove through the tunnel that crossed over into northern Italy, looked at the beautiful lake country over to Switzerland where I saw the marvelous Monte Sissone again.

Africa had always been another point of dramatic interest for me. Even before I went to South Africa for the first time, I was intrigued by the country—its government and culture; so I subscribed to a South African financial weekly. When I first visited, I found that the English-language publications were published by a company called Argus Printing and Publishing Company, Ltd. The publishing company also produced the Cape Town and Johannesburg newspapers.

Of course, I had to look into the finances. Argus shares were traded on the Johannesburg Stock Exchange, and to my surprise I found they were selling at six and a half and seven times earnings. This was at a time when comparable American newspapers were selling at fourteen to twenty times earnings. At that time, the South African Rand was around a dollar fifteen.

I asked our London office to find out if there were some way to buy these shares out of South Africa. To my amazement, they not only came back with an answer, but said they could buy a block of the shares—I forget exactly how many, but it was a lot more money than I would normally invest, something like seventy-five to eighty-thousand dollars. For some reason, I simply said, "Go ahead and buy them." So I bought the shares in Argus Printing and Publishing Company through the London office, and a new certificate came through.

It turned out there were two kinds of Rand: A free Rand and a frozen Rand. You could buy a frozen Rand at a significant discount, which the London office bought for me, so my cost of the Argus shares was significantly reduced. I think the frozen Rand sold at about a twenty-five percent discount from the free Rand.

As problems in South Africa continued to mount, the Rand kept declining, but Argus shares kept going up-up-up! Argus brilliantly got into the broadcasting business and spun off one company, I think, to give the black South Africans the opportunity to have some interest in the publishing business. Argus shares split a couple of times.

Then I saw the shares of the spun-off corporation had gone way up in price. I sold those, and even with the frozen Rand came out very well indeed. But the shares of the other company kept going up-up-up as well. Finally one day, following the end of apartheid, the Rand was freed up and the shares rose significantly in value. I asked if I could sell them and when I finally *could* sell them, went over in the summer and got an excellent price for the shares.

The transfer was a bit of a hassle, but I earned well over a million dollars in cash from that deal. I haven't followed it recently, but I think the Rand has gotten down to about fourteen cents. I think the Rand was around sixty-five cents when I sold out.

During my second trip there, I had long talks with a young, black South African in the hotel bar. Apartheid was still very much a part of the culture. The young man had studied accounting in high school, but no accounting firm would hire him. He couldn't get an accountancy license, even though he had worked in the profession for a number of years.

At the time, CBS had a television crew there. The government accused CBS reporters of trying to start trouble with the black people. My newfound friend led me through some of the black tribes from the Hosas to the Zulus. We discussed the black tribes of the neighboring African countries who were immigrating to South Africa and taking jobs that should have been given to qualified, decent black people. How I was allowed to take pictures in the South African gold mine and in the miners' quarters, I'll never know. That was something no American mining company would have allowed. Unfortunately, once I came home, I ruined the pictures by using the wrong developing technique.

More recently, I wanted to go to South Africa again. So much had happened in the past several years, I wanted to experience the change. So I arranged a trip for John, Mindy and me to go to Johannesburg. Unfortunately, I got sick and couldn't make the trip, but John and Mindy went and had a wonderful, wonderful time. Then I planned a trip to Saudi Arabia with People to People, my doctor forbad me to go. I ended up with a trip to the hospital instead, to have my pacemaker installed.

Mindy and I enjoying Hana, Hawaii

On the airplane en route
to Hong Kong

Mindy and I
Napa Valley

John and I in Hong Kong
(below) I'm enjoying a brew in Manzanillo, Mexico
Mindy and John are posing by a sea wall

April 2002:
The Enron and Arthur Anderson Scandal
-Corporate America Loses its Integrity-

I am witnessing firsthand the much-publicized demise of corporate integrity. Last night, C-Span broadcast the U. S. Senate hearings on the Enron scandal. I began listening to them at the very beginning of the hearings - it must have been around nine o'clock. I finally went to bed after two in the morning. They are absolutely fascinating to me because of my vast experience as a director of various companies.

When I finally gave up and went to bed I couldn't get to sleep. I was thinking about all the things I had heard and how I agreed or disagreed with many of the issues that were brought up by various senators. Early the next morning, I lay in bed thinking about how I would have reacted under similar circumstances and how those circumstances played to the very companies of which I have been a director over the years.

I thought back about my experience with International Chemical and Nuclear Corporation - ICN Pharmaceuticals. Their board of directors reflected so much of the issues that are now going on with the Enron board.

Our chief financial officer was from our accounting firm Peat Marwick whose guys always pushed the envelope as far as they could. A couple of the directors were patsies. One fellow was a hotshot from New York. I forget his name, but he was very fashion conscious and quite self-promoting. There was a man from a local university, the Seventh Day Adventist School - east of us in Pasadena, and a couple of non-entities that were completely under Milan Panic's thumb. I was the *dirty SOB* who detected things all the time!

And just the other day, it came out in the financial news that Panic was still at it—again! He had arranged a spin-off from a subsidiary of ICN Pharmaceuticals for a huge fee. Here he was, the president of the company doing the job he's supposed to do, and spinning off of a subsidiary. And he got a huge fee for it. What makes it worse is that his board of directors went along with him. I couldn't believe that!

I thought about how careful we were in our board meetings of United Cities Gas, the Dominguez Water Company, even Far West Financial, which eventually became Westminster Capital. Although I disagreed with the Belzbergs of Far West, at least they didn't cheat anyone or cut any corners in that regard, though they were greedy so-and-sos! We always had internal auditors; the board met solely with the internal auditors, asked them one-on-one questions; then we met solely with the CPA firm and asked them one-on-one questions as well. I was chair of audit committees through the years for several organizations. We rode herd on audit reports!

Of course, with Measurex, we went back and forth and made sure no sale was ever booked until the order was shipped out of the plant to the customer or was shipped to a warehouse. There had to be an order for a customer to put the product in the warehouse and the customer would take effective delivery at the warehouse. We found some shaving of expense accounts and things of that nature in France and when we did, we changed the management there in a hell of a hurry.

With United Cities, we had a long, legitimate argument with the IRS. The question was, of course, had we been paying enough taxes? One SOB came in to audit the firm and said that we were over-depreciating our assets. He said that we were under-claiming revenues because we didn't cut off revenues at exactly midnight on December 31.

First of all, we used the metered reading at the end of the month, and estimating from our Italian gas purchases as to what the sales should have been, we won most of that argument, but the IRS agent retired after finishing the United Cities job. He was in our offices for a whole year and caused us unbelievable annoyance and hardship by simply moving into our space and taking over an entire office. But through all my years, especially with the reputation as Dr. No, I never made a decision that comprised my integrity.

Going back to the senate hearings, the first three people on the stand were Enron executives, none of whom who had claimed the Fifth Amendment. They were all long-time board members. One was head of the Audit Committee; one was head of the Compensation Committee, and I forget what the principle responsibilities of the third was, but they were all obviously very senior, quite knowledgeable professionals. They all read from position papers and then were cross-questioned by the panel, which was comprised of members of the Finance Committee of the United States Senate.

They all claimed to have asked the right questions. And they all stated that they had been given the wrong answers by various people at Enron. To my mind, however, they never really asked the same questions I would have asked had I been in their positions. I know that Enron had Arthur Anderson as internal auditors. But Arthur Anderson was an outside auditor, in my book. And I always firmly believed that under no circumstances should a company ever have its internal audit work done by its external public accounting firm. It isn't possible to maintain the objectivity and separation necessary.

In addition, of course, there was a vast amount of consulting work done. I believe Enron was Arthur Anderson's second largest client. Their fees for the most recent year, I think, were fifty-two million dollars for internal audit, external audit and consulting work. Enron had these weird partnerships that were designed to take debt off the balance sheet but they were leaving liabilities there theoretically without risk, because they could pay off the debt by delivery of Enron stock.

But they never disclosed what was supposed to happen if Enron stock dropped sharply in price. For example, if it dropped to forty dollars a share, which is unthinkably low, there would only be 5.6 percent dilution of the existing shares to extend a billion dollars of debt, or something of that sort.

They claimed that these various partnership risks were hedged. Well, they were not hedged but the *hedging*, such as it was, was with Enron stock. Enron had a code of conflict and conflict of interest developments, but the board specifically approved a senior financial officer of Enron to work both sides as a general partner in one of these limited partnerships in which he incurred over a billion dollars in debt.

An earlier one was designed to promote some money for Enron . Enron had formed a limited partnership and borrowed five hundred million dollars from, I believe, the Chase Bank in New York, then borrowed a billion dollars from the partnership, which means they were really drawing out five hundred million dollars of new money. That particular one they paid off; they sold for another limited partnership, raised the five hundred seventy-thousand dollar capital to pay off the first partnership owed to Chase Bank, but incurred even more debt with the new partnership. The Enron financial officer, who was allowed to become general partner of some of these partnerships, was both general partner and an officer of Enron, which means he was carrying water buckets on both shoulders.

One might expect that that might be a conflict of interest that could be resolved by limiting his compensation to a nominal amount for the nominal amount of work he actually did supposedly conducting the limited partnerships. But no, it seems he took out an enormous amount of money from those partnerships for those duties as *general partner*, gleaning an override of some sort. Obviously, he had a conflict of interest there. But the board never asked of him what kind of compensation he was going to have. Neither did they restrict him to a nominal amount of compensation.

Enron's Chief Executive Officer Ken Lay, talked the board into giving him a five million dollar open line with the company, which means he could draw money out of the company by just asking a trader to write him a check up to that amount. (It was later increased to seven million.) But it turned out that Lay ended up drawing seventy-seven million dollars out of Enron.

At the end, God knows how much more he may have drawn out, but he paid those debts off by giving Enron stock back to Enron which mean he was getting cash from Enron—Enron was only getting back their own paper!

I remember in my first finance class at the Harvard Business School, we had a case that highlighted the premise that your own stock in your own company is *not* cash! I never forgot that lesson. The board members obviously never fully understood all the things

Enron was doing, particularly the vast foreign investments, which were big losers. They never looked very hard into those. Some of those were hidden in the so-called limited partnerships but their reliability was on the Enron name.

Enron acquired Portland General Electric Company and I hope it was acquired for cash, because if Enron had acquired it with stock, and the electric company's employees had 401k investments, my heart really goes out to those poor guys if those shares had been converted into Enron stock.

The Enron employees who had money in Enron stock were already on board the ship and should have known more about what was going on, although Enron claimed there were only a few people who could understand the company's income and losses. Their losses were always so well hidden.

Enron's largest investment was a big power plant in India where GE, and I think Bechtel, ran small participations, but Enron had over eighty percent ownership. The plant ran into all kinds of trouble complicated by typical Indian legalese, and the electricity coming out of the plant was far too costly. Enron also had made substantial investments in Venezuela and Brazil, both of which were losers. Another one of Enron's *winners* was a water investment here in California that turned out to be an enormous amount of water for the desert, which they could never get title to, and of course never could use.

One of the Enron directors and some British Lord had an audit committee meeting in London. Enron took Arthur Anderson and some of their own people to this meeting in London. My God, what an expense that must have been! Of course, there was a discussion on the games Enron was playing with its electrical service to California and how they formed up capacity shortages and things of that nature. That story is still unraveling. I do know that along with El Paso Gas Company, Enron had some capacity limitations, which helped push up the price of natural gas here in California.

A lot of these cans of worms are still to be opened before we see where the blame really lies. There is no question but that the shenanigans were scandalously real. The silly thing is that if the business had kept clean as it was until eight or so years ago, it would have had no problems at all and it could have made excellent money.

But like so many of these guys, Milan Panic and the rest, the people at the top were greedy sons-of-bitches.

As the public came to discover, three of the directors of Enron were insiders who were being compensated at the rate of three hundred fifty thousand dollars a year *plus* stock options! All three claimed they didn't sell their Enron stock. And it is anybody's guess as to what will happen with Arthur Anderson.

The Circle is Complete

It is ironic that as I was in the final chapter of dictating my autobiography, the telephone rang. It was a cold call from a woman at UBS Paine Webber who wanted to know if I were a man who might be interested in investing. We had a nice long conversation. I explained that I had begun my professional career with Eastman Dillon fifty years ago. I went through the history of all the financial firms I had been with up to UBS Paine Webber, for which I am currently Senior Vice President. I doubt she'll call again.

Looking Forward to the Future

The next trip I'd like to take will be to go up to San Francisco, pick up Mindy and fly off to London on a 777 captained by John E. Baum! We will spend a week in London, go to the theatre, wander around London a little bit, and fly back on a return flight - also piloted by Captain John E. Baum! Unfortunately, I have to get my wind back and walk a bit more steadily before I can permit myself to go. Mindy and John and I certainly would have a wonderful time in London together for a week…at the Stafford, of course!

Epilogue

Dwight C. Baum died of pneumonia on June 19, 2002 as he was completing this book. His ashes were interred in Syracuse, New York on Oct 3, 2002.

A reading from *Into the Sunset* by S. Hall Young was offered at the service. This is an excerpt:

Let me die, working.
Still tackling plans unfinished, tasks undone!
Clean to its end, swift may my race be run.
No laggard steps, no faltering, no shirking;
Let me die, working!

Photo by Alex Berliner/BEIMAGES

Dwight C. "Bill" Baum, Dwight J. Baum II, President George Bush and Judy Baum
enjoying a discussion about flying at the 2000 USC building dedication.

This generous man's philanthropy enabled the National Federation of the Blind to establish a program in Los Angeles that offered the blind telephone access to the Los Angeles Times, New York Times and other major metropolitan newspapers. He was a benefactor to Cornell University, his alma mater, assisting with numerous projects including recent funding for nanofabrication research. The University of Southern California has benefited from his gifting for construction of a new engineering and multimedia building. These are just a few of the educational institutions and organizations Baum sought to assist.

ABOUT THE AUTHORS

Dwight C. "Bill" Baum was born in Syracuse, NY in 1912, the son of celebrated architect Dwight J. Baum. He graduated from Cornell University and Harvard Business School. Baum was involved in some of the most fascinating mergers and acquisitions the country has known. He traveled extensively and stories of his family trips are heart-warming.

Kate Kitchen is a seasoned journalist whose features have profiled Stephen King, Rita Moreno, Joseph Califano, Jean-Michel Cousteau, Miss America Jackie Mayer and Time Magazine Editor-in-Chief Henry Grunwald. This is her second book. Kitchen recently published her first novel - *Family Shadows.* She is in the process of completing a new novel: *Willow, Weep for Me (fiction)* and *The Strength of Grace* - biographies of former Miss Americas.

Printed in the United States
R1141500001B/R11415PG27178LVSX00003B/6}